T0046131

ADDITIONAL PRAISE FOR

THE SECOND AMENDMENT

"A welcome addition to the ongoing debate over gun rights and gun control in America."

—*The Buffalo News*

"An insightful look at both the historical foundation of the Second Amendment . . . a welcome re-injection of historical context into the present debate over the rightful role of guns in American culture."

—*Chicago Tribune*

"Terrific."

—Nicholas Kristof for *The New York Times*

"Compelling."

—*The Washington Post*

"Rigorous, scholarly, but accessible book."

—*The New York Times*

"Waldman relates this tale in clear, unvarnished prose and it should now be considered the best narrative of its subject."

—*Publishers Weekly*

"Waldman offers historical perspective on the fierce debate. . . . A lively and engaging exploration."

—*Booklist*

"Thoughtful, accessible . . . useful to anyone arguing either side of this endlessly controversial issue."

—*Kirkus Reviews*

"The ongoing debate about the Second Amendment and the right to bear arms continues to set off multiple explosions in the blogosphere. Waldman's new book will not make the most zealous NRA advocates happy, but for anyone who wants his or her history of the Second Amendment straight-up, this is the most comprehensive, accessible, and compelling version of the story in print."

—Joseph J. Ellis, author of *Founding Brothers*

"From the founding of the Republic to the Newtown massacre of elementary school children, and beyond, Michael Waldman vividly portrays the evolution of a nation's passionate debate over the right to keep and bear arms. Activist, conservative justices on the U.S. Supreme Court may have thought they ended that debate in 2008, but with rich detail and crisp narrative, Waldman shows how it continues to reverberate across the landscape with important lessons for all Americans."

—Marcia Coyle, author of *The Roberts Court*

"Through most of American history, the Second Amendment guaranteed the right to be a citizen-soldier, not an individual vigilante. With wit and erudition, Michael Waldman tells the story of how the Amendment's meaning was turned upside-down and inside-out."

—David Frum, author of *The Right Man: An Inside Account of the Bush White House*

"Michael Waldman gives us the turbulent life story of the Second Amendment. If one clause of the Constitution better deserved a quiet retirement, it is our right to keep and bear arms, a vestige of the Founding Fathers' concern with the role of the militia in a republican society. Yet today the Second Amendment has become one of the feistiest, most disputed clauses of the Constitution, and Waldman vividly explains why this obscure, minor provision has become so controversial."

—Jack Rakove, author of *Original Meanings*

"Partisan pseudo-histories of gun regulation and the Second Amendment abound. Michael Waldman's excellent book slices through the propaganda with candor as well as scholarship. It advances an authentic and clarifying history that will surprise and enlighten citizens on all sides of the issue. Here is a smart and cogent history that performs a large public service."

—Sean Wilentz, author of *The Rise of American Democracy*

"Anyone interested in the hot button issue of guns and their place in our society will find this book a helpful tool for ongoing discussion."

—*The Decatur Daily* (Alabama)

"*The Second Amendment* is a smart history of guns and the US . . . his calm tone and habit of taking the long view offers a refreshing tonic in this most loaded of debates."

—*Los Angeles Times*

"Waldman's detractors would do well to read the book, which focuses less on taking a position on gun control and more on explaining what the Founding Fathers intended when they approved the amendment and how subsequent decisions from the U.S. Supreme Court and elsewhere have transformed that intent. . . . Seeing the subject discussed and dissected in untypically calm, scholarly tones, then, is a refreshing development."

—*Miami Herald*

ALSO BY MICHAEL WALDMAN

*My Fellow Americans: The Most Important Speeches of America's
Presidents from George Washington to Barack Obama*

A Return to Common Sense

POTUS Speaks

Who Robbed America? A Citizens' Guide to the S&L Scandal

Who Runs Congress? (with Mark Green)

THE
SECOND
AMENDMENT

A Biography

Michael Waldman

SIMON & SCHUSTER PAPERBACKS

NEW YORK   LONDON   TORONTO   SYDNEY   NEW DELHI

Simon & Schuster Paperbacks
An Imprint of Simon & Schuster, Inc.
1230 Avenue of the Americas
New York, NY 10020

Copyright © 2014 by Michael Waldman

All rights reserved, including the right to reproduce this book or portions thereof in any form whatsoever. For information address Simon & Schuster Paperbacks Subsidiary Rights Department, 1230 Avenue of the Americas, New York, NY 10020.

First Simon & Schuster trade paperback edition May 2015

SIMON & SCHUSTER PAPERBACKS and colophon
are registered trademarks of Simon & Schuster, Inc.

For information about special discounts for bulk purchases, please contact Simon & Schuster Special Sales at 1-866-506-1949 or business@simonandschuster.com.

The Simon & Schuster Speakers Bureau can bring authors to your live event. For more information or to book an event contact the Simon & Schuster Speakers Bureau at 1-866-248-3049 or visit our website at www.simonspeakers.com.

Interior design by Akasha Archer

Manufactured in the United States of America

2 4 6 8 10 9 7 5 3 1

The Library of Congress has cataloged the hardcover edition as follows:

Waldman, Michael, 1960–
The Second Amendment : a biography / Michael Waldman.
pages cm
Includes bibliographical references and index.
1. United States. Constitution. 2nd Amendment—History.
2. Firearms—Law and legislation—United States—History.
3. Constitutional history—United States. I. Title.
KF3941.W35 2014
344.7305'33—dc23
2013051339

ISBN 978-1-4767-4744-6
ISBN 978-1-4767-4745-3 (pbk)
ISBN 978-1-4767-4746-0 (ebook)

To my family

CONTENTS

INTRODUCTION

On March 1, 1792, Secretary of State Thomas Jefferson issued a terse announcement. Congress had established the post office. It had passed a new law governing fisheries. And the states had ratified the first ten amendments to the Constitution: the Bill of Rights.

Jefferson's deadpan proclamation belied years of drama and conflict. The amendments were the product of a fierce debate over government's role and the rights of the people, one that unfolded since the start of the American Revolution. Even today, Americans know some parts of the Bill of Rights by heart. We cherish the First Amendment, with its guarantee of freedom of religion, speech, and the press. We debate the Fourth Amendment, with its requirement for a search warrant. All know about the right to avoid self-incrimination ("taking the Fifth").

For two centuries, however, the Second Amendment received little notice. Few citizens understood its provisions. Scholars paid it little attention. Lawyers rarely raised it in court. In recent years, of course, the Second Amendment has been thrust to the center of controversy. Politicians declare themselves its "strong supporters." News reports speculate about gun laws and whether they will pass muster. It has become a synonym, in powerful unspoken ways, for America's gun culture.

The Second Amendment is one sentence. It reads in its entirety:

A well regulated militia, being necessary to the security of a free state, the right of the people to keep and bear arms, shall not be infringed.

Its foggy wording and odd locution stand out in the Constitution. Lawyers and scholars debate its commas and clauses. For 218 years, judges overwhelmingly concluded that the amendment authorized states to form militias, what we now call the National Guard. Then, in 2008, the U.S. Supreme Court upended two centuries of precedent. In the case of *District of Columbia v. Heller,* an opinion written by Justice Antonin Scalia declared that the Constitution confers a right to own a gun for self-defense in the home. That's right: the Supreme Court found there to be an individual right to gun ownership just a few years ago. Now, when we debate gun control we do so in the context of a Supreme Court ruling that limits what we can do (though we don't yet know how much).

Far from a dry set of words scratched on parchment, then, it turns out that the story of the Second Amendment can tell us much about how our country has changed and grown, how we see ourselves and our government, how we balance the rights of individuals and the need for safety.

Part One of this book begins in the tumultuous years of the American Revolution and its aftermath. The Constitution was drafted in secret by a group of mostly young men, many of whom had served together in the Continental Army, and who feared the consequences of a weak central authority. They produced a charter that shifted power to a national government. "Anti-Federalists" opposed the Constitution. They worried, among other things, that the new government would try to disarm the thirteen state militias. Critically, those militias were a product of a world of civic duty and governmental compulsion utterly alien to us today. Every white man age sixteen to sixty was enrolled. He was required to own—and bring—a musket or other military weapon.

Debate still burns about the Framers' intent and the original meaning of the Constitution. Surprisingly, there is not a single word about an individual right to a gun for self-defense in the notes from the Constitutional Convention. Nor with scattered exceptions in the records of the ratification debates in the states. Nor on the floor of the U.S. House of Representatives as it marked up the Second Amendment. James Madison's original proposal, in fact, included a provision for conscientious objectors.

People ask: who is right? Did the Second Amendment protect militias, or an individual right to a gun? The answer: both, and neither. It protected the individual right to a gun . . . to fulfill the duty to serve in a militia. To the Framers, even our *question* would make little sense. To us, today, their *answer* makes little sense.

As the nation spread west, guns grew abundant. (After all, one of those young Constitution writers, Alexander Hamilton, was killed in a duel!) In the years immediately following the Civil War, the authors of the Fourteenth Amendment wanted to make sure that former slaves could arm themselves to protect against organized violence from white vigilantes. But gun control laws were prevalent, too. An iconic photo of Dodge City—that legendary frontier town—shows a sign planted in the middle of its main street: "The Carrying of Fire Arms Strictly Prohibited." In the twentieth century, Americans demanded a stronger government as they surged into crowded cities. Amid Prohibition and the Depression, modern gun control laws sought to rein in gangsters and the heat they packed. And, again, the courts stayed out. Chief Justice Warren Burger—a rock-ribbed conservative appointed by Richard Nixon—articulated the consensus when he called the idea of individual gun rights in the Constitution a preposterous "fraud."

Part Two tells the story of how that changed: how a remarkable, concerted legal campaign toppled two centuries of precedent.

One thread, of course, is the rise of the National Rifle Association. The group brags of its ballot box victories. Starting in the 1970s, the organization also quietly—but emphatically—backed a jurisprudential campaign to enshrine gun rights in the Constitution. Its legal allies insisted that for two centuries judges simply got it wrong. They managed to persuade a substantial part of the public, and after that the courts. The road to *Heller* was paved by one of history's most effective, if misleading, campaigns for constitutional change.

Heller shows something more: how a generation of conservative judges and scholars transformed the way we interpret the Constitution. "Originalism" asserts that the only legitimate way to interpret a constitutional provision is to ask what the Constitution meant at the time it was enacted, in the late 1700s. Its influence has peaked in the Supreme

Court led by John Roberts. He assigned Scalia the 2008 gun case. Lawyers arguing before the Supreme Court now brandish obscure historical texts like graduate students defending a particularly opaque dissertation. This section will suggest that reverence for the "text" can be just a pretext for a particular political view.

What now? Part Three will trace *Heller*'s impact as we struggle again to curb gun violence. As before, spasms of violence spur calls for new laws. (Today, we are sickened by massacres such as the one in Newtown, Connecticut, rather than the political assassinations that prompted action before.) This is the first time, though, that Americans have debated firearm safety proposals with an individual right to own a gun enshrined in the Constitution. Will new doctrine deflect new laws? Will we all have the right to carry a weapon and stand our ground? We will examine the cases since *Heller*, and find a surprise: despite the hoopla surrounding the case, courts upheld nearly all gun rules. Individuals have a right to a gun, judges have found, but society has a right to protect itself, too. Yet that assumption may be premature. As Justice Robert Jackson said, the Supreme Court is not final because it is infallible, but infallible because it is final. Inevitably the Court will speak again. But the High Court's imprimatur has given new strength to Second Amendment fundamentalism. Increasingly the debate over guns resembles less a contest over crime policy, and more a culture war over core values.

Through it all, we see how the great themes of American history rise and recur: the role of government. Race. Freedom. The singular power of the Supreme Court. Most strikingly, the fact that our view of the Second Amendment is set, at each stage, not by a pristine constitutional text, but by the push-and-pull, the rough-and-tumble of political advocacy and public agitation.

But first, we should start by understanding why we have a Second Amendment in the first place. That story begins in the heat of revolution, sixteen miles outside Boston.

PART
ONE

PART
ONE

ONE

Patriots' Day

On April 18, 1775, Boston was an occupied city. Ringed with checkpoints and sentries, jammed with imperial troops of the world's strongest army, the town of sixteen thousand was swollen with five thousand British soldiers. It was also latticed with spies and revolutionary committees. That afternoon, word came from several sources: the British regulars would march the next day. Dr. Joseph Warren, a Patriot organizer, hurried to verify this with the rebels' best-placed informant, presumed by historians to be the American wife of British general Thomas Gage. She confirmed: the army regulars would leave town that night. They would cross the Back Bay, and march through the villages outside Boston. They would seek to arrest John Hancock and Samuel Adams, two garrulous Patriot leaders, in hiding in the countryside.

Most important, the British would come for the colonists' guns: the store of gunpowder, cannons, and weaponry carefully stored by the local militia in the town of Concord, sixteen miles northwest of Boston. Because weapons rusted easily at home, and because black powder could explode, the colonists kept arms in a common area, easily accessible to the militia for drilling and use.

We know of the ride that night of the silversmith Paul Revere: the lighting of two lanterns on the steeple of North Church. (An Anglican church, so a dissident minister slipped Patriots into the steeple past the senior minister.) The trip across the Charles with muffled oars. The dash across the hills. Revere did not ride alone. In fact, he and several others set off an elaborate chain of messengers, at least thirty in all. It was known as the Lexington Alarm. When a messenger reached a village, the leaders of the town government would assemble and vote on the next steps. Some of the militias were organized as "Minute Men," trained to muster within seconds at the sound of the alarm.

The next morning, eight hundred British Army regulars marched two by two in resplendent red through the hills, toward the arms depot at Concord. As they advanced, they heard echoing gunfire, church bells, the sound of a countryside on alert. Militia members from the village of Lexington had gathered at one in the morning, standing guard for an hour. When the British failed to show, they repaired to a tavern. After several hours, possibly worse for wear, they heard unnerving news: the British were coming, after all. As the regulars marched past Lexington, seventy somewhat ragged men stood ready on the green. A rattled British commander rode back and forth before the rows of farmers, brandishing his sword. One witness heard him yell, "Lay down your arms, ye damned rebels." The Americans began to straggle away. Someone, perhaps a bystander, fired a single shot. Amid confusion, the regulars gunned down eighteen colonists. Firing a victory volley and bellowing three cheers customary after a successful battle, the regulars continued their march to Concord. This time, to their astonishment, militias from across Middlesex County had streamed to the hillsides surrounding the town. The colonists repulsed the British and drove them back. As the soldiers retreated to Charlestown, militiamen assailed them on a harrowing seven-hour march.

Today, our picture of that moment focuses on solitary individuals. The villager, roused from bed, grabbing a musket. Stodgy British troops harassed by patriotic shopkeepers defending their homes. "The farmers gave them ball for ball," Longfellow wrote, "From behind each fence and farmyard-wall." That image lives on in the statue of the Minute Man on Lexington Green, or the Daniel French statue in Concord. (In recent years, the National Rifle Association mailed its life members a tiny replica of the Lexington statue.)

But behind this portrait of the solitary fighting farmer stood a far more complex reality. The militia of April 19, 1775, was a well-organized military force, well trained, and woven firmly into the fabric of colonial government. Historian David Hackett Fischer explains in his authoritative study: "The fighting on this day was not merely an open running skirmish along the Battle Road. It was also a series of controlled engagements, in which the Middlesex farmers fought as members of formal military units." General John R. Galvin, former U.S. commander of NATO, studied the battle. He estimates that four thousand militiamen from fourteen regiments attacked the British that day—part of the fourteen-thousand-man Massachusetts military force that marched toward Boston as the alarm spread.

In its first weeks, as the Revolution matched the British Army against the colonial militias, the militias' prestige soared. Word spread of their feat against the world's most fearsome army. To many Americans, this was not only a moment of high pride and patriotic fervor. They saw their worst fear unfolding: a tyrannical standing army, pitted against a phalanx of citizen soldiers. For Americans of that time, "hearing the Lexington Alarm" froze memories, akin to recalling where you were when you first learned of Pearl Harbor or the terrorist attacks of 9/11. This was the apogee of the well regulated militia, comprised of farmers and innkeepers, that not only defended their towns but defined the republican ideal of active, virtuous citizenship.

THE WELL REGULATED MILITIA

With its odd syntax, the Second Amendment gives the whiff of an urgent, impassioned point being made in a long forgotten argument. Why does it start with homage to the "well regulated militia"? How does that relate to the "right to keep and bear arms"? Who are "the people"? To understand the history of the Second Amendment, we start by understanding the role of those militias—and just as important, what Americans thought of them. The Second Amendment is after all a product of a particular time and place: a world with clear, plain distinctions between militias ("well regulated" and otherwise) and armies. It comes to us from a moment when ordinary citizens were expected to bear arms for the community. Few parts of the life of Revolutionary Era Americans seem more distant.

Given the intense debate over the Second Amendment today, it is striking to see the tactical, even offhand maneuvers that led to its enactment. The young men who crafted the Constitution were the first American political leaders to feel the force of public distrust. They did what politicians do when faced with a difficult electorate: they weaved, and retreated, and gave up as much as necessary and as little as possible.

At times we squint in search of a missing character. Where is the grand conversation about the individual's right to own a gun? Two centuries later, details and meaning can seem murky. The Framers, we know, cared about posterity. Still, they might well be startled to see and hear how later generations read, and misread, their goals and tactics as they pushed a new constitution into being.

First, some definitions. Militias were military forces drawn from the citizenry—largely the yeoman farmers who owned their own property and worked their own land. In England, and then even more so in the colonies, militia service was a universal expectation. Men from sixteen to sixty were required to join a company, and train intermittently. They were expected to own and bring their own gun. They were not *allowed* to have a musket; they were *required* to. More than a right, being armed was a duty.

Militias had a long history among the English-speaking peoples. The idea of a sturdy social class of property-owning militia members was far from fanciful. Compared to the Continent, with its foppish aristocrats and vast numbers of unhappy peasants, British law and custom led to a wider distribution of property. Over time, the idea of the militia anchored a full-fledged political philosophy. Historians called it civic republicanism, and it played a larger role than we realize in the formation of the American colonies. Niccolò Machiavelli's ideas were widely influential. In *The Art of War* he promoted the idea of an armed force drawn from citizenry. So, too, were those of the philosopher James Harrington. He wrote what can only be described as a book of science fiction about a commonwealth called Oceana. His book lauded the imaginary land where the infantry was made up of the "yeomanry or middle people."

We have long imagined that the colonists were scrappy individualists, focused on a notion of personal freedom that would put them at home in our century. Historians Bernard Bailyn and Gordon S. Wood have forcefully shown us a different picture: the colonists believed powerfully in duty and civic responsibility. They were heavily influenced by so-called radical British political thought, developed during struggles between Parliament and the king in the century before 1775. They took with deadly seriousness the ideas of no taxation without representation, the rule of law, and the dangers of a standing army. Before the Revolution, that took the form of a devoted, even exaggerated fealty to the political ideas of a country few colonists had ever visited. One crucial difference divided the British militia from its bumptious American cousin. In England, the most dependable people were culled into a select militia— a "trained band"—for ongoing service. In the colonies, militia service was for everyone. (All white men, that is.)

For today's readers, it can be slightly dizzying to read the raptures induced in colonial era writers by the ideal of a militia. Sir Francis Bacon, in 1622, wrote, "England, though far less in territory and population, hath been (nevertheless) an overmatch; in regard the middle people of England make good soldiers, which the peasants of France do not." Adam Smith in *The Wealth of Nations*, writing in 1776, intoned, "In a militia, the character of the labourer, artificer, or tradesman, predominates over that of the soldier: in a standing army, that of the soldier predominates over every other character." Americans ladled it on even more thickly.

Another institution stood as the self-evident opposite to virtuous, egalitarian militias: a standing army.

In Britain and elsewhere, the king commanded the army, which stood alongside the militias. Soldiers were paid. They were professionals who signed up for a fixed time, were drilled in discipline and obedience, and had no job beyond their military service. Few property owners would dream of enlisting for such a tour of duty. The king could send his army across the country or overseas. One writer explained that regular army soldiers were "a species of animals, wholly at the disposal of government." Unlike the yeoman farmers who became intermittent militiamen, army soldiers were the "dregs of the people." Forced through punishment into submission, they survived on discipline. Armies were also expensive. Parliament raised taxes to support them. Give a king an army, it was thought, and he would find a war to fight. One colonist explained, "Money is required to levy armies, and armies to levy money; and foreign wars are introduced as the pretended occupation for both." People of 1775 did not see the army the way we might today—as a noble embodiment of patriotic spirit, or a force that binds a nation together. They saw the army as tyranny in the making, authoritarianism on the march. To the people of Boston, under military occupation, the British Army was not a representative of "us" but an oppressive force sent by "them."

Since the arrival of English settlers in the New World, militias organized by colonial governments provided security and order. Colonists formed militias as soon as they arrived. A colonial era writer explained that for New Englanders, the "near neighbourhood of the Indians and French quickly taught them the necessity of having a well regulated militia." From the earliest settlements in Plymouth and Massachusetts Bay Colonies, every male automatically enlisted in the militia when he turned sixteen. They were required to bring their own gun. (If they could not afford one, they could buy one on credit.) They mustered often, drilled frequently, and were called up at the service of the colonial governor. At times of emergency, the militias could "impress" or draft ablebodied men to go off and fight. At first, throughout the colonies, militias included nonwhite men. As the slave population grew, though, Southern colonies decided to limit membership. In New England, militias elected their commanding officers, and often decided tactics (such as whether to join in a battle) after ample discussion and a vote.

Sturdy, virtuous, calling forth the patriotic efforts of a nation of farmers: that was what colonial Americans told themselves about their militias. Even then, much mythologizing mixed with fact.

Despite the valorous imagery, the militias were often a rusted instrument of defense. At times they were balky. The French and Indian War of 1754–63 required an invasion of Canada; some northeastern militias refused the king's call. Connecticut Colony's governor even supported the militia's opposition to action.

And though the militias were supposed to be universal, in fact the wealthy and well-born could wriggle out of service. Some paid others to do their time. Exemptions and excuses abounded (the kind that would be familiar in a later era): those in college, or "with important business" could stay home. During the French and Indian War, all able-bodied men were supposed to join a militia. One military historian notes "it seems never to have crossed the introspective mind of young John Adams that he was exactly the right age to serve."

Another problem reared often: too few guns of the right type. Weapons were not cheap, and most Americans allocated their scarce resources to guns that were lighter to carry and more useful for shooting birds or killing vermin. Colonial legislatures repeatedly passed laws requiring able-bodied men to obtain military-quality muskets, and repeatedly nothing happened. In some colonies, militia members demanded that government provide guns. They were hard to keep in working order, and their aim was inaccurate. The colonies had few gun factories. Many militiamen showed up at Lexington Green without military weapons.

In the decades before the Revolution, militias had declined in importance. "When no danger was in the offing," historian Edmund Morgan recounts, "training day was a boisterous holiday, accompanied by light talk, heavy drinking, and precious little training." Some urged greater discipline. "But most Americans were content with the festivity and the easier, looser variety of subordination that went with training days, when the soldiers delighted in surrounding a pretty girl and firing their muskets in the air, while officers dashed about in glittering uniforms that bespoke social rank more than military prowess."

Britain's Stamp Act of 1765 changed that. London had sent the army to secure the western frontier in the French and Indian War. Now it sought to pay for it. Parliament, frustrated by resistance from across the Atlantic, began to ratchet up taxes and punitive laws. What followed was a cascade of miscalculations, with new taxes and rules from London, increasingly bold resistance by colonists, retreat and newly tightened imperial screws by the crown. Suddenly the colonial militias were vital, even dangerous. Whig militias, opposed to the crown, began to elect Whig officers. Training, recruitment, maneuvers, and marching stepped up. Britain imposed an arms embargo. Colonists began to buy and collect guns, smuggling them from the Continent. In 1774, Parliament passed the Coercive Acts, designed to tighten pressure on New England. Massachusetts's Provincial Congress responded. It formed the Committee of Safety, stockpiled arms, and required all men between sixteen and fifty to "enlist." Some communities formed "Minute Men." Gunpowder (some of it stolen from the British) was stored as "common stock." In Lexington, for example, townspeople kept the powder beneath the pulpit in the Congregational meetinghouse. Throughout 1774, Americans gathered in large, patriotic militia parades up and down the colonies.

By the clash at Lexington and Concord the next spring, the militias had revived as an established system of defense. Many men had fought in the war against the French, or had been engaged in battle on the fringes of empire. They drilled in tactics learned in a century of combat. Now as panic spread throughout New England, militias from neighboring towns and colonies mobilized and descended upon Boston. Some twenty thousand citizen soldiers from throughout New England ringed the hillsides overlooking the city. Two months later, the British Army tried to break out of Boston by seizing Breed's Hill in Charlestown. After two tries, the regulars took the high ground, but they won a Pyrrhic victory in the battle named after the proximate Bunker Hill, with staggering losses. The revolutionary government of Massachusetts enacted a law strengthening the requirement that men between sixteen and fifty enroll, train, and join their militia. They were required to bring their own weapons and equipment. The colonies were swept up in what a French visitor called a *Rage Militaire,* an infatuation with the militias that led even noncombatants to dress in rough-hewn militia garb.

In these first days of revolution, Americans reveled in the thought that "the people" were at last facing off against a monarch. As we grapple with the thought of the Founding generation, it can be hard to reckon with the degree to which this notion of the whole people takes on a misty, sentimental quality. One is reminded of the homages to "the people" in, say, Popular Front folksongs of the 1930s. "The people" were sovereign, and not only were the source of legitimacy for the government, but were expected to carry the burden of making—and defending—the government, too. The set of ideas we now know as "liberalism"—an efficient and strong government, chosen by the people but not intimately involved with them, with individual liberties being protected above all in a continent-wide market economy: that lay in the future.

In a time when political equality was only vaguely embraced, the militia was one way for colonists to express a yearning for democracy. The revolutionaries who assumed control of state governments in 1775 and 1776 wrote new constitutions, many enshrining the militia, and making clear that ordinary citizens were to bear arms in its service.

Consider the Declaration of Rights passed by the Virginia legislature in the spring of 1776. This document famously began by declaring, "all men are by nature equally free and independent, and have certain inherent rights . . . namely, the enjoyment of life and liberty, with the means of acquiring and possessing property, and pursuing and obtaining happiness and safety," language borrowed (and edited) by Thomas Jefferson for the Declaration of Independence a few weeks later. Virginia's declaration continued, explaining the role of the militia and army in this new constitutional vision:

> *That a well-regulated Militia, composed of the body of the people, trained to arms, is the proper, natural, and safe defence of a free State; that Standing Armies, in time of peace, should be avoided, as dangerous to liberty; and that in all cases the military should be under strict subordination to, and governed by, the civil power.*

In the Old Dominion, plantation owners ruled. It was assumed that the "better" men would predominate. What about states beyond Virginia? Pennsylvania's new government was far more radical. Dominated by western backwoodsmen and "mechanics" from Philadelphia, it gave the vote to all male adults, even those without property. Military service spanned all classes: so should political power. A Philadelphia editorial explained that the vote should belong to "every man who pays his shot, and bears his lot." Pennsylvania's charter provided for military service, but omitted homage to the "well-regulated militia." Instead, it declared "that the people have a right to bear arms for the defense of themselves and the State." John Adams principally drafted the new Massachusetts constitution. It included elaborate procedures for election of militia officers, and revised Pennsylvania's language to make clear that citizens could "keep" as well as "bear" arms, but only in the "common defence." (John was the attorney Adams. He had seen the power of rampaging mobs, used to such effect by his cousin Samuel in the years before the Revolution.) Of note, these declarations of rights were appended to the state constitutions. They amounted to exhortations, rather than legally binding commands. As such, they open a window on the thinking of the colonists as they became citizens of a new country.

That spring of 1775 marked the high point for militias, and for the vision that a citizen force—of men pulled away from home, carrying their own weapons—could match the professionalism of a trained fighting force. For a few months, at least, that seemed plausible. Reality soon intruded.

THE FORGE OF THE REVOLUTIONARY WAR

Wars change many things. They reorder thinking, teach hard lessons, jumble social classes. Certainly the American Revolution did that. Among other things, it instantly began to school its leaders in the limits of the much romanticized militia system and the role of the citizen soldier. The men who wrote the Constitution in 1787 were not the same men they were when they rebelled against the crown in 1775.

Weeks after the bloodshed at Lexington and Concord, the Second Continental Congress convened in Philadelphia. It was a war Congress; its principal challenge, to raise and maintain a fighting force. Immediately it struggled with how to wage a continent-wide conflict against a professional army with a ragtag force of temporary militias.

Virginia congressman George Washington started the conflict already a skeptic. He had been a leader in the Virginia militia, even as he built his plantation and expanded his businesses. As a young man, Washington even took part in the bumbling first expedition to the Ohio Valley that kindled the French and Indian War (which became a global conflict, known in Europe as the Seven Years War). This early unhappy experience marked and humiliated Washington. Like many colonials, he chafed when treated poorly by British regulars. He never received the officer's commission in the British Army he craved. But the militias proved as frustrating. When he procured uniforms for that expedition, his troops promptly sold them. Fewer than one in ten of the Augusta County militiamen summoned into action actually showed up. George Washington began the Revolution with fewer illusions than most.

Still, he arrived at the Continental Congress incongruously clad in a flashy blue and gold militia uniform. This profoundly impressed his new colleagues. John Adams wrote his wife, Abigail, "Colonel Washington appears at Congress in his uniform, and by his great experience and abilities in military matters is of so much service to us." Dr. Benjamin Rush explained to a friend, "He has so much martial dignity in his deportment that you would distinguish him to be a general and a soldier from among ten thousand people. There is not a king in Europe that would not look like a valet de chambre by his side." Congress saw political wisdom to have the fighting force at Boston led by a Virginian. It elected Washington commander in chief of a new national army.

Washington quickly traveled north. He arrived at Cambridge, determined to transform the patchwork of New England militias into something more. Congress had formally incorporated the local forces into an "American Continental Army." To his new troops, Washington proclaimed that soldiers drawn from the colonies were "now the troops of the United Provinces of North America and it is hoped that all distinctions of colonies will be laid aside." But as he rode through the camp he found chaos. Militia units were paralyzed by debate. Few gave orders, or followed them. Conditions were filthy. He wrote his brother despairingly that he had found an "army of provincials under very little command, discipline, or order." Washington was unnerved to learn that the New England militias elected their officers. Shopkeepers and farmers predominated. He expressed his surprise that Massachusetts officers "are *nearly* of the same kidney with the privates." He could not persuade Congress to appoint the officers, instead of allowing the governments of each state to do so. In vain he tried to obtain enough cloth to make a common uniform.

Washington's troops scored a decisive early victory when they captured fifty-nine cannon from Fort Ticonderoga in upstate New York and dragged them three hundred miles to Boston. The sudden arrival of artillery pointed at the city from Dorchester Heights panicked the British, who abandoned Boston and relocated to New York. Perhaps a force of militiamen, carrying their own arms and drawn from civilian life, might be enough to prevail after all. But the next year taught harsh lessons. Men deserted en masse. "Whole divisions," reports biographer Ron Chernow, "scampered away in fear." When enlistments expired, usually after one year, militiamen simply left for home. The militias barely escaped the disastrous Battle of Brooklyn when the British pushed them across the river into Manhattan. From the heights of Harlem, preparing to evacuate once again, Washington wrote Congress in September 1776:

> To place any dependence upon Militia, is, assuredly, resting upon a broken staff. Men just dragged from the tender scenes of domestic life; unaccustomed to the din of arms; totally unacquainted with every kind of military skill ... [are] timid and ready to fly from their own shadows. Besides, the sudden change in their manner of living ... produces shameful, and scandalous desertions. ... Certain I am, that it would be cheaper to keep

50,000 or 100,000 men in constant pay than to depend upon half the number, and supply the other half occasionally by militia.

Washington's frankness was not universal. Others flattered the citizen soldiers in public, and scorned them in private. General Charles Lee was a rival for power; even today, Fort Lee stares across the Hudson at Washington Heights. At first, the British-born Lee curried popular favor with his homages to the militia. In 1775, he wrote letters designed for newspaper circulation praising the grit and skill of the Americans, "the zeal and alacrity of the militia." By the next year, he, too, had changed his tune. "As to the Minute Men," he now wrote privately, "no account ought to be made of them. Had I been as much acquainted with them when they were summoned as I am at present, I should have exerted myself to prevent their coming."

Lawmakers fitfully tried to help. Congress drafted the Articles of Confederation to govern the new nation. "Every State," they intoned, "shall always keep up a well-regulated and disciplined militia, sufficiently armed and accoutered, and shall provide and constantly have ready for use, in public stores, a due number of field pieces and tents, and a proper quantity of arms, ammunition and camp equipage." Little happened. Conscription, explains historian Charles Royster, "remained primarily a technique for determining who would hire a substitute rather than for allotting military service." Pamphleteers continued to churn out paeans to the civic spirit of the militiamen, each bearing their own musket brought from home. But only one third of the American forces that won the Battle of Yorktown and ended the war were from the militia. The ranks of the Continental Army were filled with the poor, including black men, indentured servants, and city dwellers. Commissary General Jeremiah Wadsworth reported to Congress that the Continental Army was comprised of "very idle and very worthless fellows, which did not hinder them from doing their duty."

Other revolutionary leaders quickly grew disillusioned with the idea that militias would be enough. The firebrand Samuel Adams, who had been at Lexington, now fretted, "Would any Man in his Senses, who wishes the War may be carried on with Vigor, prefer the temporary and expensive drafts of militia to a permanent and well-appointed army!" Thomas Jefferson, serving as governor of Virginia, despaired about the weakness of the militia. Men refused to leave their state, and discovered sudden maladies. "I had as many sore legs, hipshots, broken backs etc. produced as there were men ordered to go," he groused.

For the Americans on the home front, though, the militias' prestige remained high. They provided security, serving as an internal police force. Militias kept order, rousted (and punished) Tory sympathizers, and warded off Indians on the frontier. In parts of the country they harassed British troops in guerrilla warfare for years, skirmishing with as few as a dozen troops and then melting into the countryside. Whig (Patriot) and Tory (Loyalist) militias flailed at each other throughout, pillaging and engaging in brutal atrocities on both sides. The ferment of war posed special challenges in the slave society of the South. The British had offered freedom to slaves owned by rebels who escaped and crossed the lines to fight with the British Army, and thousands did so. The threat of slave rebellion hung heavily. In the South, militias were beefed up to enforce the plantation system.

For Washington and the young men around him, the war began a lifelong project to forge a national army and a national identity. "In the early stages of this war," he later wrote, "I used every means in my power to destroy all kind of state distinctions and labored to have every part and parcel of the army considered as continental."

"THE CRITICAL PERIOD"

With the war's end, public distrust of a strong government reasserted itself. Not for the last time, Americans found themselves ambivalent about the army that had just fought on their behalf. Communities celebrated with giant feasts, but to use a phrase familiar from later less popular wars, there were no victory parades. Congress disbanded the Continental Army. Demobilization unfolded in near chaos. Promised pensions went unpaid. States began to squabble about who would pay the veterans. There was an undertow of possible conflict between the military and civilians.

By March 1783, mutinous Continental Army officers edged close to staging a putsch. Outraged by Congress's unwillingness to provide back pay and promised pensions, they prepared an armed march on Philadelphia. Washington surprised the mutineers at a meeting in Newburgh, New York. This, he told them, was not what they had fought for. He implored the still skeptical officers not to "open the flood Gates of Civil discord, and deluge our rising Empire in Blood." The restive troops sat unmoved. Then Washington, an avid theatergoer, turned to drama. Fumbling to read a letter, the fifty-one-year-old general reached into his pocket and put on reading glasses. His men gasped: few had seen Washington wear them before. "Gentlemen," he said gravely, "you must pardon me. I have grown gray in your service and now find myself growing blind." The meeting dissolved in tears and protestations of loyalty to Washington. Historians often cite the incident as evidence of Washington's forceful if opaque character—his willingness to forgo power, thus gaining it. To contemporaries, the Newburgh Conspiracy, quickly so dubbed, underscored something more: the dangers to republicanism posed by men on horseback. General Washington saw the threat, even if his rum-fortified officers did not.

Newburgh offered evidence of what could happen when professional soldiers were set adrift after a war. It was not the only omen. When news finally arrived from Paris of the peace treaty with Britain, recruits deserted and stormed the Pennsylvania State House, demanding payment. Congress fled to Princeton, New Jersey. After the peace, former army officers formed the Society of the Cincinnati. Membership would pass on to their sons. Conspiracy-minded civilians fretted the group could be an aristocracy in the making, or a cabal ready to seize control. Mercy Warren, an early American historian, wrote a London acquaintance bemoaning the influence of the Society of the Cincinnati. In America, she reported, "the young ardent spirits . . . cry out for monarchy."

Washington returned to private life. Before he left he sketched out a plan for a Continental Militia, enlisting all adult men but requiring a small group of the best to serve for one month a year. The idea went nowhere. Neither did other proposals. In Virginia, Washington persuaded the state's governor—the legendary patriotic orator Patrick Henry—to find appointments for Continental Army veterans as officers of the militia. Furious local dignitaries, deprived of the status that came from officer rank, howled. The next year the legislature repealed the law and gave the epaulets back to the civilians.

Meanwhile, the weak central government under the Articles of Confederation began to fray. States could and did veto federal action. Taxes went uncollected. States competed with each other for commerce and land. The Articles themselves could not be changed without unanimous agreement among the states. Twelve states agreed that Congress should have the power to levy a 5 percent impost tax on imports to pay war debts and fund the government. Rhode Island vetoed it. John Quincy Adams, delivering the commencement address at Harvard College in 1787, called it the "critical period."

A portent of anarchy came in 1786. Farmers faced ruinous debts as the economy plummeted after the war. States raised taxes to levels far higher than before independence. Foreclosures and bankruptcy followed. In rural Western Massachusetts, protesters led by Daniel Shays refused to submit to the power of the judiciary. They formed a movement called the Regulators (how that phrase would change meaning!) that marched on the state courts to prevent bankruptcy proceedings. When the Bay State governor ordered the militia to break up the mob, it refused to do so. "Notwithstanding the most pressing orders," the local officer reported, "there did appear universally that reluctance in the people to turn out for the support of government." A few weeks later, the governor ordered militiamen to march into Great Barrington, after protesters seized the courthouse. This time, the citizen soldiers took a vote. Most joined forces with the protesters. Finally, early in 1787, the governor found it necessary to raise a special militia, funded by Boston merchants. When an agrarian army of 1,500 farmers tried to seize the federal government's armory in Springfield, the state's rump military force did battle and suppressed the Regulators.

Shays' Rebellion and the feeble response to it sent shivers. Militias represented the new country's military force. But if they could not put down civil unrest—or be counted on not to switch sides—how could the nation hold together? Delegates to a conference in Annapolis, Maryland, called to revise the tariff policies, already had proposed a new gathering to meet in Philadelphia. The clashes between the farmers and the militia alarmed Washington. Friends sent him an increasingly frenzied and often inaccurate stream of reports about Shays' Rebellion and its implications. Properly rattled, Washington agreed to travel to Philadelphia for the new federal conclave, giving it the legitimacy it needed. It would become the Constitutional Convention.

THE CONSTITUTIONAL CONVENTION: THE ARMY VERSUS THE PEOPLE

One young man could not wait for the convention to begin: Virginian James Madison arrived early, ten days before any other out-of-town delegate.

Slight, sickly, Madison made his way in life through study and ingratiation. He had traveled to attend college at Princeton, New Jersey, where he read deeply in the classics. He was a painful public speaker, tending to mumble, and was a bit of a hypochondriac. Madison never served in the military. But as a state legislator in Virginia, he made himself useful to Washington, and became a protégé, one of the great man's succession of surrogate sons. He was far advanced in thinking about rights, and fought for religious freedom in Virginia. But he was alarmed by the collapse of governmental authority in the new country. Together with New York's Alexander Hamilton, another young nationalist, he maneuvered to have the convention called, to drum up attendance, and to make sure it was seen as a major turning. And once it had been scheduled, he drove himself to study world political systems, trying to understand how republics rise or fall. Thomas Jefferson sent him two hundred books from Paris for the cram session. Even before arriving in Philadelphia, Madison had sketched out a new approach, one with a strong central government and power divided among three branches: legislative, executive, and judicial. (In a letter he confessed to Washington he had not thought much about the executive branch, except that the new government should dominate the militia.) Madison had come to believe that power checked power, and that a muscular government could be consistent with liberty if structured properly. Above all, he felt it vital that national government "enlarge the sphere." A government that spread across territory would be less likely to fall prey to faction. Congress, not the states, would reign. Only it could "control the centrifugal tendency of the states; which, without it, will continually fly out of their proper orbits," he said at another point. It was a vision that could horrify older Americans who believed that virtue would be enough to prevent tyranny, if government were kept small.

Madison and the other Virginians closeted themselves at the Indian Queen Tavern in Philadelphia, and put in writing a blueprint for a new national system that echoed Madison's ideas. Introduced by the state's governor, Edmund Randolph, it became known as the Virginia Plan, and it formed the basis for the new government of the United States of America.

Delegates gathered in the same room on the ground floor of the Pennsylvania State House where independence had been declared: even then, symbolically powerful territory. Most newspapers worried they would not go far enough, given their charge merely to look at the Articles of Confederation and recommend changes. The convention voted to elect Washington as its president, and to deliberate in secret. The doors closed. Even windows were shut, to avoid eavesdropping, leading to stifling heat in an otherwise cool summer. Not until a new proposed constitution was released publicly four months later did word leak of the convention's work.

Washington sat impassively in the chair, facing the rows of delegates. Madison sat just below him, intently taking notes. Historians long have sifted motives behind the calling of the Constitutional Convention. Were the Framers patriots stopping the slide toward a failed state? Did the delegates wrest power in a creditors' coup, seeking to protect their investments, as Progressive Era historians alleged? Regardless, as Madison scanned the high-ceilinged room, he could see that those who sought a strong national government were present in force. Young men who had served in the great cause dominated the gathering. Fully one third had served as officers in the Continental Army. In the eventual fight for ratification, many of the most influential backers of the Constitution were a decade younger than those who opposed it. Repeatedly, on issue after issue, a core of delegates led by Madison thrust toward the creation of a more powerful central government. Madison, though hardly alone, was among the most ardent. If he had had his way, the federal government would have had a veto over laws passed by the states. (Many who laud him as "Father of the Constitution" might strip him of the title if they knew what he actually favored.) Others struggled to balance their desire for order and national energy with older, deep distrust of centralized power.

Through the summer of 1787, the delegates crafted a series of intricate compromises. Never before had a nation built its new political institutions entirely from scratch, sketching the structure in writing long before it took shape in reality. Repeatedly delegates picked at vexing questions about the nature of the new government: What power to levy taxes would it have? How to apportion representation? Small states insisted that they retain equality in the new government, as they had in the Articles of Confederation. Virginia would have abandoned equal standing among the states and replaced it with a system based on proportional representation according to population. (New Jersey's rival plan would have retained the country as a league of sovereign states. It was defeated.) Midsummer, delegates brokered the Great Compromise, which created a House elected by the people and a Senate representing states. The thicket of questions were handed off to a deliciously named Committee of Detail, which worked for two weeks and offered a draft constitution. Delegates still referred to it as "the plan," as if calling it something more would reveal the audacity of their work.

As the delegates pored over the document, a particularly elaborate section addressed the question of the new nation's armed forces. As ratified, the Constitution gives Congress the power:

> *To raise and support Armies, but no Appropriation of Money to that Use shall be for a longer Term than two Years;*
>
> *To provide and maintain a Navy;*
>
> *To make Rules for the Government and Regulation of the land and naval Forces;*
>
> *To provide for calling forth the Militia to execute the Laws of the Union, suppress Insurrections and repel Invasions;*
>
> *To provide for organizing, arming, and disciplining, the Militia, and for governing such Part of them as may be employed in the Service of the United States, reserving to the States respectively, the Appointment of the Officers, and the Authority of training the Militia according to the discipline prescribed by Congress.*

As we read the Constitution today, it is easy to skip over this oddly precise language. To the Framers, these paragraphs were exceedingly important. Some delegates sought to move decisively toward an army—paid, trained, professionalized. Others clung to the belief that state militias were more representative of the people, and provided a check on a possibly overweening central government. Most were torn: they yearned for an effective national force, yet felt protective of the state militias, and were eager to profess their continued fealty to the ideal.

They envisioned a complex dual system. The country's safety could still be trusted to the militias, rooted in the thirteen states, with their citizen soldiers and stashed-at-home weapons. But the president could command the militias when the Congress called them into federal service. Congress would set the rules for discipline and arming the militias, even though they were state government functions. And there could be, when necessary, an army. This was, in one degree, a radical shift from traditional republican theory: moving ultimate command of the militias from the states to a national government. A division of military authority among the president, the Congress, and the states would check danger.

To the delegates, fear of a standing army was not abstract. The British Army had sailed away just five years before. That dread, and the earnest belief in militias as an alternative, permeated the records of the Constitutional Convention. When it spilled out into public debate, it led directly to the Second Amendment.

Delegates tried to counter the possible abuse of federal power in several ways. For example, they limited funding for an army to no more than two years. This time limit was designed to prevent establishment of a permanent force, with an endless drain on the treasury. Constitutional scholar Akhil Reed Amar notes, "The particular two-year cutoff meshed perfectly with the gears of the Constitution's electoral clock, which would bring the entire House membership before the American electorate every two years." The Constitution imposes a similar funding curb on no other governmental function. Congress, too, has the power to declare war (not the president). Of note, the Constitution also tried to harness federalism as a check on centralized military power. If a president on horseback or a rampaging Congress were tempted to use a U.S. Army as an oppressive force, the state militias—made up of armed freemen— would stand in their way.

But some delegates still found the role of the national military to be unchecked and unbalanced. This fear of a standing army, and reverence for the militias, flashed into one of the most intense debates late that summer, after the most significant issues of representation had already been resolved. The most passionate critic was Elbridge Gerry of Massachusetts. As he comes to us through history, he was excitable, at times a crank. Much constitutional history can be read, among other things, as an effort—at first polite, increasingly frustrated—to placate Gerry and fend off his interjections.

Throughout the summer, Gerry assaulted the new Constitution's military order, each fusillade noisier than the last. At one point he proposed that the Constitution prohibit a standing army larger than "two or three

thousand" men. George Washington had sat immobile through nearly
the entire summer. Reportedly he turned and in a stage whisper proposed the Constitution include a provision declaring "no foreign enemy
should invade the United States at any time, with more than three thousand troops." Perhaps jolted by the great man's rare intervention, the delegates rejected Gerry's motion. Gerry's pithiest attack does not appear in
Madison's straight-faced notes, but comes to us through oral tradition.
"A standing army is like a standing member," he supposedly gibed. "An
excellent assurance of domestic tranquility, but a dangerous temptation
to foreign adventure." Still, despite Gerry's demands, the Constitution
nowhere actually barred a standing peacetime army—a sign of how far
its center had shifted from traditional republican ideas.

The provisions governing militias proved even more contentious.
Would states still run them, or would control shift to the federal government? Just a few years after a devastating war, months after Shays'
Rebellion, fears were raw. The committee draft gave Congress power to
summon the militia to "subdue a rebellion in any state on the application
of its legislature." One delegate proposed letting the national government step in without state approval. Gerry held back little. "One senses
the excitement in this slight, nervous man, the frown etched deeply, the
hands stiff with tension," writes Catherine Drinker Bowen in *Miracle
at Philadelphia*. Borrowing an image from Homer's *Iliad*, he warned of
the risks of "letting loose the myrmidons of the United States on a state
without its own consent. More blood would have been spilt in Massachusetts in the late insurrection [Shays' Rebellion] if the General Government had intermeddled." As Gerry fulminated—a performance that
still leaps off the pages of Madison's deadpan notes—New Yorker Gou-
verneur Morris replied calmly. "We first form a strong man to protect us,
and at the same time wish to tie his hands behind him." Eventually the
requirement for state legislative approval was removed.

Originally the August 6 draft gave Congress the power to "call forth
the aid of the militia" but not to set its rules. Virginia delegate George
Mason repeatedly urged that more power over the militia be given to the

general government. "Thirteen states will never concur in any one system, if the disciplining of the militia is left in their hands." Madison made clear he thought the national government had too little authority over the state military establishment. Others recoiled. John Dickinson of Pennsylvania proposed that no more than one quarter of the militia be under federal control at any one time. Connecticut's Oliver Ellsworth defused the conflict with an aside. "The states will never submit to the same militia laws. Three or four shillings as a penalty will enforce obedience better in New England, than forty lashes in some other places." (Jokes about skinflint Yankees and sadistic slave owners counted as ethnic humor in 1787.)

On August 23, tempers frayed as the delegates engaged in their most direct debate over the role of the military and an armed citizenry. The drafting committee now had proposed to give Congress power to "make laws for organizing, arming & disciplining the militia." To let the national government set rules and organize the militia, the notes show Gerry insisting, "is making the states drill-seargents. He had as lief let the Citizens of Massachusetts be disarmed, as to take the command from the States, and subject them to the General Legislature. It would be regarded a system of Despotism." Madison looked up from his notetaking to reply: he "observed that 'arming' . . . did not extend to furnishing arms. . . . The primary object is to secure an effectual discipline of the militia." Already, states "neglect their militia. . . . The Discipline of the Militia is evidently a *National* concern, and ought to be provided for in the *National* Constitution." Madison proposed that the national government be able to appoint senior militia officers. This, to Gerry, posed an ultimate threat to state sovereignty. "Let us at once destroy the State Govts," he declared with heavy sarcasm, "have an Executive for life or hereditary, and a proper Senate, and then there would be some consistency in giving [this power] to the Genl Govt."

The debates showed how far the war and especially its aftermath had scrambled traditional thinking. Previously all republicans assumed that militias, locally controlled, would be closer to the people, less prone to corruption and abuse. By 1787, though, it became clear that local militias might side with local troublemakers, as they had during Shays' Rebellion. Even the militias, scholar David Williams notes, might become seditious. The shift to a national army, with federal control over the militia, was both logical and radical. To the men of the convention, an effective government required it, however humbly they tipped their tricorn hats to the public's pride in its hometown fighting forces.

As the deliberations drew to a close, opponents realized with mounting alarm that their chances to make substantial changes were dwindling. George Mason had declared earlier in the summer he would "sooner chop off his right hand than put it to the Constitution as it now stands." He scribbled a list of objections on the back of a draft that had been produced by the Committee on Style, seeking to persuade the Maryland delegation to oppose the plan: where was a bill of rights? In the last week before the final vote, Mason rose to complain to the full convention. A bill of rights "would give great quiet to the people; and with the aid of the State declarations, a bill might be prepared in a few hours," he insisted. Gerry backed him.

The convention rejected the idea of a bill of rights. Every state voted no. The architects of the new government thought it unnecessary. How could they have made such a misjudgment? In part, the delegates shared Madison's view that such declarations were mere "parchment barriers," meaningless verbiage that would prove much less important than the goodwill of legislative majorities. Madison's study of successful governments persuaded him that institutional arrangements, checks and balances, would far better protect minority rights. Others embraced a different argument, in some ways contradictory. James Wilson of Pennsylvania offered the most influential explanation a few weeks after the convention ended. No bill of rights was needed, Wilson explained, because Congress had no power to take away those rights. All power not stipulated as given to the national government remained with the states. Consider "the liberty of the press, which has been a copious source of declamation and opposition—what control can proceed from the federal government to shackle or destroy that sacred palladium of national freedom?"

Regardless, it was to prove a costly political mistake, and nearly undid the Constitution. It is worth noting there is no evidence—from James Madison's notes or those of any other participant—that the delegates in the Constitutional Convention had the slightest inkling that private gun ownership was viewed as being at risk and required inclusion in a bill of rights. *It simply did not come up.*

Delegates had kept discord from spilling out into public view by strict adherence to the rule of secrecy. Now those debates erupted in public view.

TWO

Ratification

The publication of the Constitution was one of the most spectacular moments in American history. George Washington, Benjamin Franklin, and dozens of the leading men of the thirteen states had vanished for weeks, with rumors and speculation swirling. In Philadelphia, the *Packet* reported breathlessly in early September, "We hear that the Convention propose to adjourn next week. . . . The year 1776 is celebrated for a revolution in favor of Liberty. The year 1787 it is expected will be celebrated with equal joy, for a revolution in favor of government." Many Americans had no idea a new constitution was coming.

The document—printed in full in dozens of newspapers within days—burst far beyond the expected. And the young men of the convention realized they had limited time to push through the new charter. The audacity of their project was heightened by the way they tried to ram the product toward ratification. They knew the Convention had greatly exceeded its mandate. And they wanted to move quickly. They chose a distinctly democratic method of approval to win legitimacy: the new Constitution should be ratified by the people—by special conventions elected for that sole purpose—rather than the state legislatures. Instead of allowing any state to veto, as under the Articles of Confederation, the Constitution would take effect if nine of thirteen states ratified it.

Existing state legislatures would have to authorize the calling of conventions. The Confederation Congress, still meeting in New York, played a muddled role. Rather sourly its members "Resolved unanimously" to send the document to the states, without comment. Historian Pauline Maier notes that this savvy wordsmanship gave the public a mistaken impression of unanimous support. The people of the states were given a stark choice: all or nothing, up or down.

In the fight over ratification Americans engaged in one of history's great public debates. A frenzy of politicking broke out, as people ran to be elected delegates, petitioned the various bodies, churned out articles and pamphlets. "Brutus," "The Federal Farmer," "Catiline," "Publius," and other pseudonymous authors contended at an exceptionally high level of erudition. Charges and countercharges, arguments and responses, flew so rapidly that it can be hard to discern patterns. "In reading through this immensity of writings, ranging from lampooning verses and jingle-jangle squibs to scholarly treatises and brilliant polemical exchanges," historian Bernard Bailyn observed, "one easily loses track of any patterns or themes."

We forget that the classic of political theory, *The Federalist*, was produced in a fury by partisan writers—arguments that today would find a home on an op-ed page or perhaps an eloquent blog. Often Publius focused on a seemingly obscure topic because an unseen debating counterpart had brought it up. Sometimes, we have to wonder if the authors believed all their own arguments. Through it all, Americans realized they were embarking on something different. "This is a new event in the history of mankind," the governor of Connecticut declared at the time. "Heretofore, most governments have been formed by tyrants and imposed on mankind by force. Never before did a people, in a time of peace and tranquility, meet together by their representatives and, with calm deliberation, frame for themselves a system of government."

With support from Franklin, Washington, and the able pens of Hamilton and Madison, the Federalists were formidable. Newspapers also overwhelmingly backed ratification. Yet opponents of the new government rallied. They warned that the new system tilted far too dramatically to the national government. Their objections were varied, sometimes contradictory, and often reactive. Many arguments bordered on shrill. Smelling conspiracy, they saw the new document as allowing the return of monarchy or worse. In an early example of deft spin, those who backed the Constitution—which yanked power away from the states—dubbed *themselves* the "Federalists." Their opponents, they insisted, were "Anti-Federalists," shorthand rejected by the critics themselves. In the welter of charges and counters, with articles published and meetings held, there were several broad arguments. Most frequently, the federal government would have the power to levy taxes. The Constitution trampled the role of the states. The means of representation was set wrongly: senators would become aristocrats, while House districts were too large to be truly democratic. Wasn't that what the Revolution was fought against? States would be swallowed up by the new government, in contrast to the Articles of Confederation, which had restricted the national government only to specific delegated powers. When individual rights were weighed, the Constitution offered no protection for free speech or religious liberty.

Amid this contention, one loud argument held that this new, overpowerful central government could wield a standing army and crush the citizen militias that were so central to liberty. Luther Martin, the attorney general of Maryland and a convention delegate, sketched a typically dystopian vista in a speech to his legislature that fall. Congress could "march the whole militia of Maryland to the remotest part of the union, and keep them in service as long as they think proper," with no permission from the state. Its citizens could be "subjected to military law, and tied up and whipped at the halbert like the meanest of slaves." A pamphleteer named "Philadelphiensis" demanded: "Who can deny but the president general will be a king to all intents and purposes, and one of the most dangerous kinds too; a king elected to command a standing army?" In Boston a pamphleteer echoed Martin's worries. "It is asserted by the most respectable writers upon government, that a well-regulated militia, composed of the yeomanry of the country, have ever been considered as the bulwark of a free people. Tyrants have never placed any confidence on a militia composed of freemen."

It quickly became plain that the convention had made a significant political error when it failed to include a bill of rights. Seven state constitutions already had such declarations, though most were little more than vague statements of basic freedoms that the government ought to respect. Most protected the militia. Four states out of thirteen protected the right to bear arms; only one (Pennsylvania) for personal self-defense.

This criticism, these debates, focused on the militia—if they touched on military matters at all. We know that the militia drew on ordinary citizens, who were expected to bring military weapons from home. What about the broader role of guns—was that a principal worry for those who criticized the Constitution?

Guns abounded. The western frontier, especially, experienced a nonstop series of raids and reprisals with Indian tribes and their French allies. There were few restrictions on hunting game. In towns and cities, no police forces had been established to protect public order. And, of course, there was the duty to serve in the militia, however intermittently it was followed.

Yet at the same time, gun regulations were common. The historian Saul Cornell has traced some of the most significant: Boston made it illegal to keep a loaded gun in a home. Laws governed the location of guns and gunpowder storage. New York, Boston, and all cities in Pennsylvania prohibited the firing of guns within city limits. States imposed curbs on gun ownership. People deemed dangerous were barred from owning weapons. Pennsylvania disarmed Tory sympathizers. Residents had to swear a loyalty oath. Other states imposed restrictions less defensible to modern eyes. Before the Revolution, Maryland had prevented Catholics from owning guns. Most states banned African Americans, even freemen, from joining the militia; some from holding weapons at all. A variety of gun rules pertained to militia service. For example, Rhode Island conducted a house-to-house census—an early American form of a gun registry. In the middle of the ratification fight, in fact,

Pennsylvania recalled all the militia guns in the state to be inspected and cleaned. (The state's citizen soldiers had allowed the weaponry to rust and decay.)

In general, gun use was governed by common law, handed down from England and enforced by judicial decisions. Everyone had the right to self-defense. A citizen threatened by another had a right to protect himself. The British legal scholar William Blackstone was highly influential among colonists. In studying the English common law, he identified "the natural right of resistance and self-preservation," which was effectuated by the right "of having arms for their defence, suitable to their condition and degree, and such as are allowed by law." But judges weighed this right against other long-standing rules and practices. For example, the misdemeanor of *affrighting*, dating from medieval times, prohibited carrying a weapon in a way that menaced others. (That covered clubs and maces as well as guns.)

To be sure, Americans expected to be able to own a gun, just as they understood they had a right to own property—another cherished freedom subject to regulation and the states' police power. They just did not expect the Constitution to address an issue that clearly had no relevance to federal authority. The Anti-Federalist Brutus, for example, explained, "It ought to be left to the state governments to provide for the protection and defence of the citizen against the hand of private violence, and the wrongs done or attempted by individuals to each other." The Federalist Tench Coxe reassured, "The states will regulate and administer the criminal law, *exclusively of Congress.*" The police power of the states would not be diminished under the new Constitution, he explained, and the individual states would continue to legislate on all matters "such as unlicensed public houses, nuisances, and many other things of the like nature."

To modern readers, one area of confusion comes from the fact that weapons were far less powerful than today. Nelson Lund, opposed to gun control, notes, "Technological advances have created a sharp distinction between military weapons and the less lethal weaponry customarily kept by civilians for self-defense. This change, along with the firmly established

practice of maintaining large peacetime standing armies, has created the
need for legal distinctions that the Framers had no cause to consider. For
them, there was no difference between military and civilian small arms."
The Framers focused on the military purpose of bearing arms, but the
weapons in question were muskets, not bazookas (or drones).

In any case, the debates over rights focused far more prominently on
protections for speech, or the right to trial. Perhaps if the Constitution
had included such guarantees in the first place, public anxiety would
have found a different target. As it was, the new document provoked
almost existential panic among many foes.

FEDERALISTS AND ANTI-FEDERALISTS

The Federalists' high-handed drive to rush the Constitution forward did
little to assuage concerns.

The first test came in Pennsylvania. The Constitutional Convention
had been meeting on the ground floor of the State House. With the
document now publicly revealed, delegates dashed up the broad steps
to the second floor, where the state legislature was in session, to break
the big news. The next day supporters read the document aloud, and demanded that lawmakers quickly call a state ratification convention. Benjamin Franklin implied strongly that if Pennsylvania acted fast, it would
be chosen the new capital. Philadelphia area politicians who backed
the Constitution, many Quaker, dominated the legislature. Opponents
drew support from the western part of the state. These legislators were
more rural, less commercially connected, less educated. On the farthest
frontier, they waged constant war with neighboring Indian tribes. In
the decade before the Revolution, they had complained bitterly that the
Quaker-heavy Assembly would not give them guns or organize a militia to fight Indians. The two factions long struggled for control. (Some
patterns start early: Barack Obama was not the first urban politician to
complain that rural Pennsylvanians "cling to guns or religion.")

Opponents tried to stall the bid for quick action by refusing to return after lunch, thus denying a quorum for a vote. After several days hunting legislators in boardinghouses, sergeants at arms forcibly dragged two to their desks. An ominous crowd blocked their escape. Quorum achieved, the Pennsylvania legislature sent the U.S. Constitution to a convention for ratification.

The same fights played out in the state's ratifying convention. Federalists, backed by most newspapers and commercial interests, rammed the document past the objections of backcountry delegates. On the last day of the convention, opponents proposed that the decision be postponed. They lost. Just before a final vote, Anti-Federalists presented a lengthy list of proposed revisions. The most significant curbed Congress's taxing power. Others guaranteed trial by jury, required congressional elections every year, and constrained the power of the federal courts. One proclaimed, "the people have a right to bear arms for the defence of themselves and their own state, or the United States, or for the purpose of killing game; and no law shall be passed for disarming the people or any of them, unless for crimes committed, or real danger of public injury from individuals; and as standing armies in the time of peace are dangerous to liberty, they ought not to be kept up; and that the military shall be kept under strict subordination to and be governed by the civil powers." Another amendment guaranteed the *right* to hunt. (This may have been a response to the actions of earlier British kings, who restricted game licenses as a way of disarming the militias.)

Pennsylvania delegates never debated these changes. The Federalists refused to allow it. Instead they voted down the amendments as a block, and then voted in identical numbers to ratify the Constitution. They even refused to print the proposals in the official journal. Pennsylvania was convulsed as anti-Constitution gangs attacked supporters of ratification. The dissidents printed their own unofficial minority report (including the rather incoherent set of amendments), which was circulated widely within the colonies. Federalists mocked the pamphlet. Noah Webster—decades before he compiled his landmark of American usage—suggested an additional provision assuring "that Congress shall never restrain any inhabitant of America from eating and drinking, at seasonable times, or prevent his lying on his left side, in a long winter's night, or even on his back, when he is fatigued by lying on his right." He mischievously suggested that citizens be *required* to hunt, too.

By mid-January 1788, Delaware, Pennsylvania, New Jersey, Georgia, and Connecticut had ratified the charter with overwhelming support. Outside the conventions, debaters parried fiercely.

Then Massachusetts took its turn. Anti-Federalists seemed to hold the majority of the state. Delegates voiced the same concerns as elsewhere: taxes, representation, juries. Delegates seemed poised to reject the whole document. Two canny politicians made a decisive stroke. We first met them hiding in the Middlesex County countryside twelve years before. John Hancock now served as governor of Massachusetts. His flamboyant self-satisfaction comes to us through his large and flowery signature. Hancock's theatricality proved decisive in 1788. The governor had not yet declared his position on the Constitution, using illness as an excuse for silence. On January 30, servants carried Hancock into the meeting room from his sickbed, and before a riveted audience he announced his position. The old Patriot would support the Constitution, urging a "yea" vote. But he proposed that Massachusetts also vote to send a list of recommended amendments to serve as a bill of rights for Congress to enact in its first term.

At first, Pauline Maier recounts, Hancock's triangulation seemed to recoil on the Constitution's proponents. If the document needed no change, why support amendments? But the topics seemed carefully chosen to avoid structural alterations. Then the Bay State's other silent Revolutionary Era legend stepped in. Samuel Adams had refused to attend the Constitutional Convention in Philadelphia, fearing it would centralize governmental power. Now he declared he would support the Constitution after all, while recommending amendments. In early February, Massachusetts narrowly ratified the Constitution (187 to 168). The delegates recommended that Congress enact nine amendments ranging from a bar on direct taxation to a requirement for jury trials in civil cases. Adams proposed additional changes, but the delegates rejected them, including one to prevent the disarming of "peaceable citizens." In the end no recommended amendment mentioned the militia or the right to bear arms. These were the first official, proposed changes: the first with the color of authority.

Now a template for victory in large states seemed set. Backers would defend the Constitution and all its provisions. At the last minute, grudgingly, they would agree to append a bill of rights, which would pronounce (with varying degrees of vagueness) assurances that the new government would not, after all, impose tyranny. A cascade of small states ratified. First, Maryland unanimously endorsed with no amendments. Then South Carolina recommended minor wording changes to the Constitution. It shrank from embracing a bill of rights, though, perhaps because these often began with a proclamation that "all men are created equal." In June 1788, New Hampshire ratified, essentially adopting the Bay State's list of proposed changes. It urged that a standing army require a vote of three quarters of each house of Congress, and added: "Congress shall never disarm any Citizen unless such as are or have been in Actual Rebellion."

Nine states in: the Constitution, formally, had taken effect. But two major states had not yet ratified: Virginia, the home of the presumptive first president, and New York, then the capital. Anti-Federalists seemed to hold the majority in each. Debate intensified even as momentum tipped toward ratification.

First up was Virginia, the largest state. Patrick Henry no longer served as governor, yet he dominated its politics. Henry first gained fame in 1776 demanding "give me liberty, or give me death," in support of raising a militia to fight the British. Now he trained his eloquence on a constitution he saw as tyrannical. He was willing to see Virginia break away, and even sent feelers to other states and to France. Never far beneath the surface surged issues of slavery and fear of revolt. The ratification convention is rich with that distinct Virginia blend of high-flown tributes to liberty, honeyed testimonies of personal distaste for slavery, and venomous appeals to race prejudice. The new constitution would give Congress too much authority, Henry warned. "They'll take your niggers from you," he said to laughter.

Henry and George Mason picked at the document, line by line. Madison wearily responded for days. Principal objections, as elsewhere, came on the issues of taxes and religious freedom. But military power rattled, too, touching underlying fears of civil unrest.

George Mason focused with vehemence on the idea that Congress could call up the militia. During the war they kept order and forestalled any hint of slave revolt. The new Constitution gave Virginia power to appoint officers. But Congress could decide who would serve, how they would be disciplined, and whether they were properly armed. Congress could even leave Virginians defenseless by calling its men into service and marching them across the country. That should be barred without the Virginia legislature's consent, he insisted. In reply, a Federalist leader again obliquely raised the threat of slave uprising. It was the Southern states "from their situation" who were in fact most likely to need help from elsewhere.

Attacks grew ever more personal. At one point Henry and the current governor, George Randolph, reportedly prepared for a duel.

More than most, Mason personified the genteel hypocrisy of Virginia's gentry. He earnestly opposed slavery, but owned one hundred slaves. He had written the ringing language declaring all men created equal. He tiptoed to the edge of the issue. "The militia may be here destroyed by that method which has been practised in other parts of the world before; that is, by rendering them useless by disarming them," he worried. "Under various pretences, Congress may neglect to provide for arming and disciplining the militia; and the state governments cannot do it, for Congress has an exclusive right to arm them." Madison responded that the power to arm the militias was concurrent, that both Congress and the state could do so. The new Constitution would make sure the militia was properly armed. Madison apparently made that argument up on the fly.

Henry pounced. "The militia, Sir, is our ultimate safety. We can have no security without it," Henry proclaimed. The state should have responsibility to arm it. Otherwise it could lead to the boondoggle of both levels of government paying for arms, or neither.

*So that our militia shall have two sets of arms, double sets of regimentals,
&c. and thus, at a very great cost, we shall be doubly armed. The great object is, that every man be armed. But can the people afford to pay for double sets of arms, &c? Every one who is able may have a gun. But have we
not learned by experience, that necessary as it is to have arms, and though
our Assembly has, by a succession of laws for many years, endeavoured to
have the militia completely armed, it is still far from being the case? When
this power is given up to Congress without limitation or bounds, how will
your militia be armed?*

Henry's plaint would be quoted wildly out of context two centuries later.
As the vote neared, Federalists gained momentum. Like a ham actor
turning up the volume as he realizes he is losing his audience's attention,
an increasingly frenetic Henry broke even the South's taboo. "Slavery is
detested" elsewhere, he declared. The state's black men could be called
into federal military service, and then freed. Congress has "the power in
clear, unequivocal terms, and will clearly and certainly exercise it." Henry's
fevered speech revealed that the tide had run against the critics. By a vote
of 57 to 47, the convention ratified the Constitution. It then appointed a
committee to recommend amendments, as other states had done.

Most of the proposed changes drew from Virginia's Revolutionary
Era constitution, adopted in 1776. That document had included pledges
to support freedom of speech and religion, habeas corpus, and other
rights. It also paid tribute to the militia. Now the ratification convention
rewrote that provision slightly. Its proposed Seventeenth Amendment
proclaimed:

*That the people have a right to keep and bear arms; that a well regulated
Militia composed of the body of the people trained to arms is the proper,
natural and safe defence of a free State. That standing armies in time of
peace are dangerous to liberty, and therefore ought to be avoided, as far as
the circumstances and protection of the Community will admit; and that
in all cases the military should be under strict subordination to and governed by the Civil power.*

A proposed Nineteenth Amendment also allowed "any person religiously scrupulous of bearing arms" to avoid military service "upon payment of an equivalent to employ another to bear arms in his stead." Thus
a right *not* to bear arms for Quakers and others was seen as an essential
balance against the *obligation* to bear arms.

Virginia's recommended Bill of Rights would stand separate from the
body of the Constitution, possibly at the beginning as in several states.
The committee also proposed numerous tweaks and rewrites to the
central document itself. Further addressing worries about the militia, it
insisted that each state "shall have the power to provide for organizing,
arming and disciplining its own Militia, whensoever Congress shall omit
or neglect to provide for the same."

Madison served on the committee that drafted the proposed amendments. To him, one possible change stood out as a particularly dangerous
threat. The Constitution gave Congress the power to levy taxes directly,
without the consent of states. Only in this way could a national government hope to fund its activities. Virginia recommended an amendment
that would prohibit this. Madison was aghast, he reported to Washington
and Hamilton. They knew this was what later generations would call a
"starve the beast" strategy. Without revenue, the government would grow so
weak it could be (as we now say) drowned in the bathtub. As the focus over
ratification and amendments rolled toward its conclusion, Madison grew
ever more convinced this change would doom the new country's chances.
Throughout the rest of the fight over ratification and amendments, one of
his chief goals was to avoid it. Other amendments paled in his eyes.

Next came New York, still serving as the nation's capital.

If anywhere seemed like ripe territory for backers of the Constitution,
it would be the shipping and commercial hub at the mouth of the Hudson. How could New York say no? Yet ratification proved surprisingly
hard, again. Here, too, the urban versus rural, upstate versus downstate
conflicts that linger two centuries later arose. Also, tariff revenues from
New York City's port had flowed to the state after the British evacu-
ated. The state's ambitious governor, George Clinton, was able to keep

property taxes low, and had no interest in giving up the flow of funds to a new federal government. The convention convened at Poughkeepsie, a day's ride north from the city.

Polemicists debated in New York City with tabloid intensity. Madison had decided to stay in Manhattan to manage the pro-Constitution forces there. By the time the state convention prepared to meet, journalists and pamphleteers had published broadsides against and for ratification. Madison, together with Alexander Hamilton and John Jay, published *The Federalist* in the *New York Independent Journal* and two other papers. The topic of the new military system did not come up until the twenty-ninth article in the series. Hamilton took the first swing. It was only right, he asserted, that the new national government would take at least partial control of the militias. "If a well-regulated militia be the most natural defense of a free country, it ought certainly to be under the regulation and at the disposal of that body which is constituted the guardian of the national security," he wrote. Make the militias a success, he wrote, and that would do more "to render an army unnecessary . . . than a thousand prohibitions on paper."

The anonymous pundits of *The Federalist* were engaging in a day-by-day public argument. "The Letters of Brutus" parried with Publius in a rival newspaper. Brutus warned that citizens should fear the new military system. Two mighty nations, renowned for liberty, had seen a standing army "subvert the government": Britain and Rome. And it almost happened here. George Washington had quashed the Newburgh mutiny. But the vigorous young soldiers had been ready for a coup d'état. The call to action "affected them like an electric shock." Had their commander "been possessed of the spirit of a Julius Caesar or a Cromwell," Brutus warned, the republic would have ended shortly after the war.

Madison volleyed back a few days later. In *Federalist* 46, his frustration seems palpable. "Let a regular army, fully equal to the resources of the country, be formed; and let it be entirely at the devotion of the federal government; still it would not be going too far to say that the State governments with the people on their side would be able to repel the danger," he insisted. If a standing army were formed, he wrote, it would not grow larger than 25,000 to 30,000 men. "To these would be opposed a militia amounting to near half a million of citizens with arms in their hands, officered by men chosen from among themselves, fighting for their common liberties and united and conducted by governments possessing their affections and confidence. It may well be doubted whether a militia thus circumstanced could ever be conquered by such a proportion of regular troops." He added, "Americans have the right and advantage of being armed—unlike the citizens of other countries whose governments are afraid to trust the people with arms."

Madison's and Hamilton's arguments proved increasingly effective. New York did not wish to be a lone holdout among big, commercially vital states. But its convention did not just ask for amendments. Instead, it demanded a Second Constitutional Convention. (Madison resisted, but Hamilton thought this a necessary concession.) After all, the new U.S. Constitution stipulated such a convention could be called to propose amendments. But to reconvene delegates so quickly would freeze the new government in its infancy. Madison now had to head off the most dangerous threat of all. Again, the Constitution was ratified, again with a request for amendments—and this time through a means that could prove fatal to the national authority.

The Constitution approved, the new government began to take form. But the fight had been far closer than expected. North Carolina would soon reject the Constitution unless amended. Vermont and Rhode Island had not acted at all. All told, six of the ten states had recommended specific amendments. The states had proposed over one hundred distinct changes (and at least a hundred more that overlapped or mirrored them). They would limit a president to two terms, turn state courts into lower federal courts, bar marching the militia out of state, require a two thirds vote for commerce regulations, prevent any American from accepting a foreign title, create a presidential advisory committee, require printing of a congressional record, and more. If they were ever debated in Congress, one contemporary observer wrote, they would "immediately like Swift's books, give battle to each other, and soon destroy themselves." Of note, in a country founded on a tax revolt, much discussion focused on Congress's new power to raise revenues.

It was a momentous debate, a rare and consequential moment of government making. Thousands of speeches, dozens of pamphlets, hundreds of articles, thousands of words, debated the new document and its risks and advantages. Rarely mentioned was the idea that the new national government would threaten private gun ownership for personal protection.

Thomas Jefferson, writing to Madison from Paris where he served as envoy to the Court of Louis XVI, opened a window on what the Founders thought was important in the Bill of Rights. He liked much of the Constitution, he told his protégé. "I will now add what I do not like. First the omission of a bill of rights providing clearly and without the aid of sophisms for freedom of religion, freedom of the press, protection against standing armies, restriction against monopolies, the eternal and unremitting force of the habeas corpus laws, and trial by jury in all matters of fact triable by the laws of the land and not by the law of Nations." Even Jefferson, more enamored of individual rights than his peers, who had once proposed an individual right to bear arms in an earlier version of the Virginia state constitution, appeared unconcerned by its omission from the new document.

With the Constitution ratified, debate subsided with surprising swiftness. Most opponents retreated from public life. Many others shrugged and ran for office, seeking power in the new arrangement. A bill of rights might easily have slipped off the agenda—but for the quirks of one congressional contest in the first election.

THREE

The Tub to the Whale

J ames Madison was eager to take his place in the new government he helped shape. At a time when honor demanded that leaders act disinterested, he might expect that his national prominence would garner him a seat representing Virginia. How to act as Cincinnatus, summoned reluctantly to serve, if the people never call? As winter approached, cooped up in New York City, he realized that if he wanted to win a place in Congress, he would have to work for it—hard.

At first, Madison yearned for a Senate seat, with its leisurely six-year term. But under the original Constitution, voters did not choose senators; states did. Patrick Henry still dominated Virginia, and still opposed the Constitution. George Washington wrote regretfully to Madison, "The edicts of Mr. Henry are enregistred with less opposition by the majority of [the legislature] than those of the Grand Monarch are in the parliaments of France." Henry warned legislators that Madison's election to the Senate would result in "rivulets of blood throughout the land." Madison's Senate bid fell short. Instead, he chose to run for the House of Representatives, the body closest to the people (and the only one directly elected by them). More shocks awaited.

First, Henry pressed the legislature to pass a law requiring candidates for the House to live in the district for twelve months prior to the election. This flatly violated the Constitution, only three months old. It meant Madison could not search for a friendly electorate. Then Henry's allies appointed Madison to serve in the lame-duck Confederation Congress, soon to expire but still meeting days away by coach in New York City. "Henry did not arrange Madison's reelection to Congress because of his admiration for his legislative skills," historian Richard Labunski noted dryly.

Being stuck in Manhattan was the least of Madison's troubles. Virginia's new Fifth District had been carefully drawn to exclude pro-Constitution voters. It would be two decades before the term "gerrymandering" was coined, when Elbridge Gerry drew a congressional district so misshapen it was said to resemble a salamander. But that is what Patrick Henry did to James Madison: gerrymandered before Gerry. Madison found himself running in a hostile district with few friendly voters other than his hometown of Orange. The Virginian made it as far as Philadelphia, where he stayed to recuperate from hemorrhoids. Now he received urgent pleas from friends: if he wanted to win, he had better come home, fast.

In December 1788 Madison dashed back to Virginia for a compressed six weeks of fierce campaigning. He faced James Monroe, an old friend and business colleague who was skeptical of the Constitution and now supported a bill of rights. (Principle aside, Monroe nursed a grudge: he believed Madison had blocked him from serving as a delegate to the Constitutional Convention.) On campaign platforms in the district, the two posed a sharp contrast. Madison was bookish, diffident, and physically slight. Monroe was gregarious, athletic, a charismatic war hero who carried a British musket ball in his lung. He had little recorded evidence of intellectual attainment. The farmers of the Fifth District assuredly would rather "drink a cider" with Monroe.

Madison found himself thrown on the defensive. Monroe's supporters charged that Madison was "dogmatically attached to the Constitution in every clause, syllable and letter."

The charge, strictly speaking, was not entirely untrue. Madison's notes show him remaining silent when fellow Virginian George Mason demanded a bill of rights at the Constitutional Convention. He opposed amendments in the Confederation Congress, too. Patrick Henry bitterly suspected Madison had stealthily supported amendments at the state ratifying convention, but the records show little. Privately, Madison thrashed out the issue with Thomas Jefferson. Madison explained he would be for a bill of rights so long as it did not accidentally imply greater power for Congress than intended. "At the same time I have never thought the omission a material defect," he confided, "nor been anxious to supply it by *subsequent* amendment, for any other reason than that it is anxiously desired by others. I have favored it because I supposed it might be of use, and if properly executed could not be of disservice." Bills of rights, he believed, did little to stop the tendency of legislative majorities to abuse rights. Madison wrestled with his position. In another letter he told Jefferson that he supported a bill of rights, so long as it did not change the balance of power between the states and the federal government. A few paragraphs later, he returned to the topic, now insisting that he was all for a bill of rights in part because it would "give to the Government its due popularity and stability."

Finally Madison decided he had no choice: he needed to declare his support for amendments to change the Constitution he had just spent so much time crafting, and for which he had argued so effectively in public. The simple reason: an appeal to swing voters. White Southern Baptists became a reliable conservative voting bloc in later centuries. In 1789, they were the freethinking unaligned vote. The governing Episcopal Church long had oppressed the Baptists. In years past Madison had stood up for the Baptists. Now they wavered; Monroe, after all, supported a constitutional amendment to guarantee religious freedom. Madison found himself one of the first American politicians to pirouette, in the course of a campaign, from a deeply held view to its opposite—all the while insisting (and trying to convince himself) that he had not changed his view at all. The Bill of Rights was born of a pander to a noisy interest group in a single congressional district.

Madison executed this pivot with deft "message discipline." In 1789, political figures communicated with the public in "private" letters published in newspapers and circulated widely. Madison wrote a missive to a local Baptist clergyman explaining that he had not really changed his position. True, he noted, "I opposed all previous alterations as calculated to throw the States into dangerous contentions." That was then. "Circumstances are now changed: The Constitution is established," he explained. Now, he declared, "It is my sincere opinion that the Constitution ought to be revised, and that the first Congress . . . ought to prepare and recommend to the states for ratification the most satisfactory provisions for all essential rights, particularly the rights of Conscience in the fullest latitude, the freedom of the press, trials by jury, security against general warrants & c." Done right, these might "serve the double purpose of satisfying the mind of well-meaning opponents, and of providing additional guards in favour of liberty." One chronicler of the First Amendment called this "read-my-lips pledge . . . one of the most important campaign promises in American history."

Madison campaigned furiously through unusually harsh weather. One evening he suffered from frostbite on his nose. His switch of position proved just enough, and he won by 336 votes.

MADISON PROPOSES A BILL OF RIGHTS; CONGRESS YAWNS

In spring 1789 Madison was now thirty-eight years old, but already had performed enough public roles to last a lifetime: architect of the Constitution and pseudonymous articulator of its purposes, organizer of the campaign to ram it to passage, survivor of a harrowing campaign for Congress. He wrote George Washington's Inaugural Address, the House's reply to Washington, and Washington's reply to the House. Now he served in effect as majority leader of the new House of Representatives. At a time when William Pitt the Younger guided the fortunes of George III, Madison was George Washington's de facto prime minister. In the primordial soup of American politics, before party blocs had hardened, Madison flitted to and fro, assembling majorities and steering legislation to passage.

To his great frustration, he could not seem to get anyone to pay attention to the need for a bill of rights. He promised his constituents; the others had not. Other matters loomed larger, such as establishing the judiciary, forming the navy, and raising revenue. To be sure, Madison still thought revisions unnecessary. He worried to a friend that it was time to finish "the nauseous project of writing amendments." The Constitution had been in effect for only months—why not let it work and see what the problems were? But he had a keen political sense. He feared, above all, a call for a second convention—or, just as bad, an amendment that could prevent the federal government from levying taxes and funding itself. A bill of rights could blunt such a move.

Remarkably, both proponents and foes saw amendments as a tactic—a political feint.

Madison faced two distinct voting blocs: Federalists scorned amendments. They had just run in support of the Constitution, and had won a landslide. When newspapers around the country printed Madison's proposal, previously supportive editors turned on him. One writer sneered anonymously, "if we must have amendments, I pray for merely amusing amendments, a little frothy garnish."

Anti-Federalists were not happy, either. They viewed amendments as a distraction from the thorough overhaul they wanted: they insisted on a new convention. A political cliché of the time drew from maritime lore (the way a pundit today might glibly talk of "throwing someone under the bus"). Foes and allies likened the amendments to a trick used by sailors, who would throw a tub into the water to distract dangerous whales. "Like a barrel thrown to the whale, the people were to be amused with fancied amendments, until the harpoon of power, should secure its prey and render resistance ineffectual," one wrote. Amendments would just confuse citizens who should be demanding structural change to restore power to the states. Writers and speakers repeated this metaphor, each relishing its use as if thinking of it for the first time. It became an easy way to get under Madison's skin.

Weeks dragged by. Congressmen still straggled into town, and there was no quorum until April. George Washington took the oath late that month—well past the date set in the Constitution—and obliquely urged action on amendments in his first Inaugural Address.

The week after Washington took the oath, Madison reminded his colleagues: it was time to act. Others felt less urgency. "The storm has abated, and calm succeeds," New York's John Vining would later counsel. The House postponed the discussion until three weeks later. The next day, May 5, Madison's own state of Virginia formally submitted its call for a new convention, joining New York. That unnerved. Worse, the most vulnerable part of the Constitution remained Congress's power to levy taxes. This would pose a lethal threat to the new government. On May 25, Madison tried again, only to see the matter postponed.

On June 8, Madison rose to speak again. He faced a skeptical audience. "I hope the House will not spend much time on this subject, till the more pressing business is dispatched," one lawmaker commented. Madison insisted that the debate take place in public, through the mechanism of the House acting as a committee of the whole to draft changes. Otherwise, drafting would take place in a committee session closed to the public. Others winced at the prospect of a lengthy open debate. "It strikes me that the great amendment which the Government wants," retorted John Vining, "is expedition in the dispatch of business." Congress had "done nothing to tranquilize that agitation" stirred by the Constitution, yet the public had calmed down and moved on. Why bother with amendments?

Having endured his colleagues' hazing, Madison introduced his proposed amendments. His lengthy, clotted speech is the closest we have to a "manager's statement" on the Bill of Rights. At the time, the House of Representatives was the only part of the government directly elected by the people, and the only one that held its deliberations in public. It was the only show in town. Its galleries were often crowded with onlookers, and we can assume they were there this day. They would have had to lean in to hear Madison's talk.

If the Congress kept postponing discussion, he cajoled, "it may occasion suspicions, which, though not well founded, may tend to inflame or prejudice the public mind against our decisions," he explained. "They may think we are not sincere in our desire to incorporate such amendments in the constitution as will secure those rights, which they consider as not sufficiently guarded." Madison's motive—at least as expressed to a House dominated by fellow Federalists—was frankly therapeutic: "to quiet that anxiety which prevails in the public mind."

Two years before, ever the student, he had gathered the world's constitutions and classics of philosophy to prepare the Virginia Plan. Now he unreeled his list of amendments from the overlapping, voluminous compendium of proposals forwarded by state conventions.

Faced with strenuous calls to alter the structure of the new government, he reached for amendments that did not change the Constitution in its essentials. He ignored the call for a two thirds vote for a standing army, proposed by Virginia, or to declare war, urged by New York. "There have been objections of various kinds made against the constitution," he explained. Some were structural, such as concerns about the Senate's power to advise and consent to the president, or because it gives the federal government too much power. "I know some respectable characters who opposed this government on these grounds; but I believe that the great mass of the people who opposed it, disliked it because it did not contain effectual provision against encroachments on particular rights, and those safeguards which they have been long accustomed to have interposed between them and the magistrate who exercised the sovereign power."

Madison proposed twenty changes, hoping they would be interwoven in the existing Constitution. Americans are accustomed to thinking of the Bill of Rights as a Decalogue, akin to the commandments carried by Moses from Sinai. We would find his original list jumbled, lacking totemic power.

Madison first included a declaration that power remained with the people. His second amendment discussed the proper size of congressional districts. The third would block the effective date of congressional pay raises until after the next election. Then, a string of changes to be inserted into the section on Congress's power. It started with protection for speech and religion. Then, two amendments dealing with military issues. The first read:

> *The right of the people to keep and bear arms shall not be infringed; a well armed and well regulated militia being the best security of a free country; but no person religiously scrupulous of bearing arms shall be compelled to render military service in person.*

Why did Madison phrase it this way? *We don't know.* He never explained the amendment, either in the written record of his floor speech or in any other forum. His notes for his talk indicated amendments referred "first to private rights," though it is unclear whether that described all the amendments or just some. The notes refer, too, to the English Bill of Rights and its restrictions on arms bearing to Protestants. Plainly he had cut, pasted, and slightly rewritten the Virginia recommendation. The focus on the militia, and the reference to conscientious objectors, suggests a military purpose. Most likely he wanted to reassure citizens who were anxious about armies and enamored of militias, but to do so while making the slightest alteration to the Constitution itself. The other proposed amendments were far more precise.

In any case, he quickly moved on to another military amendment, one that prohibited troops from being quartered in people's homes. Madison also passionately urged an amendment declaring: "No state"—not just Congress—"shall violate the equal rights of conscience, or the freedom of the press, or the trial by jury in criminal cases." Madison called this "the most valuable amendment in the whole list."

As Madison dutifully trudged through his compendium, we mourn the absence of C-SPAN. Still, the sense of eye rolling comes through. Some colleagues, at least, found the whole exercise droll. Fisher Ames, a Federalist congressman from Massachusetts, acidly reported to a friend:

"Mr. Madison has introduced his long expected Amendments. They are the fruit of much labour and research. He has hunted up all the grievances and complaints of newspapers—all the articles of Conventions—and the small talk of their debates." Ames detailed the myriad changes Madison proposed, from trial by jury to freedom of speech. "There is too much of it— O. I had forgot, the right of the people to bear Arms."

Ames paused in his letter and added, "Risum teneatis amici." Translated from the Latin, "Stifle laughter, friends."

Newspapers reported on Madison's speech. The arms amendment drew little notice. The Federalist writer Tench Coxe summarized the array of amendments in one account. He devoted a few sentences to explain that the arms amendment sought to deflect oppression. "As civil rulers, not having their duty to the people duly before them, may attempt to tyrannize, and as the military forces which must be occasionally raised to defend our country, might pervert their power to the injury of their fellow-citizens, the people are confirmed by the next article in their right to keep and bear their private arms." He sent the article to Madison, who issued a polite but noncommittal reply.

In the end, the House decided to send Madison's proposed amendments to a committee, which met in secret to redraft them. Each state sent one representative. Madison spoke for Virginia. Lawmakers drafted amid frantic effort to set up the new government, squeezing in sessions at night or between other responsibilities. Finally, on August 17, the panel brought the amendments before the full House. It was a streamlined list. The panel subtly altered the militia amendment (now fourth on the list). It moved the explanatory clause to the beginning. It made clear the protection afforded was not to the "country" but the states. It deleted the provision that the militia be "well armed." And it inserted a call for the citizen soldiers to be drawn from the full populace:

A well regulated militia, composed of the body of the People, being the best security of a free State, the right of the People to keep and bear arms, shall not be infringed, but no one religiously scrupulous of bearing arms, shall be compelled to render military service in person.

Once again, Elbridge Gerry was quick to his feet. "This declaration of rights, I take it," he began, "is intended to secure the people against the mal-administration of the government. . . ."

Now I am apprehensive, sir, that this clause would give an opportunity to the people in power to destroy the constitution itself. They can declare who are those religiously scrupulous, and prevent them from bearing arms.

What, sir, is the use of a militia? It is to prevent the establishment of a standing army, the bane of liberty. Now it must be evident, that under this provision, together with their other powers, congress could take such measures with respect to a militia, as to make a standing army neces-sary. Whenever government means to invade the rights and liberties of the people, they always attempt to destroy the militia, in order to raise an army upon their ruins.

Gerry had found a new topic about which to fume. The government, he warned, could simply declare classes of people to be conscientious objectors, and thus prohibit them from bearing arms. Gerry likely was thinking about what happened in Britain a century earlier, when the Catholic King James II had declared Protestants could not join the militia. At the very least, Gerry asked, the language should be confined to people who were actually members of a "religious sect, scrupulous of bearing arms." Madison and Gerry and the other congressmen knew that such a sect dominated one state: Pennsylvania's Quakers were so influential the state never formally had a militia until 1776. (Quakers were pacifists who would not engage in any warlike actions. They could shoot guns to hunt for food, and used them to kill vermin, but would not hunt for sport.)

Tellingly, debate revolved around the conscientious objector language. Thomas Jackson of Georgia averred that while he "did not expect that all the people of the United States would turn Quakers or Moravians [a small Protestant sect]," in case of invasion it would be unjust if some served and others sat it out. The amendment should have an additional clause requiring a conscientious objector to hire someone in his stead.

A South Carolinian noted that in his state and Virginia, men could be excused from the militia if they could find a substitute. Roger Sherman of Connecticut cut this down. "It is well-known that those who are religiously scrupulous of bearing arms, are equally scrupulous of getting substitutes or paying an equivalent." In any case, it should be up to each state how it would run its militia. Besides, he said serenely, he was confident that in case of invasion, many Quakers would "defend the cause of their country."

Finally a New York congressman urged that the whole conscientious objector clause be struck out. Why not leave the question to "the benevolence of the legislature," he asked. He presciently warned, "If this stands part of the constitution, it will be a question before the judiciary, on every regulation you make with respect to the organization of the militia, whether it comports with the declaration or not?" The House narrowly voted to retain the "religious scruples" language, by a vote of 24 to 22.

Gerry was not done. He objected (bless him!) to the vagueness of the amendment, "the uncertainty with which it is expressed." If a well regulated militia is the "best security of a free state," then that implied a "standing army was a secondary one." The amendment should protect "a well regulated militia, trained to arms," thus imposing a duty on Congress to ensure that the state militias alone would protect order. This time Gerry found no support. The debate ended. But not before another lawmaker proposed yet again that the amendment include an outright ban on a standing army. He "could not help himself," he explained. Two days later, even after the amendment was passed, two lawmakers tried one last time. If the amendment did not require conscientious objectors to pay for a replacement for militia service, "a militia can never be depended upon. This would lead to the violation of another article in the Constitution, which secures to the people the right of keeping arms, and in this case recourse must be had to a standing army."

Here it was, on the floor of the House: the purpose of the right of "keeping arms" was to strengthen the militia and thus ward off the specter of an army. Twelve congressmen joined the debate. None mentioned a private right to bear arms for self-defense, hunting, or for any purpose other than joining the militia.

The Committee of the Whole voted to refer the amendments. Now the full House of Representatives would require a two thirds vote for passage. And after all the agonizing work, Madison still was short of votes. No doubt he found it necessary to play his biggest card: Washington himself. The president had written a letter saying he thought some of the changes were of minor importance, but "are necessary to quiet the fears of some respectable characters and well meaning men." Adding that he did not foresee "any evil consequences that can result from their adoption, they have my wishes for a favorable reception in both houses." Not a roaring endorsement, perhaps, but enough. Federalist votes swung behind the plan. On August 29, 1789, the House passed a version of the Bill of Rights that included seventeen amendments.

The United States Senate then took up the topic. In its first days, the Senate met in secret. We do not know what the senators said in their debates, nor do contemporary records explain the reason for any edits. Tantalizing reports leaked, some jarring. One claimed a majority of the Senate had voted "for not allowing the militia arms & if two thirds had agreed it would have been an amendment to the Constitution. They are afraid that the Citizens will stop their full Career to Tyranny & Oppression." That seems far-fetched. Perhaps it is a garbled attempt to report that the Senate considered but rejected a ban on a standing army in time of peace. We know it considered but rejected the idea of inserting "for the common defence" in the amendment.

The Senate reworded and reordered the amendment to its final form:

A well regulated militia, being necessary to the security of a free state, the right of the people to keep and bear arms, shall not be infringed.

Of note, the senators removed the description of the militia as being "the body of the people." Future Congresses could determine who would serve, including the possibility of a "select" militia. And they deleted entirely the provision allowing conscientious objectors to avoid service.

We do not know why these changes were made. Many other amendments were rewritten, always to trim words, tighten syntax, and combine thoughts. (Two separate amendments, dealing with religion and speech, were combined into one, for example.) It is also true that the Senate, chosen by state legislatures rather than voters, was designed to be a more aristocratic body than the House. Its members were overwhelmingly Federalist, and less inclined to give ground to public clamor. Its debates were secret, shielded from public view. Did the Senate hope to nudge the Constitution away from the idea that the full citizenry armed and ready for service was the way the new nation would organize its military? Again, we do not know.

The amendments were sent to the states. Legal historian Bernard Schwartz picks up the story. "It is amazing, considering the crucial significance of the Bill of Rights, that we know practically nothing about what went on in the state legislatures during the ratification process. At the time, there was nothing in the states comparable even to the *Annals of Congress*, which reported, however sketchily, proceedings and debates in the federal legislature. Even the contemporary newspapers are virtually silent on the ratification debates in the states." There must have been some controversy: a few amendments failed to pass. (The original Second Amendment, which stopped congressmen from voting themselves a pay raise, did not pass until 1990.) Of the few remaining fragments of the debate, none concern the amendment on the "well regulated militia" and "the right of the people to keep and bear arms."

On March 1, 1792, Secretary of State Thomas Jefferson made his laconic announcement. He informed the states he was sending along "an Act concerning certain fisheries of the United States, and for the regulation and government of the fishermen employed therein; also of an Act to establish the post office and post roads within the United States; also the ratifications by three fourths of the Legislatures of the Several States, of certain articles in addition and amendment of the Constitution of the United States, proposed by Congress to the said Legislatures."

WHAT DID IT MEAN?

Modern readers accustomed to hyperventilation about the Second Amendment might pause. Wasn't the debate that led to the Second Amendment a debate about gun ownership? So what did the Framers think the Second Amendment meant? We are faced with a maddening paucity of explanation. Yes, plainly, lawmakers were thinking of the militias, and the urgent need, as they saw it, to protect the system of citizen service against the threat of an overpowering federal military. But was there more? Did they, in fact, want to use the United States Constitution to protect the right to bear arms for citizens for reasons other than service in the militia?

As we have seen, it can be hard to derive one clear answer to the question of what the Framers meant. The amendment was the product both of political leaders who pushed for a stronger central military authority, and angry citizens who opposed it. It did not give the Anti-Federalists the structural changes they sought, but rather steered public energy into something else. Stanford historian Jack Rakove notes, "Understanding this aspect of the politics behind the Bill of Rights is critical to an originalist inquiry because it indicates that the final decisions about Madison's proposals fell not to those who were most ardent for the cause of amendments but to those who doubted that such amendments were even useful, much less necessary."

Gun rights proponents today point to another set of rights, suffusing the thinking of the Framers, that would justify an interpretation of the Constitution that the nature of the right protected was private. After all, Americans of that era spoke passionately of their belief in natural rights—rights that could be recognized by government, but not created by government. Gun proponents highlight the English Bill of Rights, enacted a century before. A previously little known historian, Joyce Lee Malcolm, writing in a tone of having discovered a lost hieroglyph that explains everything, declared in an influential book, "The right of individuals to be armed had become, as the [English] Bill of Rights had claimed it was, an ancient and indubitable right. It was this heritage that

Englishmen took with them to the American colonies and this heritage which Americans fought to protect in 1775." Perhaps that is the right the Framers were seeking to protect. It is far less clear that the Founders understood their English heritage this way.

Some background is in order. One hundred years before the American Revolution, England went through one of its periodic upheavals. The Glorious Revolution of 1688 marked the decisive moment that the absolute monarchy devolved power to Parliament. King James II was a Catholic, a recipe for trouble in overwhelmingly Protestant England. He sought to disarm the kingdom's Protestants, through their militias and at times in their homes. When his wife gave birth to a son (who could carry on a Catholic throne), Parliament shuddered. It reached out to a Protestant prince from Holland, who was married to one of James's daughters, and invited him to invade and seize the throne. William and Mary set sail for England. When they arrived, James dithered, panicked, and abdicated. A nearly bloodless revolution had occurred. But Parliament did not offer the crown without conditions. A hurriedly cobbled together Declaration of Rights—designed to confer legality and win support from all parties—purported to codify existing English rights. It complained that the king had disarmed some of the Protestants, while allowing "Papists" to have weapons. Instead, the declaration guaranteed "That the subjects which are Protestants may have arms for their defence suitable to their conditions and as allowed by law." What did this mean? We believe it meant that all Protestants—in other words, nearly all Englishmen—could have arms. But there were those curious qualifiers. "Suitable to their conditions" meant that arms were actually limited to upper-class Englishmen. The government limited gun ownership by limiting hunting. And "as allowed by law" meant that Parliament, not the king, could limit gun ownership. The declaration was not interpreted in England as prohibiting strict gun laws. The same Parliament that approved the Declaration of Rights opposed allowing Englishmen to all have guns in their homes. Such an idea "savours of the politics to arm the mob, which . . . is not very safe for any government," one member of Parliament warned.

Perhaps this was a background right, something the Framers intended to include in the Constitution, without ever quite saying so. There are some tantalizing clues: James Madison's notes for his speech to Congress introducing the Bill of Rights refers to the "English Decl. of Rts." and mentions "arms to Protestants" as one of its provisions. He may have been favorably contrasting a more universal right to the sectarian English version. But aside from that enigmatic scrawl (the report of his speech makes no mention of it, or of much else in the notes), there is no mention of the provision on arms from the English Declaration of Rights in the records of either the Constitutional Convention, the Congress, or the state legislatures that ratified the Bill of Rights.

However, we can draw some conclusions about what the Framers thought they were doing.

Let's be clear: the eloquent men who wrote "we the people" and the First Amendment did us no favors in the drafting of the Second Amendment. One reason it was ignored for so long is that it is so inscrutable. As later generations pore over the text, peering at stray commas and fuzzy wording, it is worth noting a few things about the text itself.

Start with those commas. The Founding generation believed in freedom to punctuate. Spelling and capitalization seemed an afterthought. Standardized rules did not take hold until the next century. Still, we must cope with the oddly choppy grammar, so unlike the other amendments to the Constitution. The version passed by Congress (and on display in the National Archives) stutters: "A well regulated Militia, being necessary to the security of a free State, the right of the people to keep and bear Arms, shall not be infringed." Law professor David Yassky, arguing in a brief in a federal court case, noted that a modern reading of this might be that "A well regulated militia . . . shall not be infringed."

Then there is the opening clause: "A well regulated militia, being necessary to the security of a free state." We know that the debate among the Framers revolved around this point: the survival and role of the militia. We know, too, that originally drafts included "and well armed" and made clear that militia service was universal. What was the significance of moving this clause to the beginning of the amendment? Did it render it merely throat clearing before the declaration of the right? Did it limit the right? Or did it explain the meaning of the right? It is worth noting that in the eighteenth century, "preambles" or "explanatory clauses" at the beginning of legal declarations had force: they were to be read as limiting what came after. John Jay wrote in an opinion in 1791, "A preamble cannot annul enacting clauses; but when it evinces the intention of the legislature and the design of the act, it enables us, in cases of two constructions, to adopt the one most consonant to their intention and design." Linguists point to the Framers' familiarity with Latin, and call the first clause an "ablative absolute"—it provides "the conditions under which the rest of the sentence is valid." At a time of intense public argument about constitutional first principles, the preamble aimed to communicate with ordinary Americans in their town meetings and taverns. Some argue that the operative clause is the "right" in the next section. The fact is that the Second Amendment is the only one of the ten in the Bill of Rights that has an explanatory clause of any kind. The First Amendment does not say, "Robust debate being necessary to sound public policy, Congress shall make no law . . ." We must take the preamble seriously.

Many modern readers are brought up short by "well regulated." Regulation, as we imagine it now, necessarily implies governmental rules and control. In the 1700s, not so much. "Well regulated" seems to have connoted internal balance, self-control, and good decorum. To Alexander Hamilton, it appeared to mean a "select" militia of only the most ardent men. In the Articles of Confederation, it seemed to mean a militia with enough weaponry. It may be that "well regulated" means "well disciplined." (The Constitution itself gives Congress the power to regulate commerce, which has a more modern meaning.) Some have asserted that a "free state" is a generic term, referring to republican government generally. But every other time that word is used in the Constitution, it refers not to "government" but states. (New Jersey, Georgia—those kinds of states.)

Then, the magisterial phrase: "the right of the people." Set aside the

question of what constitutes a right. Who are "the people"? The phrase
dots the Bill of Rights. Today those on both sides of the issue take it to
recognize an individual right of some kind, whether for personal protection or militia service. When we look at the rest of the Bill of Rights, the
meaning blurs a bit. The Fourth Amendment, for example, protects "the
right of the people to be secure in their persons"—but goes on to protect
their "houses, papers, and effects, against unreasonable searches and seizures." The First Amendment protects "the right of the people peaceably
to assemble, and to petition the Government for a redress of grievances."
The Ninth Amendment reserves rights to "the people," as distinct from
the Tenth Amendment, which reserves them to "the states."

More frequently, the Framers used "the people" to mean something
close to what we would call "the body politic." "We the People" formed
the Constitution. (Not "we the persons.") An interesting clue to their
thinking comes from the transcript of the Virginia ratification convention. In that contentious session where Madison and Henry and Mason
debated the militia, speakers used the phrase "the people" fifty-four
times, touching on other issues as well. Every single one referred to
the collective mass of Virginians, the voters, or the population generally. There is one exception: Madison seemed to regard "the people" as a
synonym for "the militia." He was asked why Congress would be given
the power to call forth the militia. Madison replied that resistance to the
laws obviously must be overcome. "This could be done only two ways;
either by regular forces, or by the people. By one or the other it must unquestionably be done. If insurrections should arise, or invasions should
take place, the people ought unquestionably to be employed to suppress
and repel them, rather than a standing army. The best way to do these
things, was to put the militia on a good and sure footing, and enable the
Government to make use of their services when necessary."

Finally, what did "keep and bear arms" mean? Of course, modern
Americans debate this phrase. There is no certain answer. Some find
this to refer to carrying guns in an individual capacity, for self-defense.
The official records of the time offer a strong clue of what the Framers
meant. David Yassky notes:

Searching a Library of Congress database containing all official records of debates in the Continental and U.S. Congresses between 1774 and 1821 reveals thirty uses of the phrase "bear arms" or "bearing arms" (other than in discussing the proposed Second Amendment); in every single one of these uses, the phrase has an unambiguously military meaning. The Continental Congress, for example, approved a prisoner exchange with the British conditioned on the returned prisoners being forbidden to "bear arms" for a specified period, and the Twelfth Congress debated legislation concerning prisoners taken "whilst voluntarily bearing arms in the service of Great Britain."

Another scholar looked at databases containing all surviving books, pamphlets, and newspaper articles from the period. He found 202 uses of the phrase in a military context, eight otherwise. In 2013, the National Archives launched a searchable database of all the writings and papers of six key founders (Washington, Adams, Jefferson, Hamilton, Franklin, and Madison). A search for the phrase "bear arms" produces 153 mentions—again, all in the military context or simply repeating the amendment's text.

One possible reason for the muddle is that the amendment itself was a bit of a holdover. The other amendments pointed forward; the Second Amendment, backward. Throughout this period we see a push-and-pull between the worldview of colonists who savored order and duty, and the newly emerging market-focused nation that cherished individual rights. The Second Amendment in some respects is a last vestige of "civic republicanism" in a list of liberties more drawn from the natural rights philosophy articulated by John Locke.

We cannot truly know what the Framers intended. But one would have to look far to find evidence that their principal concern was the risk that government would enact gun safety laws, or disarm farmers. They may have thought widespread gun ownership obvious or necessary, but thought it equally obvious that laws could protect public safety, too. (The Tenth Amendment, after all, reserves to the states the power they already had, which emphatically included criminal laws.) And yet: yes, they sought above all to protect the militias. But the militias, as they understood it, were drawn from all the people. The militias required an armed citizenry. Again, militia members were expected to own a military gun. It was not just a military draft, claiming all white men from sixteen to sixty, but a requirement to be armed for the good of the community. That was understood, and assumed.

Like using bleeding for medical care, wearing wigs, and keeping slaves, many practices and common understandings of the Founding Era are hard to fathom, or translate, today.

FOUR

Arkansas Toothpicks, Beecher's Bibles, and the Fourteenth Amendment

In any case, not long after the passage of the Second Amendment, the militia system it protected began to crumble.

We have an early clue about what the Framers meant by a "well regulated militia." A few months after the Second Amendment took effect, Congress passed the Uniform Militia Act of 1792. It followed the first-ever congressional probe of executive branch incompetence. A militia force led by General Arthur St. Clair had attacked Indians in the Ohio Territory, and lost nearly half its men. George Washington convened his cabinet and invented the idea of executive privilege to justify refusal to turn over documents to lawmakers. In the course of the controversy, Congress decided it was time to put some teeth into the militia system.

The new federal law required "each and every free able-bodied white male citizen" between eighteen and forty-five to enroll in a state militia. More significantly, it required them all to buy a gun.

Every citizen, so enrolled and notified, shall, within six months thereafter, provide himself with a good musket or firelock, a sufficient bayonet and belt, two spare flints, and a knapsack, a pouch, with a box therein, to contain not less than twenty four cartridges, suited to the bore of his musket or firelock, each cartridge to contain a proper quantity of powder and ball;

or with a good rifle, knapsack, shot-pouch, and powder-horn, twenty balls
suited to the bore of his rifle, and a quarter of a pound of powder; and
shall appear so armed, accoutred and provided, when called out to exercise.

This provision—in effect, a universal draft and a requirement that all free white men buy guns—reflects a profound degree of governmental intrusion in the country's early days. It reflects, too, the idea that citizens had a duty to participate in the governing of the country.

The public largely ignored the law. Enlistments were spotty. Fines were levied ($10, over $9,000 in today's dollars), but imposed seemingly at random. All told, "compulsory military service disintegrated during the early years of the republic."

Congress even established a nationwide registry of privately owned guns for militia use, called a "return." Officers were to catalogue the military-grade guns owned by the militiamen, and report to the central government. (Early American paperwork.) Presidents Washington and Adams essentially ignored the rule. President Jefferson—trying to revive the militia—ordered a "return" to catalogue the military guns adult American militiamen owned. He was disappointed that the bureaucracy's work was incomplete.

In 1791, the year before the Militia Act, Alexander Hamilton—now treasury secretary—searched for a source of revenue for the new government. He prodded Congress to enact an excise tax on whiskey. This hit some hard: with the Spanish-controlled Mississippi closed to American shipping, backcountry farmers were busy distilling grain into spirits to ship east. Western Pennsylvania farmers rebelled and took up arms. President Washington decided to make clear this Whiskey Rebellion was not the "well regulated militia" he had in mind. He mobilized fifteen thousand militiamen, with Hamilton at their head, to restore order. Most of the federal militiamen lacked guns of their own, and the national government had to buy them. By the time the federal posse showed up, most of the whiskey rebels had scattered. With a show of federal force, the new government established its authority.

The new nation even flirted with something more than militias. A few years later, the United States found itself entangled in a "quasi-war" with France. President John Adams reluctantly called for formation of that terrifying institution, a "standing army." Congress, authorizing it, euphemistically called its ten thousand troops a "Provisional Army." Hamilton took effective command, the ambitious man on horseback so feared by republican theorists. Adams brokered peace with France before the army could mobilize.

Soon, though, the militia system began to sputter. In 1812, trade disputes with Britain led to an ill-conceived war. Northeastern states refused even to authorize their militias to defend the coastline. British soldiers landed in Maryland. Seven thousand militiamen stood between them and the capital. The British brushed past. Quickly they burned the White House, now the home of none other than James Madison. Two historians dryly wondered "whether Madison took this occasion to reflect on his famous comment in *The Federalist* about the invincibility of a nation boasting a militia of 500,000." Not present that day was Madison's vice president: yes, Elbridge Gerry, who died a few months later.

As the country changed, expanded, grew more democratic and more rambunctiously individualist, the duty-bound concept of militia service withered. Fewer people showed up. Popular illustrations of militia musters no longer showed heroic farmers lined up for their patriotic service. Instead, they lampooned tipsy villagers, clad in shoddy clothes, slouching and lounging.

In the era we call "Jacksonian democracy," gun violence rose sharply. In the West and South, Americans dueled, drank, brandished weapons, and took ready offense. Andrew Jackson himself fought numerous duels, and killed at least one man who had insulted his wife. States began to pass the first modern-style gun control laws, focusing on easily concealed pistols or knives. (One could not conceal a musket.) In response to these laws, for the first time, some Americans began to argue that the "right to bear arms" protected individual gun ownership. For example, numerous state constitutions included "mirror" provisions of the national charter. Those dating from the Founding period tended to protect "the right to bear arms for defence of *themselves* and the state." By the mid-1800s, new state provisions had an individualist cast: "Every citizen has a right to bear arms, in defence of *himself* and the State." Even so, courts generally ruled that "the right to keep and bear arms" referred to militias, not an individual right. In 1820, a Kentucky state court overturned a law that barred the carrying of concealed weapons. (The defendant had been accused of hiding a sword in a cane.) Kentucky stood apart. Arkansas's court ruled that the Second Amendment and similar provisions in state constitutions only protected militias. Two models emerged: one calling the right a collective one, the other an individual right.

Over time, the "Arkansas doctrine" limiting the constitutional right to the militia became the standard interpretation. It was pungently expressed by the Supreme Court in another frontier state, Tennessee. A law there prohibited the carrying of a "Bowie knife or an Arkansas toothpick," weapons that were easily concealed. A man convicted of brandishing a knife claimed a violation of his right to bear arms. In an 1840 ruling, the state's high court explained that the provision was modeled on the English Bill of Rights and the Second Amendment. "The object, then, for which the right of keeping and bearing arms is secured is the defense of the public," it explained. A key was the phrase "bear arms," which was understood to have a military meaning. "A man in the pursuit of deer, elk, and buffaloes might carry his rifle every day for forty years, and yet it would never be said of him that he had borne arms; much less could it be said that a private citizen bears arms because he has a dirk or pistol concealed under his clothes, or a spear in a cane."

FROM DRED SCOTT TO
THE NEW BIRTH OF FREEDOM

Americans view the Constitution and its provisions in the light of our times. Each generation makes its own Second Amendment. In the decades before the Civil War, Americans had more guns than ever before. More of them were angry, too. The war itself raised again the question of the militias that were the heart of the Second Amendment. Armed conflict spread widely the use of guns. It pushed forward simmering issues of racial violence. And in the end, it left the Second Amendment itself largely irrelevant as a factor in America's emerging society, new constitutional order, and gun culture.

One spur for war was the U.S. Supreme Court's notorious 1857 *Dred Scott* decision, considered the worst in American history. Roger Taney's opinion overturned the federal law that embodied the Missouri Compromise and Compromise of 1850 between slave and free states. The Court declared that freed slaves could never be citizens, even when they move into a free state. If so, it ruled, they would be entitled to "the privileges and immunities of citizens." That vague phrase sits in the Constitution, but was never defined. For the first time, the Court articulated what it saw those privileges to be. Taney explained, in a tone of horror:

> *It would give to persons of the negro race, who were recognised as citizens in any one State of the Union, the right to enter every other State whenever they pleased, singly or in companies, without pass or passport, and without obstruction, to sojourn there as long as they pleased, to go where they pleased at every hour of the day or night without molestation, unless they committed some violation of law for which a white man would be punished; and it would give them the full liberty of speech in public and in private upon all subjects upon which its own citizens might speak; to hold public meetings upon political affairs, and to keep and carry arms wherever they went. And all of this would be done in the face of the subject race of the same color, both free and slaves, and inevitably producing discontent and insubordination among them, and endangering the peace and safety of the State.*

Taney's opinion was the first time in decades the Court had struck down a congressional enactment. It did so, too, using an approach we would recognize as "originalist." Taney purported to show that the

Founders intended to prevent African Americans from being citizens, even though the Constitution did not say that. Abraham Lincoln's speech at Cooper Union was an effort to show that Taney's reading of original intent was wrong. Taney's purportedly neutral use of the Founders' views was no such thing. Taney's originalism was itself the product of intense social pressure building on the issue of slavery. The South relied more on guns, because the South was a society with millions of people in bondage who could revolt at any moment. Many laws in Southern states had disarmed free black men. Slave states were growing increasingly insistent that slavery be protected, and that it expand into new territories. They were responding, in turn, to something new: the abolitionist movement. It, too, now saw guns as part of the answer.

Throughout the 1850s many foes of slavery had abandoned pacifist ideals, gravitating toward radical action. Abolitionists and the "Slave Power" took up arms rhetorically long before shots were fired. In 1856 Free Soil and pro-slavery forces poured into Kansas, struggling over the soon-to-be-state's constitution. Guns flooded the territory as well. Reverend Henry Ward Beecher, a flamboyant sermonist, drew thousands of admirers to Plymouth Church in Brooklyn, New York. He caused a sensation when he declared "more moral power in [a Sharps rifle] so far as the slaveholders of Kansas were concerned, than in a hundred Bibles." Beecher rallied supporters to send crates of guns and Bibles to Kansas. In New Haven, Yale faculty and students excitedly raised funds to ship twenty-seven rifles. Newspapers called the carbines "Beecher's Bibles." In Kansas, pro-slavery ruffians stormed the free town of Lawrence, carrying banners declaring "The Superiority of the White Race!" and "Bibles not Rifles!" They burned the Free Soil Hotel.

In 1859, John Brown—carrying arms sent by abolitionists for use in Kansas—raided the U.S. Arsenal at Harpers Ferry, West Virginia. He hoped to ignite a slave rebellion. Brown had even drafted a proposed new U.S. Constitution encouraging all men and women "of sound mind . . . to carry arms openly." Maryland and Virginia militia units responded first. U.S. Marines, commanded by Colonel Robert E. Lee, quickly joined them. After the combined force captured Brown and killed his men, fear of armed abolitionists intensified through the South. Slave states responded by strengthening their militias. Suddenly the idea of a state-focused military system did not seem so quaint, or so benign.

When the American Revolution created a new national government, people still felt obliged to pay homage to the ideal of state sovereignty and armed citizenry. The slaughter of the Civil War left little room for such pleasantries.

After Confederates fired on Fort Sumter in Charleston, South Carolina, President Lincoln called for 75,000 militiamen to enlist for ninety days to quell the rebellion. Northerners assumed war would end quickly. The first Battle of Bull Run in Manassas, Virginia, fractured those illusions. Washington officials and spectators sojourned in the countryside to see the expected triumph. When the South broke the Northern assault, the onlookers barely escaped in a panicked retreat back to the capital. Within a week after the battle, Lincoln signed laws providing for one million men enlisted for three years. The day Fort Sumter fell, the U.S. Army comprised sixteen thousand men. By the next year, it had 700,000. In 1863, Congress authorized a draft with three-year enlistments. Nearly 200,000 soldiers were African American. An army, not militias, would grind to victory.

In the end, more than two million fought to suppress the insurrection; the South fielded another million. A vast number of men now had experience with firearms. If local gunsmiths and arms smuggled from Europe had provided the firepower for the Revolution, this time a huge and profitable arms industry arose. Once state militias had patrolled the Southern plantations to enforce slavery. Now Northern armies and militias determined to uproot the same system.

Armed political and racial conflict continued after the war, and set the contours of the next development.

On April 9, 1865, in a small house in rural Appomattox Court House, Virginia, Confederate States Army General Robert E. Lee shook hands with U.S. Army General Ulysses S. Grant. The men—the one standing tall in perfectly ironed gray, the other donning mud-caked Union blue—were to end the American Civil War. When Lee finally asked Grant to write out the terms of the Confederate States Army's surrender, he negotiated only that his men, having been without food for days, be given rations and be allowed to keep their horses and mules. The animals belonged to individual citizens in the army and, Lee argued, they would be necessary to farming after the war. It would be the first step to rebuilding their civilian lives. Grant acquiesced, and so began the rebuilding of a nation.

But havoc did not end at Appomattox. Whole cities—Atlanta, Charleston, Richmond—were destroyed. Farms lost their entire livestock, which were loaned out to war efforts. Southerners suffered. And white ex-Confederates, humiliated by defeat and disgraced by poverty, were forced to live alongside their former slaves. Hundreds of thousands of African Americans had served in the Union Army, and many now returned home (often armed).

Southern whites held to the idea of racial domination, by force if necessary. State governments passed Black Codes seeking to restore slavery in all but name. These laws disarmed African Americans but let whites retain their guns. Pitched battles left scores of freedmen dead in Memphis and New Orleans. Reports of the rogue and violent South trickled onto the floor of Congress.

> In Mississippi houses have been burned and negros have been murdered. In Alabama a new code, a slave code in fact, has been attempted to be passed, and gentlemen must have seen that in the Malboro' district, in South Carolina, the planters have recently held meetings and resolved that the military power ought to be withdrawn and the freedmen compelled to work for their old masters.

South Carolina's black citizens sent a petition demanding the right to be armed on equal terms with whites. An army general issued a proclamation suspending the state's Black Codes, declaring, "The constitutional rights of all loyal and well-disposed inhabitants to bear arms will not be infringed; nevertheless this shall not be construed to sanction the unlawful practice of carrying concealed weapons, nor to authorize any person to enter with arms on the premises of another against his consent."

Congress tried to impose order. The Freedmen's Bureau bill sought to strengthen the temporary government agency that provided employment, relocation, and protection for freed slaves. Among its provisions, it guaranteed that "the constitutional right to bear arms" would be secured to all citizens equally, "without respect to race or color." Andrew Johnson, the garrulous Democrat who became president on Lincoln's assassination, vetoed it. The Civil Rights Act of 1866 sought formally to establish nondiscrimination and racial equality. It sought to guarantee the "privileges and immunities" of national citizenship, borrowing language used by the Supreme Court in the antebellum *Dred Scott* decision. Johnson vetoed that, too. Congress overrode both vetoes.

The Radical Republicans, as they were known, did not want to see the rights of African Americans held hostage to the partisan balance in Washington. They wrote two new constitutional amendments, designed to ensure civic and political equality. The Fifteenth Amendment guaranteed former slaves the right to vote, radical enough. The Fourteenth Amendment promised a social revolution.

It clarified that anyone born in the United States is a citizen, thus overturning *Dred Scott*. It declared that no state could "deprive any person of life, liberty, or property, without due process of law; nor deny to any person within its jurisdiction the equal protection of the laws." And it declared that "no state shall make or enforce any law which shall abridge the privileges or immunities of citizens of the United States." These sweeping guarantees would appear to impose a transformative vision of equal rights. Much of the next century of constitutional law amounted to a debate over the meaning of its phrases, grand but general, and to whom they should be applied.

At times the drafters held more expansive views than those of Congress as a whole, different still from the states that ratified it. Historian Eric Foner observes, "The problem of establishing the Amendment's 'original intent' is complicated by the fact that its final wording resulted from a series of extremely narrow votes in the Joint [drafting] Committee and subsequent alteration of the floor of Congress." Still, Foner notes, despite its very specific goals, "In language that transcended race and region, it challenged legal discrimination throughout the nation and changed and broadened the meaning of freedom for all Americans."

There is some evidence in these debates that some supporters of the Fourteenth Amendment intended to assure black citizens the right to protect themselves with guns. At the very least it was designed to make sure the Civil Rights Act of 1866 could be enforced, said one lawmaker, and white and black citizens should have equal rights, including "a right to bear arms." Senator Jacob Howard, introducing the Fourteenth Amendment on the floor, explained that it sought to protect "the personal rights guaranteed and secured by the first eight amendments of the Constitution." He ran through the Bill of Rights, including the right to keep and bear arms.

Sometimes that goal was described as to assure black families the ability to ward off abusive white militias. "In Mississippi," reported Senator Henry Wilson, "rebel State forces, men who were in the rebel armies, are traversing the State, visiting the freedmen, disarming them, perpetrating murders and outrages upon them; and the same things are done in other sections of the country." Other times, proponents said the purpose was to empower black men to *join* state militias. Certainly that was the fear expressed by some opponents of the amendment. On the House floor, after the amendment passed, one lawmaker warned that Alabama's Republican government was trying to establish a volunteer militia. "Of whom will that militia consist? Mr. Speaker, it will consist only of the black men of Alabama," he warned. "The white men will not degrade themselves by going into the ranks and becoming a part of the militia of the State with negroes." He predicted a "war of races."

But the intentions of some of the Radical Republicans in Congress and the understanding of the broader public seem at odds. The amendment's supporters did not sell the controversial measure to voters by claiming it would guarantee to freedmen the right to own guns.

Some scholars, notably Akhil Reed Amar of Yale, insist the Fourteenth Amendment turned the civic right of militia participation into an individual right of defense. "Between 1775 and 1866 the poster boy of arms morphed from the Concord minuteman to the Carolina freedman," he writes. Others disagree. "Whatever its appeal might be, Professor Amar's thesis suffers from a fatal flaw," one critique noted. "It confuses what should have been done with what was done." In fact, there is little evidence from the amendment's text or the statements of its framers that it meant to prohibit state governments from passing all gun regulations so long as they applied equally to white and black citizens.

In any case, just as during the period of the Constitutional Convention, the world of the framers of the Fourteenth Amendment seems palpably different from our own (or at least, from any world we would want to inhabit). It was a time of low-grade war between the races, when pressing arms into the hands of African American families was one of the only ways to protect them.

The Fourteenth Amendment became the central issue in the 1866 congressional midterm election. Radical Republicans who endorsed it were elected in huge numbers. Now they took control of Reconstruction policy. The South was divided into military districts. Southern states were barred from reentering the United States until they ratified the Fourteenth Amendment. African Americans began to flourish, electing officials throughout the South. Whites responded with terrorism, through the Ku Klux Klan. The new Republican governments of the Southern states did not see the Fourteenth Amendment as precluding their ability to protect public safety. In Texas, armed conflict raged between white Democratic Party clubs and largely black state militia and police. General Philip Sheridan, military commander of the southwest United States, commented that if he owned Texas and hell, he would rent out Texas and move to hell. The governor persuaded the legislature to pass a law "prescribing severe penalties for keeping and bearing deadly arms." In Mississippi the governor persuaded legislators to pass a law prohibiting the "barbarous practice" of carrying concealed weapons, which he said "was almost universal among both races in the South."

Eventually the North pulled back. Reconstruction formally ended in a deal to decide the tight 1876 presidential election. To keep the White House, Republicans agreed to withdraw the U.S. Army from the South. (The disputed electoral votes came from Florida and three other states. The deciding vote was cast by a Supreme Court justice. No hanging chads were involved.) The white-dominated caste system reasserted itself. It would take nearly a century to undo the consequences of Reconstruction's ignominious end.

And the Supreme Court led the judiciary in a shameful series of cases that denied to African American citizens the protection specifically designed to be given to them by the new constitutional provisions. The *Slaughter-House Cases* were first: they gutted the "privileges and immunities" clause of the Fourteenth Amendment. Those rights described only national rights, the Court ruled, but not those given within state laws or constitutions. An even more troubling case would follow.

In 1872, as racist Democrats surged back into power across the South, Louisiana citizens went to the polls. Fraud and violence marred the election. Republicans and Democrats each swore in a governor. A federal court ruled the Republican the victor, whose writ ran about as far as the New Orleans city limits. Around the state, the two sides organized militias and dug in for a fight. In the corner of a former slave plantation sat the tiny town of Colfax (named after the Republican vice president, Schuyler Colfax) within Grant Parish (named after the Republican president). The black militia took over the local courthouse and installed Republican officeholders. On Easter Sunday, the paramilitary White League stormed the town. The league massacred one hundred freedmen, losing two white men. Most victims were murdered after they surrendered, marched to their death two by two. The *New Orleans Times* exulted the next morning on its front page: "WAR AT LAST!!" Federal prosecutors charged white defendants with violating the civil rights of the freedmen, including the right to bear arms. Only three men were convicted. They appealed.

The U.S. Supreme Court heard the case in 1876. In *U.S. v. Cruikshank*, the justices ruled flatly that the Second Amendment—like the rest of the Bill of Rights—only applied to Congress. "The Second Amendment declares that it shall not be infringed; but this, as has been seen, means no more than that it shall not be infringed by Congress." It found that the convictions of the men were unconstitutional. The majority opinion neglected to mention that the case involved a massacre. Journalist Charles Lane called his book on the case *The Day Freedom Died.*

Cruikshank stands as an ugly episode in a morally debased time. Just a few years after it was enacted, the Fourteenth Amendment had been paralyzed. The ruling hindered federal enforcement of civil rights law until the 1960s. It would be another fifty years before the Supreme Court started to "incorporate" the Bill of Rights, applying its provisions to states. (Most of the provisions were not "incorporated" until the 1960s.) As a constitutional matter, the ruling had an unambiguous impact on the jurisprudence of guns: the Second Amendment did not apply to the states. And it was the states, not the federal government, that made criminal justice policy. The Court did not opine on whether it conferred a personal or a collective or a civic right. It didn't matter: it only bound Congress. States were free to do as they wished.

STRIKING THE BALANCE: GUNS AND GUN CONTROL

Over the next hundred years, several trends were evident.

Many Americans owned guns. A scholar writing in 1890 credited the Civil War. "The increase of crimes of blood has been beyond all comparison to that of the years pervious to it. The war, in effect, demoralized and changed the habits and sentiments and conduct of thousands of the men who engaged in it on either side."

At the same time, gun control laws were ubiquitous. A photo shows the main street of Dodge City, Kansas, in 1879. The scene looks like nothing more than a movie set for a Western movie: dusty street, lined by saloons and stores, with hitching posts for wagons. One expects a gunfight to erupt at any moment. Yet in the middle of the street is a large sign: "The Carrying of Fire Arms Strictly Prohibited." Visitors to Wichita, Kansas, in 1873 were told: "LEAVE YOUR REVOLVERS AT POLICE HEADQUARTERS, GET A CHECK."

And the militia system? It had vanished. In 1903 Congress passed the Dick Act. It created what we know as the National Guard, spending federal funds to train part-time soldiers (and requiring them to muster a certain number of days). "Well regulated," yes, but a far cry from the militia as the Framers knew them: only a small number of men, who would muster for a short time every year. This is what the Founding generation would have known as a "select militia." The "standing army" so widely feared is the United States Army, created in its modern form during World War I.

Over time gun ownership and gun rights evolved with the country's spread west. Frontiersmen had guns to protect themselves, to kill for food, to hunt (and on occasion to rob each other). The crowded cities of the East were less hospitable for an armed population. By the end of the nineteenth century, many state constitutions included language protecting the right to keep a gun at home, but authorizing other kinds of gun regulations.

Modern gun laws were enacted in two great waves. The first came with the rise of cities. As the industrial revolution began to transform the country, especially in the East, farmhands and immigrants flooded into growing urban areas. Violence was a much discussed threat, though easily concealed knives and clubs were the weapons of choice. Municipal police departments, first created in the 1800s, sought to impose order. Class conflict, labor disputes, and tumultuous strikes convulsed politics. It was a time of political violence. One president was assassinated in 1881, another in 1901, and his successor, Theodore Roosevelt, was shot in 1912. He spoke for nearly an hour with a bullet lodged in his ribs. "I don't know whether you fully understand that I have just been shot," he told his flummoxed listeners. "But it takes more than that to kill a Bull Moose."

At the turn of the twentieth century, nearly as many people crammed into New York City as had lived in the thirteen states when the Constitution was ratified. Violence was commonplace. Tammany Hall, the corrupt Democratic Party machine, governed. In 1911, Tammany had chosen a surprisingly honest judge, William Jay Gaynor, to be mayor. On a cruise ship berthed in New Jersey, a dismissed city worker fired on the mayor point-blank. Gaynor survived. Firearms deaths leapt 50 percent that year in New York City. The next year, after the high-profile murder of a novelist, the city's medical examiner launched a crusade for a new state gun law.

The cause was taken up by an unlikely champion: William "Big Tim" Sullivan, a Tammany Hall politician from Manhattan's Lower East Side. Sullivan was alleged to control, or at least to protect, much of the prostitution, gambling, and peep show industry south of 14th Street. He owned a string of vaudeville houses and penny arcades, and eventually formed an alliance with William Fox, the archetypal immigrant turned movie mogul. Sullivan also was evolving toward a stance as a social reformer, pushing protective legislation for women and workers. His immigrant constituents were most likely to have (and be menaced by) concealed handguns. Others suggested the high tax for guns might keep them in the hands of his own shady allies.

In 1911, Sullivan pushed a major gun control law through the legislature. The measure required a license to own a handgun, which must be approved by the sheriff or police, and made it a felony to carry a concealed gun outside the home. Small arms factories—the first gun lobby—opposed. "In spite of opposition from manufacturers of firearms," as *The New York Times* reported, the State Senate passed the handgun ban with only five dissents. Legislative debate rings familiar. "Your bill won't stop murders. You can't force a burglar to get a license to use a gun," insisted one upstate lawmaker. "He'll get one from another state." He noted that Alabama had just repealed a similar law. "Alabama is too far away from the Bowery for me to talk about it," Sullivan snorted.

Sullivan never saw the result of his work. The next year he suffered a mental breakdown, probably due to syphilis, and was confined to a sanitarium. He escaped and was the subject of a widely publicized manhunt. His body was found at the city morgue, ready for a pauper's burial. Seventy-five thousand residents of the Lower East Side thronged his funeral. The law did not seem to bring murders down, but did curb suicides by firearms.

Other states followed New York. Within a decade a model "Revolver Act" similar to the Sullivan Law became law in West Virginia, New Jersey, Michigan, Indiana, Oregon, California, New Hampshire, North Dakota, and Connecticut.

Through all this, the federal government stood at far remove. States and cities set crime policy—whether police forces, gun regulations, or everyday criminal laws. Recall that the Supreme Court already had ruled the Second Amendment did not apply to states. (At this time, courts had ruled that the Bill of Rights only limited actions by the federal government.) The Supreme Court ruled twice more that the Second Amendment did not create an individual right to gun ownership. One 1886 case, *Presser v. Illinois*, involved an armed parade of German immigrants affiliated with the Socialist Workers Party. The *bund* faced off against the newly created National Guard, which enforced the will of employers. The radicals insisted they, too, be regarded as a militia under the Second Amendment. The Supreme Court ruled that Illinois could decide who was, in fact, in its militia. More, it reaffirmed that the Second Amendment did not apply to states—but they could not pass laws that "prohibit the people from keeping and bearing arms, so as to deprive the United States of their rightful resource for maintaining the public security, and disable the people from performing their duty to the general government." In other words, a state could not ban guns to the degree that it would interfere with the federal government's military needs. In *Miller v. Texas*, a criminal defendant argued that the state's law prohibiting the carrying of weapons violated his Second Amendment right. The court disagreed: "We have examined the record in vain, however, to find where the defendant was denied the benefit of any of these provisions."

Attitudes toward the Second Amendment continued to evolve with the country and its broader understanding of the Constitution and what it means. During the nation's first century and a half, most domestic policy was set by the states. Industrialization, followed by the Great Depression, rapidly changed that. For the first time Americans urgently wanted strong national laws to be issued from Washington. The "alphabet soup" of federal agencies—from securities law to electric power— thrust the national government far more deeply into every aspect of American life. The "constitutional revolution" of the New Deal was, in many ways, a moment of constitutional lawmaking as significant as the Civil War amendments. The modern, national American government finally took shape. The federal government began to take an active role in criminal justice, too, far beyond its earlier efforts.

Social disruption proved the spur.

Prohibition had sparked mayhem in the cities, as gangs battled to control the flow of illegal liquor. New weapons, first designed for use in World War I, made it easy for gangsters to spray bullets at their foes. Cars and paved highways let them speed across state lines. During the Depression, bank robbery replaced bootlegging as a profit center. Al Capone, George "Machine Gun" Kelly, and Bonnie and Clyde (who posed provocatively with their guns) became household names. Newly elected president Franklin Roosevelt had a two-part strategy to stem the carnage. First, he ended Prohibition, winning repeal of the Eighteenth Amendment. Then he waged a crackdown on gangsters and their guns, what his attorney general called a "New Deal for Crime." And he won passage of the first federal gun legislation, the National Firearms Act of 1934. The law imposed a heavy tax on the weapons used most prominently by gangsters and familiar to any moviegoer of the time. Machine guns and sawed-off shotguns had to be registered, and could not be transported across state lines. Originally the bill included pistols, but opposition from gun owners forced amendment. In the end the National Rifle Association—then a sportsmen's group—backed the plan. The act swept through Congress in Roosevelt's first term. The federal crackdown on guns was hugely popular. When Federal Bureau of Investigation special agents captured Machine Gun Kelly, he blurted out, "Don't shoot, G-Men; don't shoot!" The nickname for federal agents stuck. FBI director J. Edgar Hoover used the crackdown on armed gangsters to build acclaim for an agency that began with controversial Palmer Raids on radicals in the 1920s. The year the gun law passed, Hollywood motion picture studios embraced a voluntary censorship code. Among the consequences: no more enormously popular gangster movies. Instead, producers got around the code by making movies focused on government agents pursuing gangsters. James Cagney got famous playing a criminal in *The Public Enemy*; in 1935, he starred in *G Men*, one of sixty-five movies that year glorifying FBI agents. The public that embraced the assertive national government embodied by Roosevelt's New Deal social programs was untroubled by federal laws cracking down on unusually dangerous guns. Libertarian sentiments reached low ebb. By 1938, the administration sought another gun bill, extending it to all guns. This time gun owners and the NRA protested. The final bill, the second federal gun control law in four years, banned interstate trafficking in guns without a license.

The Supreme Court upheld the 1934 law in *United States v. Miller*, by far its most direct examination of the Second Amendment in its first two centuries.

The case boasted a picturesque background. Jack Miller robbed banks. He was part of a notorious crew called the O'Malley Gang that raised hell throughout the Ozarks. Miller had become an informant, sending gang members to Alcatraz and other federal prisons. The next year, police picked him up driving with a sawed-off shotgun, apparently having crossed state lines, readying his next robbery. Federal agents hauled Miller before a judge, who ruled the new gun law violated the Second Amendment. He released the defendant, who promptly disappeared. Newspapers speculated that *Miller* was set up to be a test case, designed to elicit a favorable court ruling. (One clue: far from a foe of gun control, the judge who struck down the law on Second Amendment grounds was actually a former New Deal congressman who had ardently backed such measures.) The appeal went straight to the Supreme Court. Miller's lawyer telegrammed the justices' clerk: "UNABLE TO OBTAIN ANY MONEY FROM CLIENTS TO BE PRESENT AND ARGUE CASE." Only the government spoke. Miller resurfaced a month after the justices heard his case, sticking up the Route 66 Club in Miami, Oklahoma. He was found murdered the next day.

In upholding Roosevelt's gun law, the Court made its most definitive statement yet. Justice James Clark McReynolds, no friend of the New Deal, wrote for a unanimous Court. Without evidence that a sawed-off shotgun "at this time has some reasonable relationship to the preservation or efficiency of a well regulated militia, we cannot say that the Second Amendment guarantees the right to keep and bear such an instrument. Certainly it is not within judicial notice that this weapon is any part of the ordinary military equipment or that its use could contribute to the common defense," McReynolds wrote. He added: "With obvious purpose to assure the continuation and render possible the effectiveness of such forces the declaration and guarantee of the Second Amendment were made. It must be interpreted and applied with that end in view."

It was an odd opinion; McReynolds wrote poorly. Still, in broad outline, the *Miller* decision encompassed the history of the amendment: it traced the history of the militia, and the centrality of the debate over the perils of a standing army to the purpose of the Second Amendment. Its analysis of what kind of weapon could not be banned did not, notably, say that the weapon needed to be useful to a militia in 1789—rather, the test was in 1939. The Court left little doubt where it stood on the purpose and scope of the Amendment, despite later revisionist claims to the contrary.

There it stood. Gun control laws waxed and waned. Urban violence began to climb in the 1960s and 1970s, as a huge influx of rural residents arrived north at the very moment industrial jobs began to vanish. Focus on guns would peak after a publicized act of violence, often political. When Martin Luther King Jr. and Robert F. Kennedy were assassinated in the spring of 1968, President Lyndon Johnson pressed Congress to enact the Gun Control Act of 1968. It established a federal licensing system for gun dealers and banned the importation of military-style weapons. It also prohibited certain classes of people deemed dangerous— felons; fugitives; people dishonorably discharged from the military— from purchasing or possessing guns. The NRA stayed mostly silent. The assassination attempt on Ronald Reagan led over a decade later to a new gun law. The Brady Bill—named after his wounded press secretary, James S. Brady, who campaigned for passage—required a background check and waiting period before buying a gun. The next year President Bill Clinton won passage of a ban on assault weapons as part of a larger crime bill. Most focus, though, fell on other criminal justice measures that sought to grapple with a surge of crime and drugs. Harsh drug laws, "three strikes and you're out," mandatory minimums, new policing strategies were tried and discarded. The rate of violence peaked, then began to fall steeply starting in the mid-1990s.

And through it all, the decisions were made—or not made—by democratic means. Officials were elected or defeated. Richard Nixon won vowing to the Republican convention he would appoint a "new attorney general" and seek a return of "order in America." Conversely, Democrats who voted for the crime bill lost seats in the 1994 election, helping to swing Congress to the Republicans. "Three strikes and you're out" laws spread after a referendum victory in California that same year.

The courts, in short, stayed out. As crime policy—even gun laws—was debated, few thought that some constitutional provision, long submerged, in fact could strap limits on what society could and could not do to preserve order.

The constitutional consensus was expressed pungently by Chief Justice Warren Burger, appointed by the president who ran on "law and order":

> *This has been the subject of one of the greatest pieces of fraud, I repeat the word "fraud," on the American public by special interest groups that I have ever seen in my lifetime. Now just look at those words. There are only three lines to that amendment. A well regulated militia—if the militia, which was going to be the state army, was going to be well regulated, why shouldn't 16 and 17 and 18 or any other age persons be regulated in the use of arms the way an automobile is regulated? It's got to be registered, that you can't just deal with at will.*

PART
TWO

PART

TWO

FIVE

Revolt at Cincinnati

The NRA bills itself "the nation's longest standing civil rights organization." That's not exactly how it started.

During the Civil War, Union officers had grown perturbed at the poor marksmanship of their troops. Previously, guns were inaccurate, and target practice a waste of time. Now new technology—breech-loading guns and metal cartridge ammunition—made shooting a prized skill. In 1871, militia and army veterans created a new organization to train American men to shoot safely and accurately: the National Rifle Association. General Ambrose Burnside—yes, the same gent whose name lives to describe his distinctive whiskers—served as ceremonial president for a year. Government helped: New York State bought the NRA a rifle range to hold contests. The organization nearly collapsed when the state withdrew its support. "There will be no war in my time or in the time of my children," New York's governor assured the group's leader. "The only need for a National Guard is to show itself in parades and ceremonies." So federal officials stepped in, creating the National Board for the Promotion of Rifle Practice in 1901. It gave away surplus guns to clubs sponsored by the NRA. Between the world wars, the federal government provided 200,000 rifles to NRA members at cost. After the defeat of Japan, with its membership swelled, the NRA began to shift its focus. Its publications dwelled on hunting and sports shooting, not paramilitary activity. The group lobbied, and was based in Washington, D.C., but its principal focus was bagging deer, not blocking laws. In the late 1950s, it opened a new headquarters building to house its hundreds of employees. Metal letters spelled out its purpose in 1958: FIREARMS SAFETY EDUCATION, MARKSMANSHIP TRAINING, SHOOTING FOR RECREATION.

The NRA expressed unease with gun laws. But even as its ranks grew, it did not object to the first federal gun control measure, Franklin Roosevelt's 1934 National Firearms Act, which banned machine guns and sawed-off shotguns. Its chief lobbyist testified before Congress. "I have never believed in the general practice of carrying weapons," he told a House committee. ". . . I do not believe in the general promiscuous toting of guns. I think it should be sharply restricted and only under licenses." A lawmaker asked him whether the proposed law violated any part of the Constitution. The witness responded, "I have not given it any study from that point of view."

Crime remained low, and political violence minimal, in the years of consensus during World War II and the early Cold War. The tumult of the 1960s fractured that calm. Gun violence began to assume the status of a public controversy.

In March 1963, an advertisement appeared in the NRA's *American Rifleman* magazine:

LATE ISSUE! 6.5 ITALIAN CARBINE. Only 36" overall, weighs only 5 ½ lbs. Shows only slight use, lightly oiled, test fired and head spaced, ready for shooting. Turned down bolt, thumb safety, 6-shot, clip fed. Rear open sight. Fast loading and fast firing.

A man calling himself "A. Hidell" clipped the coupon and sent $21.45 to a Chicago-based mail order house to buy the military rifle. Hidell was Lee Harvey Oswald. After the assassination in Dallas, investigations angrily focused on the fact that it was possible to buy a rifle and ammunition sight unseen through the mail. Congress considered new gun laws. An NRA official testified, "We do not think that any sane American, who calls himself an American, can object to placing into this bill the instrument which killed the president of the United States." Gun owners, however, contacted Congress to bury the bill. Lawmakers vowed an investigation of the gun lobby itself.

As the decade unfolded, political divisions took on deep cultural dimensions, pitting rural and suburban culturally conservative white voters against younger, more diverse city dwellers. Race invariably intruded. *American Rifleman* started a new column, "The Armed Citizen," which profiled vigilantes. *Guns & Ammo* magazine said supporters of tighter gun rules were "criminal-coddling do-gooders, borderline psychotics, as well as Communists and leftists who want to lead us into the one-world welfare state." As Newark, Watts, and Washington, D.C., burned in urban rioting, and leading American public figures were assassinated, Americans began to worry we were distinctly violent. Historian Richard Hofstadter ruminated on America's gun culture in a widely read article in the otherwise apolitical *American Heritage*. Gun politics deepened cultural divides, he noted. "The most gun-addicted sections of the United States are the South and the Southwest. In 1968, when the House voted for a mild bill to restrict the mail-order sale of rifles, shotguns, and ammunition, all but a few of the 118 votes against it came from these regions. This no doubt has something to do with the rural character of these regions, but it also stems from another consideration: in the historic system of the South, having a gun was a white prerogative."

In a time of backlash, the NRA grew increasingly vocal. When lawmakers trifled with it, the gun lobby showed it could retaliate at the ballot box. For years after, politicians would whisper about the intense passion of gun owners, and how they "took out" a pro–gun control senator from Maryland, Joseph Tydings, whose pelt might as well have been mounted in the NRA's waiting room.

Still, the NRA principally spoke for hunters. It did not pose in opposition to law enforcement, or government generally, and it did not routinely invoke the Second Amendment. Though it did not support the 1968 gun bill, its opposition was muted. "The measure as a whole appears to be one that the sportsmen of America can live with," the organization's president assured members. In March of that year, supporting restrictions on cheap "Saturday Night Special" handguns, *American Rifleman* told its readers the NRA "does not necessarily approve of everything that goes 'Bang!'" The magazine's cover displayed a cheery defining image. A trim and chiseled man, resembling Paul Newman with a jaunty peaked cap, pine trees towering behind, held up a recently demised mountain lion.

The stance in favor of the Saturday Night Special ban set in motion forces that would supplant that grinning hunter in the NRA's pantheon of acceptable images.

Gun group veterans still call the NRA's 1977 annual meeting the "Revolt at Cincinnati." One weekend in 1976, the NRA board fired eighty staff members. The next year, the organization's leadership decided to move its headquarters to Colorado Springs, Colorado, signaling a retreat from politics. More than a thousand angry dissidents showed up at the annual convention. Many wore orange caps, and communicated by walkie-talkie. As they sweltered they insinuated that the old guard had turned off the air-conditioning. By four in the morning, the dissenters had voted out the organization's leadership. Activists from other groups—the Second Amendment Foundation, the Citizens Committee for the Right to Keep and Bear Arms—pushed their way into power. Neal Knox, editor of *Gun Week* magazine, became the NRA's new head lobbyist. He opposed gun laws of any kind. Knox mused on whether the assassinations of the 1960s were part of a gun control conspiracy. "Is it possible that some of those incidents could have been created for the purpose of disarming the people of the free world? With drugs and evil intent, it's possible," he wrote in *Shotgun News* in 1994. "Rampant paranoia on my part? Maybe. But there have been far too many coincidences to ignore."

The NRA's new leadership was dramatic, dogmatic, and overtly ideological. For the first time, it embraced the idea that the sacred Second Amendment—not just the interests of hunters or even of homeowners—was at the heart of its concerns. The first *American Rifleman* after the revolt had a new paragraph under "What the NRA Is":

The NRA, the foremost guardian of the traditional American right to "keep and bear arms," believes that every law-abiding citizen is entitled to the ownership and legal use of firearms, and that every reputable gun owner should be an NRA member.

The NRA's lurch to the right was part of an abrupt shift across the Republican coalition.

Forget baby boomer reveries and public television music documentaries. The rebellions of the 1960s seemed earthshaking at the time. In retrospect, the response from the right (and unnerved middle-class citizens) proved more politically potent and durable. Racial fears played an elemental part, especially as millions of white Southern Democrats left the party of their ancestors to vote Republican, first for president and then more reluctantly for Congress. Once sleepy groups galvanized as conservative activists wrested control. The NRA was one. Evangelical Christian churches underwent a similar change. Southern Baptists long had eschewed organized electoral politics. In 1976, most voted for Jimmy Carter, who became the first professedly born-again president. The Southern Baptist convention was convulsed by factional fights that led to the elevation of fundamentalist leadership—ministry devoted to the idea that Scripture was inerrant. Even more politically, in 1979 television minister Jerry Falwell and other conservative activists formed the Moral Majority, a coalition of religious conservatives. By 1980 nearly three quarters of them voted for Reagan. Soon conservatives tossed around the language of insurrection with the ardor of a 1960s Weatherman. The "Revolt at Cincinnati" was followed by the "tax revolt," which began in California in 1979. Conservative activists organized to pass Proposition 13, which slashed property taxes and shrank budgets with an impact that lasted for three decades. In Arizona, Colorado, and other Western states, landowners opposed the Interior Department environmental policies in a "sagebrush rebellion." Organized business shifted, too, albeit with a less mutinous stance. Corporate lobbying had been a hushed affair, with big companies such as Procter & Gamble or General Motors wooing and contributing to Democratic and Republican incumbents alike. Power and initiative shifted to the U.S. Chamber of Commerce and other ideologically charged coalitions. In the late 1970s, the Chamber supplanted the Business Roundtable (the genteel organization of CEOs) as a free-spending lobbying organization for deregulation, tax cuts, and laws to make it harder to organize a union. Business groups became more political, more partisan, harder hitting.

The New Right stitched together causes, some intrinsically at odds with others. Social conservatives sought to restore traditional gender roles and values. Economic conservatives wanted lower taxes and a reduced regulatory role for government. Foreign policy moved Northern Catholic "Reagan Democrats" and formerly liberal Jewish "neoconservatives," especially when Democrats seemed weak in the long twilight struggle against communism. As the rights language of the social movements of the 1960s began to permeate society, conservatives began to adopt its rhetoric. Young conservatives spoke less frequently of "tradition," more of "freedom." Broad and growing disdain for government deepened the appeal. In 1958, measured by polls, 78 percent trusted the government to "do what is right" most or nearly all the time. By the late 1970s that had fallen to 25 percent.

In its new militance, the NRA fused with other conservative organizations in an overtly political coalition. Journalist Thomas Byrne Edsall, the most acute chronicler of the shift, wrote, "Over the past forty years the Republican Party and the conservative movement have together created a juggernaut—a loosely connected but highly coordinated network of individuals and organizations—with a shared stake in a strong, centralized political machine." The NRA became critical to that new machine, providing fierce energy and dedicated voters. From the time of the first urban rioting in 1964 until Ronald Reagan's first year as president, membership tripled (from 600,000 to 1.9 million).

As the NRA emphasized the Second Amendment, Reagan gave the new constitutional thrust rhetorical support. The 1972 Republican platform had supported gun control. "We pledge a tireless campaign against crime—to restore safety to our streets, and security to law-abiding citizens who have a right to enjoy their homes and communities free from fear. We pledge to . . . intensify efforts to prevent criminal access to all weapons, including special emphasis on cheap, readily-obtainable hand-guns . . . with such federal law as necessary to enable the states to meet their responsibilities." In 1975, preparing to challenge Gerald R. Ford for the Republican nomination, Reagan wrote, "The Second Amendment is clear, or ought to be. It appears to leave little if any leeway for the gun control advocate." The 1980 GOP platform now proclaimed, "We believe the right of citizens to keep and bear arms must be preserved. Accordingly, we oppose federal registration of firearms." It called for repeal of some existing gun laws. That year the NRA gave Reagan its first-ever presidential endorsement.

But the organization itself stumbled during Reagan's term. The would-be assassin who grievously wounded presidential press secretary James Brady fired his six shots under the delusion they would impress movie actress Jodie Foster. Brady and his wife mounted a long campaign to require a five-day waiting period for purchasing a handgun, to keep them out of the hands of the mentally ill and criminals. Reagan supported the move. The NRA pulled back, fired its lead lobbyist, and went through a bout of internal recriminations. Membership shrank and its finances withered. It recovered as its members demanded more militance. "'What if there had been a Brady Bill 150 years ago? What if they had to wait seven days to get their rifles to come to the Alamo and fight?' an NRA vice president . . . shouted to loud applause at the annual meeting in 1991 in San Antonio," according to a *Washington Post* account.

Bill Clinton's election as president boosted NRA membership another 600,000. Clinton had tangled with the group in Arkansas. More than most national Democrats, Clinton was acutely aware of the cultural gulf separating rural gun owners from those worried about crime in crowded urban neighborhoods. His electoral strategy appealed to Reagan Democrats who had left the party, often over cultural issues. Clinton's agenda offered a complex mix of policies and signals. Violence was at an all-time high when he ran. Campaign commercials bragged he was a "New Democrat" who supported the death penalty. In speeches to black audiences, he drew applause when he spoke of the toll of gun violence. He extemporized his best-remembered presidential speech in the Memphis pulpit where Martin Luther King Jr. preached his last sermon. Were King to return, Clinton mused, he would be pleased by racial progress. "But he would say, I did not live and die to see the American family destroyed. I did not live and die to see 13-year-old boys get automatic weapons and gun down 9-year-olds just for the kick of it." Seeking to mollify gun rights supporters, he often noted that half the people in Arkansas had hunting or fishing licenses. But he signed the Brady Bill as well as a ban on fourteen kinds of assault weapons. "Not a single hunter in America has lost a weapon or missed a season as a result," he bragged.

But the tough votes on gun measures cost Democrats dearly in the 1994 midterm elections. Rural incumbents, including Speaker of the House Thomas Foley of eastern Washington State, lost as the Republicans took both chambers. "The NRA is the reason the Republicans control the House," Clinton groused two months later. Conventional wisdom echoed Clinton's plaint, though in fact numerous factors were involved, including a tax increase. Still, Democrats developed a strong muscle memory: stay away from gun control.

Despite Clinton's sure political touch, his drawled soft sell to fellow duck hunters may have missed a step. The NRA and the gun rights movement had moved beyond traditional sporting concerns. Increasingly it took on an apocalyptic, insurrectionist tone: an organization that started as a project of Union Army officers now challenged government's very legitimacy. Clots of angry citizens had begun to form armed "militias," warning that United Nations troops flying black helicopters would soon stage raids on the heartland. An organizational resolution declared: "Although the NRA has not been involved in the formation of any citizen militia units, neither has the NRA discouraged, nor would the NRA contemplate discouraging, exercise of any constitutional right."

Wayne LaPierre had been the organization's executive vice president and chief executive since 1991. Once he had almost gone to work for liberal Speaker of the House Tip O'Neill. In 1995, he signed a fund-raising letter to the NRA's 3.5 million members calling federal law enforcement agents "jack-booted government thugs." He continued, "In Clinton's administration, if you have a badge, you have the government's go-ahead to harass, intimidate, even murder law-abiding citizens." Shortly after, domestic terrorist Timothy McVeigh killed 168 people in the bombing of the federal building in Oklahoma City. When arrested, McVeigh wore a T-shirt emblazoned with Thomas Jefferson's paean to armed insurrection at the time of Shays' Rebellion, "The tree of Liberty must be refreshed from time to time with the blood of patriots and tyrants." His co-conspirator was part of an antigovernment movement styling itself a modern militia. News accounts noted that the NRA board now included the founder of *Soldier of Fortune* magazine. Former President George H. W. Bush resigned from the group to protest its incendiary rhetoric. The NRA had plunged fully into the culture wars.

After Oklahoma City, seeking to steer a less incendiary course, NRA leaders elected Charlton Heston first vice president. He later served as its president. Heston had played Moses in *The Ten Commandments* and the chariot-racing slave in *Ben-Hur*. He had marched with King as part of the Hollywood contingent at the 1963 March on Washington. He used new rhetoric, bound up in a man's duty to stand guard:

> *I am not really here to talk about the Second Amendment or the NRA, but the gun issue clearly brings into focus the culture war that's going on.*
>
> *Rank-and-file Americans wake up every morning, increasingly bewildered and confused at why their views make them lesser citizens. . . . Heaven help the God-fearing, law-abiding, Caucasian, middle class, Protestant, or—even worse—Evangelical Christian, Midwest, or Southern, or—even worse—rural, apparently straight, or—even worse—admittedly heterosexual, gun-owning or—even worse—NRA-card-carrying, average working stiff, or—even worse—male working stiff, because not only don't you count, you're a downright obstacle to social progress. . . . That's why you don't raise your hand. That's how cultural war works. And you are losing.*

Heston framed the fight for gun rights at the heart of the long struggle for freedom. He gave a legendary speech before the NRA's 2000 annual meeting, as Vice President Al Gore ran for president. He rhapsodized,

> *sacred stuff resides in that wooden stock and blue steel, something that gives the most common man the most uncommon of freedoms. . . . When ordinary hands can possess such an extraordinary instrument, that symbolizes the full measure of human dignity and liberty.*
>
> *As we set out this year to defeat the divisive forces that would take freedom away, I want to say those fighting words for everyone within the sound of my voice to hear and to heed—and especially for you, Mr. Gore.*

He held aloft a replica of a colonial rifle, and growled to a roar, "From my cold, dead hands!"*

The NRA moved into new headquarters. Oversized letters on the facade no longer referred to marksmanship. Instead, the wall of the building's lobby was emblazoned with the Second Amendment. Visitors might not notice that the text on the wall is not quite accurate. It reads:

> ". . the right of the people to keep and bear arms shall not be infringed."

The first half—the part about the well regulated militia—was edited out.

"THE STANDARD MODEL"

Second Amendment fundamentalism was rising. But courts, scholars, and the legal community with rare unanimity for much of the cen-

---

* Close your eyes when listening to Heston's speech: the actor brilliantly mimics his own classic line from *Planet of the Apes*, "Take your stinking paws off me, you damn dirty ape!"

tury had agreed that the Second Amendment did not mean what the camouflage-clad attendees at Charlton Heston speeches said it did. There was no more settled view in constitutional law than that the Second Amendment did not protect an individual right to own a gun.

After all, the Supreme Court had considered the matter four times, and had never found a Second Amendment right to individual gun ownership. In the Reconstruction-era *Cruikshank* case, it ruled that the amendment did not cover the states. In *Presser*, it found that gun rights belonged to militias. In *Miller v. Texas* in 1894, it rejected the criminal defendant's gun right claim. In the 1939 *Miller* case, it upheld federal gun law, making clear that gun laws only could not interfere with actual, current militia service. Lower courts agreed, when they considered the topic at all. Few litigants even raised an alternative view: it was seen as frivolous, a fringe position. But by the time the Supreme Court heard another challenge in *Heller*, there was strong momentum for a different view. What happened?

One key factor was a tsunami of scholarship and pseudo-scholarship that argued the traditional view—shared by courts and historians—was wrong. These new academic advocates insisted there had been a colossal constitutional mistake. The legislatures that had passed public safety laws to address modern conditions, and the courts that had upheld those laws, had been in error. The Founders, and their words, would show us how to put it right.

One political scientist examined a century's worth of law review articles on the Second Amendment. From the time the reviews began to be indexed in 1888, to 1960, every single article concluded the Second Amendment did not guarantee an individual right. The first to argue otherwise—written by a student, who began by citing an article in *American Rifleman*—appeared in 1960. It said the amendment enforced a "right of revolution," of which the Southern states availed themselves during what the author called "The War Between the States." Throughout the 1960s, only a few articles echoed that view. Then a squad of lawyers and law professors began to churn out law review submissions at a prodigious rate. Historian Carl Bogus writes, "From 1970 to 1989, twenty-five articles adhering to the collective rights view were published (nothing unusual there), but so were twenty-seven articles endorsing the individual rights model. However, at least sixteen of these articles—about 60 percent—were written by lawyers who had been directly employed by or represented the NRA or other gun rights organizations, although they did not always so identify themselves in the author's footnote."

Among the most prominent was Stephen Halbrook. He served as a lawyer in the NRA's general counsel's office, a fact unmentioned in his biography in many of his law review essays. By one estimate, three strikingly prolific writers—Halbrook, Don Kates, David Hardy—wrote thirty law review articles in the 1990s and received a million dollars in funding to back their work on gun issues. One lawyer, David Kopel, wrote or coauthored nineteen law review articles over the decade. Funds flowed freely. The NRA Foundation provided $1 million to endow the Patrick Henry professorship in constitutional law and the Second Amendment at George Mason University Law School. The NRA Civil Rights Defense Fund's annual "Stand Up for the Second Amendment" contest offered $25,000 for the best essay. In 1992, it partly funded the founding of a group, Academics for the Second Amendment, which held conferences and filed briefs. The NRA paid one lawyer $15,000 to write a harsh book review of Saul Cornell's *A Well-Regulated Militia*, among other tasks.

It is hard to convey fully the circular nature of these writings. One after another, they plumbed the same material, extracted the same quotes, and piled up citations to one another. Soon they began to include self-congratulatory explanations of how many other articles made the same point. Joyce Lee Malcolm bragged to a magazine writer, "There is no one for me to argue against anymore." The respected libertarian law professor Glenn Reynolds in 1995 surveyed the terrain and declared there was a new "Standard Model," akin to the ones adopted by physicists or astronomers to denote a scholarly consensus.

So far, the lawyers toiled at the fringe of respectability, far from the center of constitutional debate. One law review article changed all that.

Sanford Levinson is a prominent, well-respected liberal constitutional law professor at the University of Texas at Austin. In 1989, he published an article tweaking other liberals for ignoring "The Embarrassing Second Amendment." It argued that the Founders intended to grant people the right to rebel. "For too long, most members of the legal academy have treated the Second Amendment as the equivalent of an embarrassing relative, whose mention brings a quick change of subject to other, more respectable, family members. That will no longer do." He was joined by Akhil Reed Amar. The Yale professor styled himself a liberal originalist, arguing that while the Framers focused on a militia comprised of all citizens, the Fourteenth Amendment had transformed the right into one held by individuals. (Amar makes much of the fact that militias were seen to comprise all white males. Of course, the Constitution itself gave Congress the implicit power to define who was in a militia or how it would function.) Harvard's Laurence Tribe tentatively endorsed some version of an individual rights theory in a new edition of his widely used casebook. These prominent progressives differed with one another, and offered conflicting views of the amendment and its scope. What mattered was their political provenance. (One is reminded of Robert Frost's definition of a liberal: someone so open-minded he will not take his own side in an argument.) Tribe and Amar later penned an op-ed decrying the idea that people might think the Second Amendment precludes gun regulations then before Congress.

It's important to note who did not change their view of history: *historians*. Those who spent years exploring the history, context, and meaning of the Founding Era continued to conclude, with few exceptions, that the Framers' concern about militias had animated the Second Amendment. Jack Rakove, Pulitzer Prize–winning historian and author of *Original Meanings*, notes:

> *It is one thing to ransack the sources for a set of useful quotations, and another to weigh their interpretive authority. Originalism is first and foremost a theory of law and constitutional interpretation, but its viability depends upon its approach to history and its uses of historical evidence. . . .*

[In] fact only a handful of sources from the period of constitutional forma-
tion bear directly at the heart of our current controversies about the regu-
lation of private firearms. If Americans had indeed been concerned with
the impact of the Constitution on this right, and had addressed the subject
directly, the proponents of the individual rights theory would not have re-
cycled the same handful of references to the dissenters in the Pennsylvania
ratification convention and the protests of several Massachusetts towns
against their state's proposed constitution, or to rip promising snippets of
quotations from the texts and speeches in which they are embedded.

The revisionist wave came not from historians but from lawyers, and
law professors. "Law office history" describes the practice of plucking
facts or quotes out of time or out of context to fit a legal argument. It is
a style familiar to those who write or read briefs. The revisionist writers
practiced it with gusto. It is also worth understanding the distinct, somewhat anomalous position of law review articles. Unlike similar journal
articles in, say, history, economics, medicine, or mathematics, law review
articles are not subject to peer review. Students choose and edit them.
Yet courts cite them frequently. When it comes to gun rights, the revisionist articles played a crucial role.

When one delves into the articles' historic claims, a startling number
of them crumble.

Some of the assumptions are simply funny. In his book on judicial
philosophy, Justice Antonin Scalia, for example, lauded Joyce Lee Malcolm's "excellent study" on the English Bill of Rights, noting snarkily
that "she is not a member of the Michigan Militia, but an English-
woman." Carl Bogus fact-checked the justice: "Malcolm's name may
sound British, and Bentley College, where Malcolm teaches history, may
sound like a college at Oxford, but in fact Malcolm was born and raised
in Utica, New York, and Bentley is a business college in Massachusetts."

Garry Wills strafed some of the more risible claims of the "Standard
Modelers." Stephen Halbrook, for example, consulted a Federal Era
dictionary to discern the meaning of "bear arms." The dictionary lists

"to bear arms in a coat." And only a handgun, not a musket, could fit in one's coat pocket. Thus the amendment must have meant to cover firearms carried for personal protection. "Mr. Halbrook does not recognize the term 'coat of arms,' a decidedly military form of heraldry presided over by the College of Arms (by Mr. Halbrook's interpretative standards, a medical institution specializing in the brachium)," Wills wrote.

Then there was the ringing declaration from Patrick Henry: "the great object is, that every man be armed." The eloquent patriot's pronouncement provided the title for the ur-text for the gun rights movement, Halbrook's 1984 book, *That Every Man Be Armed.* It is cited reverentially elsewhere. Glenn Reynolds pointed to it in his 1995 article excitedly proclaiming the "Standard Model." The quote adorns websites and posters. The Second Amendment professorship at George Mason University is named after Henry. A $10,000 gift to the NRA makes you a "Patrick Henry Member."

As we have seen already, that is not what Henry said. The Virginian actually was issuing a protest against the expense of two levels of government—the federal and the state—buying arms for the militia at the same time. ("At a very great cost, we shall be doubly armed.") Far from a ringing statement of individual gun-toting freedom, it was an early American example of a local politician complaining about government waste.

Advocates pluck such quotes out of context with zest known previously only to those who write movie posters. Thomas Jefferson offers numerous opportunities. Don Kates enthused, "Historical research demonstrates the Founders out-'NRAing' even the NRA. . . . 'One loves to possess arms' wrote Thomas Jefferson, the premier intellectual of his day, to George Washington on June 19, 1796." What a find! Oops: Jefferson was not talking about guns. He was writing to Washington asking for copies of some old letters, to have handy so he could issue a rebuttal in case he got attacked for a decision he made as secretary of state. Not to worry: as of 2013 the NRA website still included the quote. If all else fails, you can still go online to buy a T-shirt emblazoned with Jefferson's mangled words.

Wills concluded:

Time after time, in dreary expectable ways, the quotes bandied about by Standard Model scholars turn out to be truncated, removed from context, twisted, or applied to a debate different from that over the Second Amendment. Those who would argue with them soon tire of the chase from one misquotation to another, and dismiss the whole exercise—causing the angry reaction from Standard Modelers that they are not taken seriously. The problem is that taking them seriously is precisely what undermines their claims.

Pro–gun control scholars have one conspicuous black eye, too: Michael Bellesiles. The Emory historian took a rare stab at looking at original sources from a pro–gun regulation perspective. His book *Arming America*, published in 2000, offered a counterintuitive argument. Bellesiles presented evidence showing that early Americans did not own many guns. The gun culture, he asserted, arose only later. The book won the Bancroft Prize, the history profession's top award. The author purportedly drew on probate records and other early documents to show that Revolutionary era Americans did not own firearms in great numbers. Charlton Heston called the thesis "ludicrous." Flaws quickly emerged. Bellesiles claimed key notes had been lost in a flood. He cited others that had in fact been lost in an earthquake. Columbia University withdrew the history prize, and he resigned from Emory University. In 2012, Bellesiles turned up in Connecticut; he was teaching and working as a bartender.

SIX

Contest for the Constitution

Agitation by gun activists, even the relentless arguments of revisionist writers, would not be enough to change the way the Second Amendment was viewed. That required another simultaneous development: the rise of the judicial right.

Since the 1960s, conservative jurists have come to dominate federal courts. The Supreme Court considered its gun case at their moment of peak influence. Strikingly, this new wave of conservative judges came to rely on a novel argument: the doctrine known as originalism. They proclaimed that the only legitimate way to interpret the Constitution was to ask what the Founding generation would have thought its terms meant. This was a radically new way for courts to decide. It came to fruition in the gun case. Originalism has come to dominate the jurisprudence of firearms more than on any other major topic.

Of course, through history debates roiled over the courts and Constitution. We have a written Constitution, after all. And we have a tradition of judicial review—of judges interpreting that document, with untrammeled power to strike down laws they deem unconstitutional. That tradition makes the United States distinct. It gives judges, and the lawyers who urge them on, an anomalous place in our democracy.

Chief Justice John Marshall established the principle of judicial re-

view in *Marbury v. Madison*, when the Court struck down the Judiciary
Act of 1789. But principle aside, in fact the Supreme Court rarely overturned a federal law during the nineteenth century. *Dred Scott* was noteworthy not only for its blundering racism, but because it negated a major
congressional enactment. After the Civil War, though, federal and many
state courts began to exert a greater role. Broadly they saw themselves
as a bulwark against unwise progressive legislation, and as a force for
economic liberty. Judges concocted a theory of "substantive due process"
that forbade government from enacting health and safety regulations,
wage laws and other intrusions on the market. In *Lochner v. New York* in
1905, the U.S. Supreme Court struck down a law that limited bakers to
working ten hours a day, on the grounds that the Fourteenth Amendment protected "liberty of contract." The case was so infamous, lawyers
know the entire period as the Lochner Era. The Supreme Court was,
of course, the same judicial body that refused to apply the Fourteenth
Amendment to states to protect the rights of freedmen, and that had
just upheld segregation.

Progressives decried the use of judicially crafted theories to thwart
the democratic process. They argued powerfully for judicial restraint.
Social problems, they insisted, were best solved by the politically ac-
countable branches, drawing on experience, expertise, and compromise.
We know their names today because of what they urged their brethren
not to do. Louis Brandeis made his name as "the People's Lawyer." He
managed to persuade the conservative Supreme Court that an Oregon
law limiting working hours for women was justified. His brief on behalf
of the National Consumers League included two pages of legal theory,
and 111 pages of facts: social science studies, laws from other countries,
medical reports, newspaper clippings. To this day lawyers know a filing heavy on social science as a "Brandeis brief." The original hangs in
a public hallway of the Supreme Court. When progressive president
Woodrow Wilson appointed Brandeis an associate justice, his crusad-
ing spirit lent itself to a drive for the Court to do less. He warned other
judges "we must ever be on our guard, lest we erect our prejudices into
legal principles." He joined Oliver Wendell Holmes, who famously

wrote a friend, "If my fellow citizens want to go to Hell I will help them. It's my job."

Conservative judges' impulse to intervene against an activist government came to a head during the Great Depression. One after another, the Supreme Court struck down many of the most prominent laws of the "First New Deal." Franklin Roosevelt charged that the justices were returning the country to the "horse and buggy age." He won a huge landslide in the 1936 election, when the "nine Old Men" were a campaign issue. In March 1937, Roosevelt proposed to expand the Court's membership to fifteen justices, so he could pack it with liberal jurists. Congress rejected the plan, in the past century's most contentious fight over the courts. FDR stalled politically. Yet at the same time, the Court capitulated. Suddenly, starting with *West Coast Hotel v. Parrish*, it began to affirm New Deal laws. Wags dubbed it the "Switch in Time That Saved Nine." Social Security, the National Labor Relations Act, and more were all justified under the Commerce Clause. The Court allowed the country to move into a modern industrial era. In so doing, the justices made clear they would step back from what they had regarded as their principal task: protecting economic freedom from government intervention. Yale's Bruce Ackerman observes, "With the decisive triumph of the activist welfare state over the Old Court, an entire world of constitutional meanings, laboriously built up over two generations, had come crashing down upon the Justices' heads." What role for judicial review?

Only lawyers could relish whence came the answer: a footnote. A year after the "Switch in Time," in an otherwise turgid case known as *Carolene Products*, Justice Harlan Fiske Stone made clear that the Court would stand aside in cases involving economic regulation. But cases involving the Bill of Rights, or where the political system failed to protect the rights of a "discrete and insular minority," would be subject to more searching scrutiny.

Some footnote. It set the Court off on a course of activism and a tremendous expansion of the rights of ordinary citizens, especially racial and religious minorities. It was the era of the Warren Court: led by former California governor Earl Warren starting in 1953, the justices became

agents of social change. Most significant, they struck down school segregation in *Brown v. Board of Education* in 1954. The Court began to apply
the Bill of Rights—which *Cruikshank* had declared to bind only Congress—forcefully to the states. Within a decade, the Warren Court had
required that criminal defendants be provided counsel (*Gideon v. Wainwright*), that police needed to let suspects know they had "the right to remain silent" (*Miranda v. Arizona*), and that electoral districts must reflect
"one man one vote" (*Reynolds v. Sims*). The Court expanded protection
for free speech as well. In *New York Times v. Sullivan*, it ruled that a public figure must prove actual malice to win a libel judgment, thus greatly
expanding public debate. More controversially, the court identified and
forcefully protected a right to privacy in the Constitution. Such a right
is not mentioned in its text. However, in *Griswold v. Connecticut* in 1965,
the Court struck down a law prohibiting the sale of contraceptives. Justice
William O. Douglas said that the right to privacy could be discerned in
the "penumbras, formed by emanations" from the Bill of Rights' specific
guarantees. *Roe v. Wade* followed eight years later, building on *Griswold*.

It was a thrilling and disconcerting time in the law. Once the stodgi-
est of professions, legal liberalism seemed as if it could be a force for
justice. Justice William J. Brennan Jr., the New Jersey jurist who served
as the "playmaker" on Warren's court, passionately spoke about "human
dignity" as the goal of the law. For the first, indeed only time in American history, the Court stepped ahead of public opinion.

Through it all, in conservative eras or liberal ones, the way judges
made their decisions reflected their belief in a growing, changing country.
Judges professed to base their rulings on precedent, public philosophy,
the structure of the Constitution, and other broad principles. They acted
in a kind of constitutional common law, each case building on previous
rulings. The consensus judicial view was articulated by Justice Oliver
Wendell Holmes as early as 1920: "[When] we are dealing with words
that also are a constituent act, like the Constitution of the United States,
we must realize that they have called into life a being the development
of which could not have been foreseen completely by the most gifted of
its begetters. It was enough for them to realize or to hope that they had

created an organism; it has taken a century and has cost their successors much sweat and blood to prove that they created a nation. The case before us must be considered in the light of our whole experience, and not merely in that of what was said a hundred years ago." In deciding the case (about bird treaties), "we must decide what the country has become."

By the late 1960s, vast social change abetted by "activist" judges rattled the political consensus. In earlier decades, the Court aggressively fought with a popular president; now it extended the protections of the Bill of Rights to criminal defendants and minorities. "Impeach Earl Warren" billboards dotted the Southern states. Thoughtful progressives began to worry that the Court was moving too fast. Ruth Bader Ginsburg, long a pioneering women's rights attorney at the American Civil Liberties Union, asserted *Roe* was mistakenly decided: rather than relying on fuzzy "penumbra," the justices should have made a narrower ruling based on the explicit language of the Equal Protection Clause. Barack Obama, as a young law lecturer, spoke to Chicago Public Radio in 2001. He found one of "the tragedies of the civil rights movement, was [that] because the civil rights movement became so court focused, I think that there was a tendency to lose track of the political and community organizing activities on the ground that are able to put together the actual coalitions of power through which you bring about redistributive change. And in some ways we still suffer from that."

The backlash against judicially imposed liberalism was sharp, swift, and ultimately overpowering.

LEGAL BACKLASH: THE RISE OF THE RIGHT

Business responded first. Lewis Powell was an owlish, courtly lawyer from Richmond, Virginia, who served on the boards of eleven corporations. He wrote a strategy memo for the U.S. Chamber of Commerce urging the creation of a wide network of organizations, think tanks, political committees, and publications to push for pro-business policies. Powell sketched the map for the infrastructure of the conservative resurgence. "No thoughtful person can question that the American economic system is under broad attack," he warned. ". . . We are not dealing with sporadic or isolated attacks from a relatively few extremists or even from the minority socialist cadre. Rather, the assault on the enterprise system is broadly based and consistently pursued. It is gaining momentum and converts." Two months later Richard Nixon appointed Powell to the Supreme Court. Conservative legal academics—led by Richard Posner of the University of Chicago—sought to subject the new wave of environmental and consumer protections to cost-benefit analysis, using economic tools. Throughout the 1970s, the first wave of legal conservatism focused on curbing regulatory overreach.

Still, conservative lawyers lacked an overarching theory of how to read the Constitution—how judges should rule, and how to justify when they would not. After all, jurists seeking to slam the brakes on perceived liberal judicial activism had numerous arguments. One can read a constitutional provision based on its text, on the structure of the document (what kinds of federalism or checks and balances are being served?), on tradition and the following of precedent. Conservatives could have argued powerfully for judicial restraint: unelected judges should step aside. Or they could have embraced "judicial minimalism," echoing eighteenth-century political theorist Edmund Burke. No more grand theories: cases should be decided one at a time, with appropriate respect for precedent, traditions, and the dangers of moving too fast or far. Or conservatives could have argued that the underlying value in the Constitution is individual freedom, or private property. None of these rose to the fore of conservative legal thought, though. Each lacked emotional punch.

Instead, conservatives rallied around the newest, and most radical theory. Originalism was first given prominent public voice by Attorney General Edwin Meese in 1985. He was an unlikely intellectual provocateur. Meese looked like a cheerful Realtor. A Yale-educated Californian, he was serving as a deputy district attorney when he prosecuted student protesters who occupied Berkeley in the Free Speech Movement of

1964, one of the decade's first convulsive confrontations with authority. California's Junior Chamber of Commerce honored him for his work. He joined Governor Ronald Reagan as a legal advisor and then chief of staff. In Reagan's first presidential term, he served as a counselor in the White House—the conservative voice in the "troika" that deftly steered policy. For thirteen months after Reagan nominated Meese to be attorney general, the Senate delayed his confirmation, and he endured a five-month Independent Counsel probe. Freshly confirmed, at last he had a platform, his first address to the American Bar Association in July 1985. Most dignitaries would confine themselves to bromides. Meese launched a jurisprudential movement with a high-profile, provocative speech. He accused the justices of "roam[ing] at large in a veritable constitutional forest." Ideologically polarized voting blocs "all reveal a greater allegiance to what the Court thinks constitutes sound public policy, rather than deference to what the Constitution—its text and intention—may demand," he said. Without "a coherent jurisprudential stance," the Court risked drifting back toward "radical egalitarianism."

> *What, then, should a constitutional jurisprudence actually be? It should be a jurisprudence of original intention. By seeking to judge policies in light of principles, rather than remold principles in light of policies, the Court could avoid both the charge of incoherence and the charge of being either too conservative or too liberal.*
>
> *A jurisprudence seriously aimed at the explication of original intention would produce defensible principles of government that would not be tainted by ideological predilection. This belief in a jurisprudence of original intention also reflects a deeply rooted commitment to the idea of democracy.... Those who framed the Constitution chose their words carefully; they debated at great length the minutest points. The language they chose meant something.*

Justice William J. Brennan Jr. responded publicly four months later. Brennan was the leader of the Court's liberals, and author of some of the century's most important opinions. He long had derided the idea that his job was merely to divine the Framers' "original intent." Brennan had accepted an invitation from Georgetown University weeks before Meese spoke. His words answered Meese with force, and landed the justice on the front page of *The New York Times*.

Originalism, Brennan countered, was "arrogance cloaked as humility." Often, the intentions of the Framers were ambiguous, with gaps in the record. "Indeed, it is far from clear whose intention is relevant—that of the drafters, the congressional disputants, or the ratifiers in the states?" To choose to limit our interpretation to what we think the Framers intended, Brennan argued, is itself a choice of values. "Those who would restrict claims of right to the values of 1789 specifically articulated in the Constitution turn a blind eye to social progress and eschew adaptation of overarching principles to changes in social circumstance":

> [If] I may borrow the words of an esteemed predecessor, Justice Robert Jackson, the burden of judicial interpretation is to translate "the majestic generalities of the Bill of Rights, conceived as part of the pattern of liberal government in the eighteenth century, into concrete restraints on officials dealing with the problems of the twentieth century."
>
> We current Justices read the Constitution in the only way that we can: as twentieth century Americans. We look to the history of the time of framing and to the intervening history of interpretation. But the ultimate question must be: What do the words of the text mean in our time? For the genius of the Constitution rests not in any static meaning it might have had in a world that is dead and gone, but in the adaptability of its great principles to cope with current problems and current needs.

Three decades later, the debate between Meese and Brennan still defines the polarized judicial debate. Robert Bork was the principal academic articulator of "original intent." Only the approach of "original understanding . . . is consonant with the design of the American republic," he was to write. Two years later, President Reagan nominated Robert Bork for the Supreme Court. The U.S. Senate rejected Bork after a ferocious campaign.

Reduced to its core, originalism promises that judges can ride a constitutional wayback machine, taking orders from the esteemed Founders. There is more than a whiff of filiopiety, of worship of the ancestors. Stanford's Pamela Karlan gibes that originalists should wear a bracelet reading, WWJMD? (What Would James Madison Do?) Of course, there was something obviously, even transparently conservative in the insistence that the intent of the white men of 1789 should unthinkingly bind later generations. Among other things, the "new birth of freedom" during and after the Civil War, which produced three constitutional amendments, meant that a different group of "founders" should be consulted. These framers were called Radical Republicans for a reason. Many sought a flexible Constitution to guarantee equality.

Originalists quickly found themselves in a constitutional Catch-22: what if the Framers did not want their intent to bind so tightly later generations? James Madison, after all, kept his journals secret in large measure to keep his contemporaries from relying on the notes as a canonical text. William Blackstone, whose *Commentaries on the Laws of England* are much cited by originalists, suggested "the fairest and most rational method to interpret the will of the legislator, is by exploring his intentions at the time when the law was made, by signs the most natural and probable. And these signs are either the words, the context, the subject matter, the effects and consequence, or the spirit and reason of the law. . . . As to the effects and consequence, the rule is, where words bear either none, or a very absurd signification, if literally understood, we must a little deviate from the received sense of them." In the end, courts rarely actually used original intent, other than to confirm already determined political views. Finley Peter Dunne was a turn-of-the-twentieth-century satirist. His protagonist Mr. Dooley commented on current events in a comic brogue. Historian Leonard Levy notes, "Mr. Dooley, Finley Peter Dunne's philosophical Irish bartender, believed that original intent was 'what some dead Englishman thought Thomas Jefferson was goin' to mean when he wrote th' Constitution.'"

Quickly but subtly originalists shifted ground. They no longer urged a reliance on "original intent." Instead, they urged reliance on "original public meaning." What did the public think the words meant at the time the Framers set them to parchment? At one level, this made more sense: it was, after all, the citizens who made the Constitution law when they ratified it. But it risked even greater incoherence. Jack Rakove showed in *Original Meanings* that citizens in one state might mean one thing, Congress another; the drafters of the Bill of Rights, especially, meant something different from the desires of the public they sought to mollify. What started as a patriotic call to the wisdom of the Framers became an invitation to squint at the words of the text. This was a constitutional bait-and-switch. Instead of a robust, textured look at the historical origins and philosophical underpinnings of the Constitution, advocates now insisted that the right way—the only way—to be true to original intent was to probe the precise meanings of the words as written down. This kind of hairsplitting—of canonical disputes, endless puzzlement about words and their meaning, and the meaning of asking about their meaning—would be familiar to any denizen of a faculty lounge. Depending on one's tradition, it could be derided as Jesuitical, Talmudic, or literary criticism.

Fidelity to constitutional text had always been one of the ways we interpret the document. What was new was the argument, made increasingly by many on the right, that it was the *only* legitimate way to understand the Constitution. Unlike other dry theories of jurisprudence, this one had an undeniable power. We revere our founding documents, we stand on line to view them at the National Archives; we treat them (in Pauline Maier's words) as American Scripture. The call for a return to original understandings tapped a deep yearning among many to return to earlier values, lost sense of order and greatness. Originalism became yet another mobilizing principle for millions of conservatives.

The conservative legal movement pressed on to its next great task: filling the courts. Here is where its results have been especially impressive. Reagan and Meese deserve credit for understanding the need to populate the bench with like-minded jurists (a lesson that earlier and later administrations oddly forgot).

Meese's speech had been prepared with help from researchers and speechwriters drawn from the Federalist Society. Three conservative law students, fired by Reagan's vision and feeling isolated in elite schools, started the group in 1982. Its first gathering at Yale drew two hundred and was covered in *The New York Times*. The Federalist Society did not bring lawsuits or lobby for new policies. It was, first and foremost, a network—a nationwide cadre of similarly inclined lawyers who could boost one another and fill top jobs. Intentional or not, this proved savvy. Its first executive director explained the attitude of typical grant-making foundations: "What have you done? Well, we've helped change some of the debate on the Constitution. But what have you *done*?" Instead, the society received financial support from funders including the Olin, Bradley, and Scaife foundations, already busy building other institutions in the conservative policy infrastructure such as the Heritage Foundation. These philosophically committed backers did not demand instant governmental gratification. Theirs was patient capital. The society's first faculty advisor: University of Chicago professor Antonin Scalia.

That proved consequential. Four years after the Federalist Society held its first campus conference, and two years after Meese's broadside, one of the original student conveners was on the attorney general's staff sifting names for possible appointment to the U.S. Supreme Court. President Reagan stepped before the microphone in 1986 and announced his nomination of that faculty advisor to the Supreme Court.

"AMERICAN ORIGINAL"

Few jurists have had an impact as significant as Antonin Scalia. He has done so while winning few allies among the other justices, and authoring surprisingly few major opinions. He holds sway by relentless force of intellect. Scalia may not write the opinions, but the lawyers who appear before the justices increasingly argue in his voice.

Antonin Scalia was born in Trenton, New Jersey, in 1936. His father, an Italian immigrant with exacting standards, taught classics at Brooklyn College. Scalia commuted to Xavier High School, a rigorous Jesuit

academy, from the outer borough of Queens. All Xavier students wore
uniforms and served in Junior ROTC. A skilled shooter, Scalia toted
his rifle on the subway to Manhattan from Queens. (Unlike Justice
Brennan, Scalia never served in the military, however.) Scalia worked as
head of the Justice Department's Office of Legal Counsel in the Ford
administration, fighting Congress as it exerted new oversight power
over intelligence gathering and war making. After Ford lost, Scalia
became editor of *Regulation* magazine for the conservative American
Enterprise Institute, then moved on to the University of Chicago. He
became a high-profile advocate for the view that judges were med-
dling where they ought not, imposing their political views on society.
Early in Reagan's term he was appointed to the U.S. Court of Appeals
District of Columbia Circuit. Because it hears many cases testing the
federal government's power, the D.C. Circuit is known as the second
highest court in America. Four years later, when an associate justice
slot opened on the Supreme Court, Scalia's youth, nine children, proud
Italian American heritage (and operatic persona), lifted him past Robert Bork. Scalia's confirmation hearing came after a bruising battle over
William Rehnquist's elevation to chief justice. The Senate confirmed
Scalia, 98 to 0.

Scalia is rare among American public figures. Most are pragmatists,
incrementalists. Mario Cuomo (another Queens-raised, Jesuit-trained
lawyer of Scalia's generation), memorably said, "You campaign in po-
etry. You govern in prose." Scalia stands out for bringing to high office a
thorough, carefully crafted, controversial public philosophy, and sticking
with it. Scalia's evangelizing for the idea that the only legitimate way to
interpret the Constitution is to ask what the Framers and their generation intended in 1789 has become a dominant philosophy for debating
and litigating constitutional law.

Scalia insisted he was a "faint hearted originalist." In a cogent article
published two years into his Supreme Court tenure, he called originalism "the lesser evil." He acknowledged the inherent flaws in the approach: for example, the risk of getting history wrong. But he insisted
that judges and lawyers must be guided by a consistent jurisprudential

approach. "If the law is to make any attempt at consistency and predict-ability, surely there must be general agreement not only that judges reject one exegetical approach (originalism), but that they adopt another. And it is hard to discern any emerging consensus among the nonoriginalists as to what this might be. Are the 'fundamental values' that replace origi-nal meaning to be derived from the philosophy of Plato, or of Locke, or Mill, or Rawls, or perhaps from the latest Gallup poll?"

His philosophy appears motivated more by animus to the politically liberal interpretations he saw driving notions of the evolving Constitu-tion. "If it is good, it is so," he wrote. "Never mind the text that we are supposedly construing; we will smuggle these new rights in, if all else fails, under the Due Process Clause." He derides, for example, the way courts have interpreted the Eighth Amendment's prohibition of "cruel and unusual punishment." No sane judge, he acknowledges, would up-hold lashing or hand branding as a punishment today, even though they were common in 1789. But the way judges actually have assessed how to interpret that amendment, "the evolving standards of decency that mark the progress of a maturing society," is little more than judge-made "com-mon law."

In fact, though, throughout most of his years on the bench, Scalia shrank from writing solely based on the original intent of the Fram-ers (or even the original public meaning). Like other justices, he picked and chose when to focus on the text, when to plumb the thinking of the Founders, when to rely on precedent. He had a ready justification, charmingly set out in a 1997 book: "As I have explained, *stare decisis* [i.e., following precedent] is not *part of* my originalist philosophy; it is a prag-matic *exception* to it." Often he added, "I am an originalist. I am not a nut." (Chicago professor David Strauss countered, "That way of putting it is disarming, but it seems fair to respond: if following a theory consis-tently would make you a nut, isn't that a problem with the theory?")

Even in these writings, Scalia never quite got around to explaining why the original intent of the Framers was the guidepost to follow. More, the original intent as outlined by Meese and Bork at least had the benefit of allowing for thought, context, philosophical consistency to carry forward in time. Scalia's approach—which he called "textualism"—came to focus much more intently on the words on the page. Such an approach may make sense for those parts of the Constitution that are unambiguous. Article II says the president must be thirty-five. Nobody can argue "twenty-five is the new thirty-five." For more open-ended clauses, though, the vagueness of the text is precisely the challenge. "Due process" and "equal protection" do not become clearer the more you stare at them.

But for all Scalia's intellectual wattage, for all the influence of "original public meaning" in law schools and in lower courts, his influence on his colleagues was oddly muted, surprisingly limited. Scalia proved inflexible and abrasive in his dealings with other justices. William Brennan, asked by his clerks how the Court could have come up with one or another surprising result, would hold up his hand: five fingers. Sandra Day O'Connor had been majority leader of the Arizona State Senate. Scalia seemed to prefer to stand alone. Over time, his dissents grew vehement, even cranky. When O'Connor refused to cast the deciding vote to undermine *Roe v. Wade* in 1989, Scalia taunted: her opinion was "irrational" and "cannot be taken seriously." Veteran legal journalist Linda Greenhouse, cataloguing his episodic thrashing of colleagues, reports that she cannot think of a single time another justice was persuaded over time to join with Scalia's views. Biographer Joan Biskupic wrote that Chief Justice Rehnquist "realized soon enough that if a contentious case had been won by a single vote, he should not assign the opinion to Scalia, lest the obstinate justice lose the majority."

Then in 2005, O'Connor retired, and Rehnquist died, and Scalia was joined on the bench by two jurists who rose in the conservative movement Scalia helped create: Associate Justice Samuel Alito and the new chief justice, John Roberts. Suddenly those five fingers were on the right hand. The Roberts Court would prove willing to embrace constitutional views that broke sharply, even radically, from the consensus of the past century.

SEVEN

The Road to Heller

A militant National Rifle Association combined with a forest's worth of law review articles built inexorable momentum to press the court to change its views of the Second Amendment.

Key government agencies began to shift first. Republicans took control of the U.S. Senate for the first time in twenty-four years in 1981. Utah senator Orrin Hatch became chair of a key Judiciary Committee panel. He commissioned a study, "The Right to Keep and Bear Arms." In a breathless tone it announced, "What the Subcommittee on the Constitution uncovered was clear—and long lost—proof that the second amendment to our Constitution was intended as an individual right of the American citizen to keep and carry arms in a peaceful manner, for protection of himself, his family, and his freedoms." The cryptologist discovering invisible writing on the back of the Declaration of Independence in the Disney movie *National Treasure* could not have said it better.

A constitutional right to gun ownership, though, was still too far a reach, even for the doctrinal conservatives in Ronald Reagan's Justice Department. In part, "the individual rights claim on the Second Amendment was a New Right right," notes Yale's Reva Siegel, "at odds with judicial precedent and in tension with New Right complaints about judicial activism." It would undo the work not of judges, but demo-cratically elected legislators. In addition, libertarian law professors and insurrectionist movie actors were only part of the conservative coalition. The Justice Department spoke for law enforcement, as well, and the national agencies (such as the FBI and Bureau of Alcohol, Tobacco and Firearms) and local police were united in their desire to crack down on gun violence. Attorney General Meese, fresh from the controversy and impact of his original intent speeches, commissioned a comprehensive strategy to map a drive for jurisprudential change in fifteen areas rang-ing from the "exclusionary rule" under the Fourth Amendment to public initiatives to strengthen private religious education. *The Constitution in the Year 2000* was an audacious plan to rewrite constitutional doctrine. It did not include a strategy for the Second Amendment.

But the NRA's power to elect presidents (and the judges they ap-point) began to shift the organs of government, too. In 2000 ("especially for you, Mr. Gore"), gun activists strongly backed Governor George W. Bush of Texas. During the election, a new dispute over the meaning of the Second Amendment began to move through the courts. Timothy Emerson, a Texas doctor, was under a restraining order after allegedly threatening to kill his wife's lover. Federal law barred him from own-ing guns. He was indicted for owning a Beretta pistol. He insisted his Second Amendment right had been violated. In a letter about the case, a Justice Department official confirmed its long-held view that "the Second Amendment does not extend an individual right to keep and bear arms." NRA activists circulated it widely in West Virginia, Tennes-see, and Arkansas, states previously won by Democrats but lost by the Democratic vice president.

In 2001, newly installed Attorney General John Ashcroft announced a major policy pivot. The NRA's head lobbyist read Ashcroft's letter to the group at its convention in Kansas City: "The text and original intent of the Second Amendment clearly protect the right of individuals to keep and bear firearms." The next year, the Justice Department formally reversed its position of seven decades. A federal appeals court ruled against the Texas doctor, but made the noteworthy assertion that the

Constitution confers a right to own a gun. Solicitor General Ted Olson, who had argued the *Bush v. Gore* case that secured the presidency, urged the Supreme Court to reject the doctor's appeal. At the same time, the Justice Department argued that the Constitution "broadly protects the rights of individuals" to own firearms.

The individual rights argument was starting to win in another forum: public opinion. Citizens were sharply divided on gun laws. By early 2008, according to the Gallup poll, 73 percent of Americans believed the Second Amendment "guaranteed the rights of Americans to own guns" outside the militia. In 1959, according to a Gallup poll, 60 percent of Americans favored banning handguns; that dropped to 41 percent by 1975 and stood at 24 percent in 2012. The idea of a Second Amendment right began to become synonymous with opposition to gun control, with conservatism, even with support for the Republican Party. In 1993, for example, *The New York Times* mentioned gun control 388 times, and the Second Amendment only sixteen. By 2002, overall mentions of the issue dropped, but the Second Amendment was mentioned fifty times.

In the end, it was neither the NRA nor the Bush administration that pressed the Supreme Court to reverse course. A small group of libertarian lawyers believed other gun advocates too timid. They targeted a gun law passed by the local government in Washington, D.C., in 1976, perhaps the nation's strictest. It barred individuals from keeping a handgun at home and required trigger locks on other guns. Robert Levy was a technology entrepreneur who graduated law school at age fifty-three, then served as a clerk for two federal judges. A constitutional fellow at the idiosyncratic Cato Institute, Levy found appealing plaintiffs and bankrolled the litigation. By the time the case reached the high court, Levy and two colleagues represented Dick Heller, a security guard at the Thurgood Marshall Federal Judiciary Building who wanted to bring his work revolver home to his high-crime neighborhood. The NRA tried to sideswipe the effort, filing what Heller's lawyers called "sham litigation" to cloud the case. Worried about an adverse court ruling, it even tried to persuade Congress to nullify the District's law, which would have rendered the case moot. The D.C. Circuit Court of Appeals—the court where Justices Roberts, Scalia, and Ginsburg once served—struck down the gun law, 2 to 1.

All knew that the Supreme Court was poised to speak in a new voice on the Second Amendment. Sixty-six friend of the court briefs from scholars, lawmakers, and interest groups tumbled into the clerk's office. Linguists wrote to explain the meaning of the preamble. Early American historians explained the history of the amendment's ratification. The NAACP Legal Defense Fund, the American Bar Association, organizations against domestic violence, Jews for the Preservation of Firearms Ownership, and many others weighed in. Many expected the George W. Bush administration to speak for those who opposed the D.C. law. Instead, the brief filed by Solicitor General Paul Clement equivocated. Second Amendment rhetoric aside, the Department of Justice argued that the Appeals Court ruling would endanger bans on weapons such as machine guns. It endorsed a "reasonable" Second Amendment right, and said the Court of Appeals had not applied that analysis in striking down the ban on handguns. Conservatives pounced. Vice President Dick Cheney filed his own far more adamant brief, with a majority of members of the House and Senate, backing Heller.

At the argument before the justices, the surprise was the degree to which originalism had triumphed. There were few questions about current gun laws, or the toll of gun violence, or legislative history, or precedent: all the things prior courts relied on to make major decisions. Queries from the justices focused heavily on colonial, early American, even seventeenth-century British history. The smell of snuff could have pervaded the courtroom. Much history was fuzzy, at best. Justice Anthony Kennedy asked of the amendment, "It had nothing to do with the concerns of the remote settler to defend himself and his family against hostile Indian tribes and outlaws, wolves and bears and grizzlies and things like that?" The District's lawyer, former acting Solicitor General Walter Dellinger, explained that the debate over the amendment—all of which took place on the Eastern seaboard, far from grizzly danger—focused on militias and fighting government tyranny. Justice Stephen Breyer noted that guns kill or wound 80,000 to 100,000 Americans per year. Would it be unreasonable for a city with a high crime rate to ban handguns? "You want to say yes," Scalia instructed Heller's lawyer. He agreed.

HELLER'S PUBLIC MEANING

On the last day of the term in June 2008—in the final opinion announced before the presidential election—the Supreme Court issued its ruling.

Five to four, the justices voted to strike down the capital's gun law. Chief Justice Roberts, Anthony Kennedy, Clarence Thomas, and Samuel Alito joined Scalia's opinion. Justices John Paul Stevens, Ruth Bader Ginsburg, David Souter, and Stephen Breyer dissented. For the first time, the Court ruled that the Second Amendment recognizes an individual right to own a gun unrelated to militia service. Scalia wrote the opinion, a sure sign the Court would move aggressively to the right. Roberts had done something Rehnquist never would: he assigned Scalia the job of writing the big one. It remains Scalia's most important majority opinion.

At last, Scalia could apply his honed judicial model to a consequential case. How did he do so? A close read is instructive.

Scalia does not seek to explain the Framers' original intent: this is emphatically an opinion focused on a closely parsed text, regardless of what it meant to those who wrote and ratified it. The Second Amendment, he begins, "is naturally divided into two parts: its prefatory clause and its operative clause." But he has a surprising way to deal with that prefatory clause, the homage to the "well regulated militia being necessary to the security of a free state," so important to the Framers. *He skips right over it.* Scalia simply lops off the first half of the amendment, just as in the bowdlerized quote in the NRA headquarters lobby.

What counts is the second half. This is the right way to read the amendment, Scalia's opinion explains, because that is the way people in the past used to read constitutional provisions. In support he turns to a treatise on statutes published in 1874, nearly a century later. Other than to show off his clerks' research skills, why then? One clue is that statutes and constitutional provisions were seen differently in the late 1700s, when the Second Amendment was written. There, the proper construction was loose. Moreover, lawyers in the Founding Era knew they were seeking to win approval from ordinary citizens who played a much greater role in ratification.

Then Scalia takes the reader on an almost claustrophobic reading of the words of the amendment's second part. Who are "the people"? The majority concludes quickly that meant all members of the political community. It simply announces peremptorily: "We start therefore with a strong presumption that the Second Amendment right is exercised individually and belongs to all Americans."

Then, "keep and bear arms." As we have seen, the overwhelming public usage of "bear arms" at the time of the Constitution referred to military service. Scalia's opinion could have grappled with this in any number of ways. Instead, it mulls over each word separately (and out of sequence): "arms" and "bear" and "keep" are parsed and defined one at a time. The analysis verges on tendentious: "At the time of the founding, as now, to 'bear' meant to 'carry.'" As source material, it cites three separate dictionaries from the 1700s. It all has the feel of an ambitious Scrabble player trying too hard to prove that triple score word really does exist. At times this word search stretches credibility.

> The phrase "bear Arms" also had at the time of the founding an idiomatic meaning that was significantly different from its natural meaning: to serve as a soldier, do military service, fight or to wage war. . . . But it unequivocally bore that idiomatic meaning only when followed by the preposition "against," which was in turn followed by the target of the hostilities.

That is plainly wrong. When the Framers debated giving conscientious objector status to those "religiously scrupulous of bearing arms," Madison and Gerry were not worried about those too physically weak to lift a musket. "Giving 'bear Arms' its idiomatic meaning would cause the protected right to consist of the right to be a soldier or to wage war—an absurdity that no commentator has ever endorsed." Well, yes: that is exactly the specter that worried some Anti-Federalists: that people would be barred from serving in state militias.

Scalia fumes and fusses about the words. "Bear" must mean "carry," since "keep" means "keep." Otherwise, "It would be rather like saying 'He filled and kicked the bucket' to mean 'He filled the bucket and died.' Grotesque." Harrumph, he might have added. "Putting all of these textual elements together, we find that they guarantee the individual right to possess and carry weapons in case of confrontation."

The opinion then strolls, Wikipedia-like, through the historical background before the Founding Era: it describes England's 1688 Glorious Revolution and the limited right to arms it granted some Protestants. (The colonists changed that right in drafting the Second Amendment, anyway.) It made the powerful point that for colonists, the right to have guns was "fundamental," a "natural right." The amendment did not create a new right, but acknowledged an existing one.

> *There seems to us no doubt, on the basis of both text and history, that the Second Amendment conferred an individual right to keep and bear arms. Of course the right was not unlimited, just as the First Amendment's right of free speech was not. Thus, we do not read the Second Amendment to protect the right of citizens to carry arms for any sort of confrontation, just as we do not read the First Amendment to protect the right of citizens to speak for any purpose.*

The opinion then spends precisely two pages (out of sixty-four) on "a well regulated militia." It agrees that the Constitution defines those entities with precision, as the military forces controlled by state governments—but breezily asserts that the amendment referred to something else, meaning "all able-bodied men." The Constitution refers to "the" militia, but the amendment refers to "a" militia, which is apparently something else entirely. Scalia also declares that the word "state" connotes government generally, rather than the way it is meant every single other place it is used in the Constitution: to refer to states, such as Rhode Island or Georgia.

Glancingly, the opinion does grapple with the nub of the challenge: the fact that the Second Amendment was driven largely by the fear that many Founders had that state militias would be disarmed by the central government. The amendment thus confirmed the right to "keep and bear arms." But the opinion never really addresses the connection between that fear and the decision to respond with an amendment. It strolls through contemporary state constitutions, only one of which explicitly protected arms for self-defense at the time of the amendment's drafting—the very menu from which Madison and colleagues chose their markedly more limited language.

At its best, Scalia's opinion makes strong points: Madison was bent on reassuring Federalists that nothing would change the structure of the Constitution. Given that, how could this articulated right actually reassure those who worried about the state militias? Madison originally intended the militia provisions to be part of the Bill of Rights, rather than inserted into Article I itself. At its worst, it engages in sleight-of-hand. The opinion selectively cites later commentators from the 1800s who agree with an individual rights interpretation. It snipes at Stevens's dissent, which quotes the jurist Joseph Story in an 1833 treatise as focusing his attention on the militia. "That is wrong." Actually, it isn't. The majority opinion simply looks at an earlier section of Story's lecture than Stevens had.

It is the fog of history that rolls most notably across the pages. There are plenty of things we do not know, and many more that have lost their validity over time. Earlier Scalia wrote that to truly engage in originalism requires a gargantuan level of historical inquiry. He essentially chose to ignore the actual, stated, publicly known purpose of the amendment—focusing instead on what the words must have meant, if the right dictionaries are consulted.

Scalia professes to practice a refined form of originalism: not a futile search for the subjective "intent" of the Founders, but "original public meaning." This was the most visible opportunity he would have to apply this approach. In the end it appears to be little more than "words with friends." Even accepting, somehow, that what was meant then—in 1791—should control our actions today, "public meaning" can mean little without context. The context was the fight over the militia and the army. And that context is, basically, ignored. Such a genuine historic inquiry would not be without ambiguities. We would be uncomfortable with the idea that states could fight wars against the U.S. Army. We would recognize that the Founders expected people to have *military* weapons in their homes. (Muskets, not rocket-propelled grenade launchers, but still.) Above all, the principal fact about the world of the militias and the Second Amendment is that it is gone, both in terms of people's concerns and even the institutions they sought to address them.

The Court's ruling overturned two centuries of precedent. Usually justices acknowledge that fact, as when *Brown v. Board of Education* overturned *Plessy v. Ferguson*. Instead of being intellectually honest about that, Scalia's opinion insists it did no such thing. Most relevant is the *Miller* case from 1939, which found that the Second Amendment did not protect guns not used for "military purposes." The majority does not say it overrules *Miller*. Rather, it explains that *Miller* simply held that the sawed-off shotgun was not covered by the right: the "type of weapon at issue was not eligible for Second Amendment protection." With a shrug the justices deem it "unsurprising that such a significant matter has been for so long judicially unresolved."

But the Bill of Rights has mostly been applied to the states for a half century now. And federal gun laws began in the 1930s. Indeed, Scalia himself sat on the Court when it considered some of them. The Court's previous reluctance to find an individual right to a handgun was not an oversight, or the result of tardiness. It reflected the judicial consensus.

And then—after engaging in hyper-literal readings of words, and after pages of highly selective historical readings from two hundred years ago that ignore the history of the past hundred years—suddenly the opinion veers away from originalism altogether.

Like most rights, the right secured by the Second Amendment is not unlimited. From [the English legal writer] Blackstone through the 19th-

century cases, commentators and courts routinely explained that the right
was not a right to keep and carry any weapon whatsoever in any manner
whatsoever and for whatever purpose. . . . Although we do not under-
take an exhaustive historical analysis today of the full scope of the Second
Amendment, nothing in our opinion should be taken to cast doubt on
longstanding prohibitions on the possession of firearms by felons and the
mentally ill, or laws forbidding the carrying of firearms in sensitive places
such as schools and government buildings, or laws imposing conditions
and qualifications on the commercial sale of arms.

This eminently sensible list barges into the text, seemingly from
nowhere. Is it the price to secure a fifth vote (perhaps from Justice
Anthony Kennedy, the court's eternal swing voter)? Are these included
with an eye toward public opinion, to show citizens the courts had not
leapt fully in bed with the NRA? ("I am an originalist. I am not a nut.")
Regardless, no explanation is given why these limitations are acceptable.
And why, if these are permitted, the District of Columbia's law is not.

The opinion offers another clue for future courts: weapons that are
"dangerous and unusual" can be banned, but those that are "in common
use" cannot. Market share evidently determines constitutionality. This
fully severs the first half of the amendment and floats it off to sea. The
militia is irrelevant, Scalia writes. For "it may be true that no amount
of small arms could be useful against modern-day bombers and tanks.
But the fact that modern developments have limited the degree of fit
between the prefatory clause and the protected right cannot change our
interpretation of the right." Or, to paraphrase the justice's frequent reply
when asked about *Bush v. Gore*, "Well regulated militias? Get over it."

Having set out a broad, transformative statement of the right to bear
arms, and then limiting it with a seemingly random set of exceptions,
the opinion finally gets around to striking down the Washington, D.C.,
law. The statute, it notes correctly, was an outlier, much stricter than that
of other jurisdictions. Handguns are distinct. They are "the quintessential
self-defense weapon." The ban only applies to guns kept in the home,
where most suicides and domestic assaults take place. Nonetheless,

"whatever else [the Second Amendment] leaves to future evaluation, it surely elevates above all other interests the right of law-abiding, responsible citizens to use arms in defense of hearth and home."

Hearth and home: we've come far from "a well regulated militia" and the "security of a free state." *The New Yorker's* Jeffrey Toobin summarized it well: "Scalia translated a right to military weapons in the eighteenth century to a right to handguns in the 21st."

The opinion drew two lengthy dissents. Stevens wrote an impassioned assessment of the purpose, historical roots, and intended meaning of the amendment. Stevens found himself arguing emphatically that the militias were—and still are—the protected party. This is what has been called the "states' rights" version of the Second Amendment. "The Second Amendment was adopted to protect the right of the people of each of the several States to maintain a well-regulated militia," he declared flatly.

> *It was a response to concerns raised during the ratification of the Constitution that the power of Congress to disarm the state militias and create a national standing army posed an intolerable threat to the sovereignty of the several states. Neither the text of the Amendment nor the arguments advanced by its proponents evidenced the slightest interest in limiting any legislature's authority to regulate private civilian uses of firearms. Specifically, there is no indication that the Framers of the Amendment intended to enshrine the common-law right of self-defense in the Constitution.*

It is in Stevens's dissent that we hear at length from Madison himself, from the debates over the Second Amendment and its meaning by the men who framed and ratified it. The dissent powerfully sets out the historic record. The elderly jurist, seeing the Court begin to lurch from the caution it had displayed during most of his time on the bench, seems incredulous at the majority's blasé mien as it abandons two centuries of precedent. "Even if the textual and historical arguments on both sides of the issue were evenly balanced," he writes, "respect for the well-settled views of all our predecessors on this Court, and for the rule of law itself, would prevent most jurists from endorsing such a dramatic upheaval in the law." Stevens made a consequential strategic choice. He made a *better* originalist argument than Scalia. Plainly he believed he had the facts on his side: both original public meaning and original intent. But his focus on the doings of Framers from 1791 missed a chance to make the point that there is something amiss about allowing ourselves to be guided entirely by their choices, ignoring the intervening two-hundred-plus years of history, law, and social development.

Breyer issued his own dissent. He chose a different tack. In effect, Breyer stipulated that there was an individual right. What then? What kind of right? And how do we know when it has been violated? Historical evidence about the scope of the right is "the *beginning*, rather than the *end*, of any constitutional inquiry." To decide on a particular regulation of guns "requires us to focus on practicalities, the statute's rationale, the problems that called it into being, its relations to those objectives—in a word, the details." Breyer proposed an "interest balancing inquiry," in which judges had no choice but to weigh the costs and benefits of a particular law. And gun regulation was exactly the kind of area where democratically elected governmental bodies, such state legislatures or Congress, are "likely to have greater expertise and greater institutional factfinding capacity." Where lawmakers could draw different results from different facts, courts should defer and let them do so. Citing UCLA's Adam Winkler, he notes that hundreds of state Supreme Court decisions on firearms law took this approach. Breyer's dissent rings with the voices of Holmes and Brandeis. It also reflects the approach he set out in his own book, *Active Liberty*. In his view, the overarching theme of the Constitution is democracy, and judges had better be very careful when overturning the work of popularly elected branches. The majority brushed that idea aside: Breyer was proposing little more than a "judicial balancing test." But the people had already balanced the interests, albeit people wearing breeches in 1791. Breyer's dissent received short shrift on decision day. *The New York Times* gave it one sentence. In the real world, in subsequent years, it has had far greater impact as judges and legislatures tried to sort through *Heller*'s sepia-toned new world.

Outside the court, camera crews swarmed, protesters cheered and jeered, and the plaintiffs stood for interviews. Dick Heller answered questions, grinning in front of a handheld sign. It read, once again misquoting Patrick Henry, "THE GREAT OBJECT, EVERY MAN BE ARMED."

ORIGINALISM AS LIVING CONSTITUTIONALISM

Away from the Supreme Court steps, reactions fell along surprising lines. Politicians breathed relief. John McCain, the likely Republican nominee, applauded it; so did Barack Obama. Scalia himself later pointed proudly to *Heller* as the greatest "vindication of originalism. . . . When I first came on this Court, I was the only originalist. Counsel would not even allude to original meaning," Scalia told legal journalist Marcia Coyle. "They would cite the last Supreme Court case." Originalism once had been advanced as a way to avoid the "temptations of politics" on the Court. Now it was the basis for a 5 to 4 ruling that Velcroed snugly to the jurists' political predilections—in service of a ruling in which judges negated the decision of a local government.

The most thoughtful progressive scholars recognized that the Court was responding to a broad shift in attitudes about gun rights. For one thing, elections matter. The presidents who appointed the five justices in the majority all were themselves NRA members. In *Heller*, Yale's Reva Siegel argued in a brilliant article, "originalism" is the best recent example of "living constitutionalism." At moments, Scalia was quite frank about the source of the constitutional understanding. *Heller* let slip that even if "hundreds of judges" had relied on the Supreme Court's *Miller* case, that "cannot nullify the reliance of millions of Americans . . . upon the true meaning of the right to keep and bear arms." Another liberal academic, Cass Sunstein, noted that it can be appropriate for a court to recognize a right because it reflects a consensus. Consider this thought experiment: what would have happened if the Supreme Court ruled the other way—had it proclaimed there was no personal right to carry a gun? Certainly it would have prompted an uproar. It might well have spurred a constitutional amendment.

While citizens are split on gun control, majorities shift and attitudes change, sometimes depending on how polling questions are asked. Siegel correctly identified *Heller* as the product of something more purposeful: the long campaign by the gun lobby to create a public climate that would make a Supreme Court ruling inevitable. Siegel and other observers are tracing and quantifying what Finley Peter Dunne's "Mr. Dooley" observed a century ago when he noted, "No matter whether th' Constitution follows th' flag or not, the Supreme Coort follows th' iliction returns." This new school of liberal scholars is spelling out ways the Court responds to public opinion. Far from a principled reliance on the intent of the Framers in 1791, they suggest, the opinion's originalism is little more than "living constitutionalism" with a Southern accent. There is an unnerving risk: that judges will feel emboldened by a vague sense of public opinion, or manipulated by pressure groups. When elected bodies such as the Washington, D.C., City Council enact laws, through normal processes rife with messy compromise, they ought to be given greater weight. Even though most members of Congress signed a brief urging the Court to strike down the District's handgun law, those same lawmakers never got around to passing a law that would do exactly that, even though the federal government has ultimate power over the capital's local laws.

Liberals, in short, mostly responded to *Heller* with a practiced shrug: is it really a surprise that the Court would rule as it did, given its political alignment? For progressives, the opinion with all its pretensions was one more piece of evidence for a chastened, realistic assessment of the Court and its role in American politics.

Meanwhile, some prominent conservatives have denounced *Heller*. For them, the case marked a return of loosey-goosey constitutionalism of the kind they, and Scalia, had spent a career eviscerating.

J. Harvie Wilkinson III, a federal appeals court judge from Virginia, scorched Scalia's opinion. Wilkinson was a former Reagan official, whom President George W. Bush had interviewed as a possible chief justice nominee. (Bush grilled him on his fitness regimen.) His impeccable standing among conservatives made his words sting. *Heller*, he said, was as great an act of judicial overreaching as *Roe v. Wade*.

> *After decades of criticizing activist judges for this or that defalcation, conservatives have now committed many of the same sins. In* Heller, *the majority read an ambiguous constitutional provision as creating a substantive right that the Court had never acknowledged in more than two hundred years since the amendment's enactment. The majority then used that same right to strike down a law passed by elected officials, acting, rightly or wrongly, to preserve the safety of the citizenry.*

Wilkinson was particularly aghast at the paragraph listing permissible gun restrictions. "The Constitution's text," he wrote, "has as little to say about restrictions on firearm ownership by felons as it does about the trimesters of pregnancy" (the medical methodology used by Justice Harry Blackmun in *Roe*).

Richard Posner was even more perturbed. Posner is one of America's leading public intellectuals. (He made the list, and put himself on it, but it's true.) A rare polymath, he is a judge on the U.S. Court of Appeals for the Seventh Circuit, continues to teach at the University of Chicago, publishes a blog with a Nobel laureate economist, and churns out books on topics from the financial crash to law and literature. Posner pioneered the use of economics in law. He was anything but economical in his scorn for *Heller*. "It is questionable in both method and result, and it is evidence that the Supreme Court, in deciding constitutional cases, exercises a freewheeling discretion strongly flavored with ideology," he wrote in *The New Republic*. Perhaps, he speculated, "turnabout is fair play" after liberal decisions. Posner mourned the fact that local governments would be blocked from enacting local policies because of the political sentiments of a majority of Americans. Even the opinion's purported originalism left him cold. "The range of historical references in the majority opinion is breathtaking, but it is not evidence of disinterested historical inquiry. It is evidence of the ability of well-staffed courts to produce snow jobs."

Then things got really nasty. With a coauthor, Scalia published *Reading Law*, a 567-page treatise on how to interpret legal texts—his magnum opus arguing that the meaning of laws, and constitutions, does not change over time. Posner's review: "incoherence." "*Heller* probably is the best known and the most heavily criticized of Justice Scalia's opinions. *Reading Law* is Scalia's response to the criticism," Posner wrote. "It is unconvincing." He noted that whatever he might claim, Scalia "is doing legislative history" when he scours for "original meanings of eighteenth-century provisions." Legislative history: them's fightin' words. Scalia stammered to an interviewer that Posner's assertion is "simply, to put it bluntly, a lie." It's a good thing the two did not have guns.

Another telling critique, at least implicit, came from another conservative judge, Frank Easterbrook, also on the Seventh Circuit. His seeming slap came in an unexpected place: in the foreword to Scalia's book. "Words don't have intrinsic meanings; the significance of an expression depends on how the interpretive community alive at the time of the text's adoption understood those words. The older the text, the more distant that interpretive community is from our own. At some point the difference becomes so great that the meaning is no longer recoverable reliably," Easterbrook wrote. When that happens, the courts should "declare that meaning has been lost, so that the living political community must choose." He dryly cites *Heller* as a controversial example. Reviewing the volume, Posner noted it was hard to escape that the "living political community" in *Heller*, Richard Posner noted, "consisted of the elected officials, and the electorate, of the District of Columbia."

In effect, these three leading conservative jurists were calling out Scalia for having become what he, and they, had decried for years: a judicial activist who conjured spurious legal theories to justify Court interventions into the political process that just happened to advance their policy views and political aims.

RIGHT TURN

Heller was the first major case in which the Roberts Court upended years of precedent to move in a conservative direction. It was not the last.

Two years later, in 2010, the same five justices issued *Citizens United v. FEC.* There the Court overturned the long-standing bar on corporations and unions spending unlimited sums to defeat or elect candidates. No nod to minimalism, here. It erased decades of Supreme Court precedent. It also nullified federal law dating back to 1907, when President Theodore Roosevelt fought for a law banning corporate election spending. (He had been caught in a campaign finance scandal, and he wanted to defend his honor. Without reform, he declared, "Sooner or later, there will be a riotous, wicked, murderous day of atonement.") Neither party in *Citizens United* had asked for this result. The opinion rang with indignant tones. "The censorship we now confront is vast in its reach," wrote Justice Anthony Kennedy. "The government has muffled the voices that best represent the most significant segments of the economy." Justice Stevens dissented again. "While American democracy is imperfect, few outside the majority of this Court would have thought its flaws included a dearth of corporate money in politics."

Two years after, the Court came within inches of striking down the Affordable Care Act, the health care law popularly (and unpopularly) known as Obamacare. In the end, Chief Justice Roberts joined the majority to hold the law constitutional under the "taxing power." But the *Heller* majority justices found the statute's requirement that individuals buy health insurance violated the Commerce Clause, which gives Congress power to regulate the economy. Originalists insisted the Supreme Court got it wrong in 1937 when it dropped its resistance to government regulation of business. Some called it the "Lost Constitution." Had the Court struck down Obamacare on the grounds that it exceeded Congress's power under the Commerce Clause, it would have set in motion forces that would have toppled statutes going back to the New Deal. Dozens of laws and hundreds of prior cases could have been at risk.

Then in June 2013, in *Shelby County v. Holder*, the Court effectively overturned the key provision of the Voting Rights Act, perhaps the nation's most effective civil rights law. Again, the five *Heller* justices ruled. Again, they undercut carefully crafted laws. The original 1965 statute came after beatings of civil rights marchers at the Edmund Pettus Bridge in Selma, Alabama, galvanized President Lyndon Johnson and Congress to act. It was reauthorized three times. In 2005, the Senate voted 98 to 0 to reauthorize it, and the Supreme Court upheld it, as it had repeatedly. At oral argument, Scalia declared that the Voting Rights Act perpetuated "racial entitlement." "Even the name of it is wonderful: the Voting Rights Act," he added. "Who is going to vote against that in the future?" In its ruling the Court effectively ended Section 5, which required the Justice Department or federal courts to approve in advance changes in voting laws in jurisdictions with a history of discrimination. The opinion drew on some imaginary originalism: it explained the law violated a constitutional rule of "equal sovereignty"—not among people, but among states. This phrase, with a murky provenance, only has ever previously applied to the terms on which states entered the Union. It poses severe challenges for other laws that are premised on the aftermath of slavery, sounding an echo of Southern complaints about Reconstruction. Faulkner would have understood: "The past is never dead. It's not even past."

Not all these rulings relied on originalism. Rather, beyond their ideological bent, they seem suffused with contempt for Congress, or more broadly for elected governments.

To be sure, Roberts displayed a canny sense when to press, and when to retreat. In spring 2009, the same five justices had made clear their itch to overturn the Voting Rights Act, but pulled back. Jeffrey Toobin reports that Roberts first sought a narrower ruling in *Citizens United*, then lost out to the emotional First Amendment soliloquy ultimately in Kennedy's opinion. The Court sprang multiple leaks to reveal that Roberts first voted to kill the Affordable Care Act, then changed his vote. If so, his switch in time saved the nine from being a central campaign issue for years to come. Roberts cannot dictate results; his role is more akin to a legislative leader heading a rowdy and ideological caucus. But he seems always to have his eye on the gauge of public respect for the Court. Given the frequent dysfunction consuming the rest of the capital, it is a pleasure to watch an institution run well. But it is running hard to the right.

Lines are not neatly drawn. The same week the Court gutted the Voting Rights Act, it also struck down the Defense of Marriage Act, also approved by an overwhelming majority of Congress in 1996. DOMA refused federal recognition for legal same sex marriages. There were crucial differences. The 2013 case was in fact the first time the Court weighed DOMA's constitutionality. More, it came in a pair of opinions where the Court actually sidestepped the need to overturn the marriage laws of four out of five states to rule that equal protection required states to allow same sex marriages. The strongest justification for overturning DOMA—powerful if largely unspoken—was that the country had evolved, progressed. Our understanding of equality has changed over time. Seen in that light, the DOMA ruling served as the most recent application of long-standing constitutional principles. Bitterly dissenting, Scalia denounced the marriage equality ruling. "[We] have no power under the Constitution to invalidate this democratically adopted legislation," he complained, an error that springs from a "diseased root: an exalted conception of the role of this institution in America." Perhaps he was being droll.

Scholars debate the intensity of the Roberts Court's activism. Ruth Bader Ginsburg, in a rare public rebuke, called it "one of the most activist courts in history." Some argue these justices are no more prone to strike down federal laws than their predecessors. That measures quantity, not quality. Not in decades has the Court overturned laws of such reach. And never over a century have the justices relied so frequently on assertions about original intent and meaning. *Heller* stood most explicitly. Prior court precedent was skimpy. That hardly explains the health care decision: it, too, focused intently on what the Framers meant by "commerce," despite myriad relevant precedents. *Citizens United*, by contrast, could not rely on history—at the time of the founding, for profit corporations of the kind we have today did not exist. And *Shelby County's* rationale appears to be "that was then, this is now." What seemed to matter most, in each of these cases, was outcomes: the political coalition of the party that appointed the justices, with gun owners, business, and white Southern voters at its heart, proved more powerful than any interpretive methodology. Perhaps this ought not to surprise.

This much is evident: after public backlash (and electoral shifts), for three decades left and right stalemated on the Court. No more. Today's justices seem constrained only by their sense of what the political market will bear. Originalism and textualism have proven no more principled as methods of interpretation than any other.

ON THE ROAD

Students, neatly pressed; faculty; alumni; journalists: over seven hundred of them filled Princeton's Neo-Gothic Richardson Auditorium the afternoon of December 11, 2012. Antonin Scalia looked out over the crowd. The Supreme Court justice, in his twenty-sixth year on the Court, had settled into his shtick: opinionated, jovial, garrulous, a hint of arrogance. It was a friendly audience, thrilled to be in the presence of a renowned jurist and not entirely unhappy with the contents of his talk, either. The James Madison Program sponsored the lecture. Its other public events the same academic year included "Left Turn: How Liberal Media Bias Distorts the American Mind" and a panel on "Benghazi: What Do We Know? What Don't We Know? What Do We Need to Know?"

Some applauded when a freshman asked the justice why he had compared homosexuality to bestiality and murder. Others applauded when Scalia pugnaciously replied, "I don't apologize for the things I raised. I'm not comparing homosexuality to murder. I'm comparing the principle that a society may not adopt moral sanctions, moral views, against certain conduct. I'm comparing that with respect to murder and that with respect to homosexuality."

Scalia was in his element. His greatest passion came when he propounded his jurisprudential vision. "I have classes of little kids who come to the court, and they recite very proudly what they've been taught, 'The Constitution is a living document.' It isn't a living document! It's dead," Scalia declared. "Dead, dead, dead!" The crowd laughed.

The Princeton speech came four and a half years after the justice proudly announced *Heller* from the bench. It was also three days before a deranged young man walked into Sandy Hook Elementary School in Newtown, Connecticut, and murdered twenty children and six adults. The nation would begin to discuss gun control again—this time in the context of a newly articulated constitutional doctrine that might limit next steps.

PART
THREE

PART
THREE

EIGHT

From Heller *to* Sandy Hook

In the year before the December 2012 massacre at Sandy Hook Elementary School, the bucolic countryside around Newtown rang with automatic weapons fire and odd explosions. Police were inundated with complaints of noisy shooting late at night and early in the morning. The din did not come from weapons for hunting deer (plentiful in the woods), or handguns stashed in a bedside night table. Residents had begun spraying targets with semiautomatic weapons. According to the police chief, some had taken to shooting up propane tanks. Others enhanced their targets with Tannerite, a mixture of ammonium nitrate and aluminum powder, which detonates with a roar when hit. At the request of police, the town council prepared an ordinance to ensure there would not be noisy shooting late at night, early in the morning, or too close to occupied buildings.

Then one hundred hunters and gun activists crowded monthly meetings and decried the zoning proposal as a violation of their Second Amendment rights. "This is a freedom that should never be taken away," one woman proclaimed. The National Shooting Sports Foundation—the firearms industry lobbying group—was headquartered in the town, and argued against the ordinance. The town council retreated. It never changed the rules. Mary Ann Jacob, the chair of the council's "ordinance committee," soon became better known: she was the heroic librarian's aide who barricaded the door to shield children at the school during the mass shooting.

A few days after the bloodbath, the National Shooting Sports Foundation website seemed frozen in place. A message from the group's president professed to being "deeply shaken and saddened by the horrible events that took place in Newtown, Connecticut, our headquarters and home." Surrounding the statement were promotions for the industry's SHOT trade show in Las Vegas, and links to the group's "Bullet Points" and "Pull the Trigger" blogs. Second Amendment fundamentalism, amped up by industry lobbying, turned even a zoning tussle into a fight over first principles: welcome to post-*Heller* America.

The Newtown massacre that punctuated 2012 was hardly the first instance of gun violence in the new millennium. Each year, thirty thousand Americans die from guns. Fifty thousand more are wounded. Over the previous two years, mass murders in Tucson and at a midnight movie showing in Aurora, Colorado, each briefly horrified. These deaths were only the most visible. Inner-city neighborhoods routinely are plagued with gangs who strafe each other and passersby with gunfire.

But the shooting at Sandy Hook cracked wide the gun issue again. Patterns have repeated over the past century: first, a wrenching, publicized atrocity. In the past, it was political violence that galvanized, from the assault on Mayor Gaynor to the murders of Robert Kennedy and Martin Luther King, to the attempt on the life of President Reagan. A spasm of remorseful legislating would follow, some more symbol than substance, all politically painful or even impossible. It has been half a century since a president was slain. The background noise of gun violence and crime has lost its capacity to spur action. But mass killings still shock. Newtown, Aurora, and Tucson were the first massacres in our current media and political age, and also the first in the era of constitutionalized litigation on guns.

Gun law, now, had become a constitutional concern, a new legal realm. New gun laws will have to comply with the new interpretation of the amendment. But rights, even core constitutional rights, face limitations in courts and in practice. In the years after *Heller*, Americans began to grapple with what that right really might mean.

JUDGING GUNS AFTER *HELLER*

In June 2008, a mere two hours after Justice Scalia read out *Heller* in the Supreme Court, gun supporters filed the first lawsuit to strike down Chicago's municipal law. By the next day, the NRA and its allies filed five suits around the country. Within months, dozens more cases were working their way through the courts. Confusing matters more, *Heller* used a novel approach, asking courts to consider tradition, long-ago history, and colonial practice in assessing thousands of state and local laws here and now. Supreme Court decisions often give lower courts precise guidance on how to interpret rights. *Heller* offered few standards at all.

So what did the monumental ruling in *Heller* actually mean for the law?

All knew the anticipated next step for gun rights advocates would be to seek a ruling that the Second Amendment's individual right applied to the states. Most gun law is found in state statutes. Washington, D.C., is federal territory, ultimately under Congress's jurisdiction; hence *Heller*. In *Cruikshank*, and then in *Presser*, the Supreme Court had been quite precise in holding that the Second Amendment did not apply to state governments. Of course, originally none of the Bill of Rights did, either. Courts began to enforce those rights throughout the twentieth century, by "incorporating" them through the Fourteenth Amendment, parts of which *did* apply to states. As of 1920, the guarantee of free speech and freedom of the press, the requirement for a search warrant, the requirement for just compensation when government seizes property, were deemed not to apply to states. By 2008, all did. Only a few provisions had not yet been "incorporated." The Second Amendment's individual right, newly proclaimed, was one of them.

So in 2010 in *McDonald v. Chicago*, the Supreme Court addressed the Second Amendment again—this time as it applied to states. Sequels rarely are as exciting as the first blockbuster. This one offered little surprise. Chicago had the country's toughest handgun law, now that Washington, D.C.'s had been negated. Once again, a sympathetic plaintiff brought suit. This time an elderly Chicago man, Otis McDonald, lived in a high-crime neighborhood and wanted to protect himself with a handgun at home. Once again, a flurry of friend of the court briefs (fewer, less impassioned). The vote among the justices, once again, was 5 to 4: the Second Amendment did in fact apply to the states. Justice Samuel Alito wrote for the majority. Alito's opinion was a judicial victory lap. It made clear there was not only a right to a workable gun in the home, but that it was "fundamental." Originalism felt less strained the second time around. After all, there was considerably more historical evidence that at least *some* framers of the Fourteenth Amendment thought it covered individuals protecting themselves with guns, as opposed to militias marching around New England village greens. The dissenters made their arguments, this time less indignantly. Justice Stevens once again wrote a demurral. He asserted that the framers of the Fourteenth Amendment, the Radical Republicans, cared first and foremost about equal treatment of white and black Southerners, rather than an amendment that would somehow block states from enforcing criminal justice policy in a neutral way. (That was a slightly queasy argument, given the way liberals rely on the Fourteenth Amendment to expand an array of rights in the Constitution.) Justice Breyer, in turn, catalogued the array of scholarly articles by historians pummeling *Heller*'s errors. In truth, all knew that if the Second Amendment now constrained Congress, which passed few gun laws, it would be markedly odd if it did not apply to states as well.

That night Wayne LaPierre and Paul Helmke, the director of the Brady Campaign to Prevent Gun Violence sparred on public television. The NRA chief pronounced *McDonald* "a landmark decision." Helmke noted ruefully, "This is good for lawyers."

Yes, it was. Now that the Supreme Court had spoken, hundreds of judges, thousands of litigants, and communities and jurisdictions around the country would have to sort out what it meant. The justices would not weigh in again soon. But the Court's rulings in *Heller* and *McDonald* just began the challenge for lower courts. The searching, if tendentious, examination of history is not easy for judges and overworked advocates who might be intrepid legal aid lawyers or harried assistant district attorneys.

All told, dozens of suits challenging the vast array of gun laws were brought. Surprisingly, courts rebuffed nearly all. In the first two years after *Heller*, federal courts considered the constitutionality of gun laws in two hundred cases. Gun laws were upheld in all but two. According to one tally, judges upheld laws requiring "good cause" for issuance of a permit to carry a concealed gun, those requiring guns to be kept in a locked container when not in the owner's possession, requiring gun owners to be twenty-one. Courts upheld laws that prevented people from buying a gun if they had a past felony conviction, or a misdemeanor domestic violence conviction, or had been involuntarily committed to a mental institution. Criminal defendants now routinely claim violation of their Second Amendment rights. These claims have been rejected, too.

Heller had proclaimed a right, one individuals can sue to uphold—but agreed that there were limits to that right. Our Constitution is replete with such rights. They are important but subject to boundaries. That begins but does not end the analysis. Judges and lawyers, assessing a constitutional right, often sought other analogies, other lines of cases that can suggest the best way to proceed. The libertarian UCLA professor Eugene Volokh showed that there were multiple justifications for gun regulations that nonetheless recognized an individual right. Some laws affected who could own a gun, where a gun could be owned, what kinds were especially dangerous, and so on. He urged courts not to simply borrow the standards of review used for other constitutional rights. Another professor, Mark Tushnet, made a bolder prediction. He suggested it likely that judges would in fact find a way to avoid knocking down gun laws like bowling pins. They would find and use existing models for how to do this.

Repeatedly courts turned to the First Amendment. The right to speak is fundamental, but is limited or regulated under myriad circumstances. You are not entitled to commit libel, or to turn up a sound truck to eleven at three in the morning. As Justice Holmes wrote, you cannot falsely shout fire in a crowded theater. The First Amendment does not enable you to stage a parade without a permit: government cannot ban your political speech, but can set rules on "time, place and manner." Courts treat campaign contributions to lawmakers as a form of speech, but have upheld limits on the size of the gift in an effort to ward off corruption.

Most courts have made a similar assessment. First, they ask whether the law affects a core Second Amendment right. What is that right? *Heller* identified the right of self-defense in "hearth and home," with a "commonly used" weapon. Then judges scrutinize the law, to see whether it goes too far to impinge on that right. Scalia wrote that D.C.'s gun law would fail under "any standard of scrutiny." *Heller* explicitly rejected the loosest standard. That would ask only whether the legislature had a "rational basis" for enacting the law, at least when it comes to handguns in the home. When courts apply this test, legislatures only must show that a given law plausibly could make a difference toward its stated goal. At the same time, judges have not been willing to apply "strict scrutiny," which asks whether a law is narrowly tailored to serve a compelling government interest. When judges apply this exacting standard on other issues, usually this means they will strike down a law.

Instead, most judges have applied "intermediate scrutiny." As one federal court of appeals wrote, in one of the first rulings just a year after *Heller*, intermediate scrutiny "need not establish a close fit between the statute's means and its end, but it must at least establish a *reasonable* fit." Consider the case of a Meadville, Pennsylvania, man convicted of obliterating the serial numbers imprinted on handguns, and selling them out of his home. His conviction, he said, violated his Second Amendment right. Because it involved a handgun in a home, the court of appeals ruled, this did implicate a Second Amendment right. But the judges found that government had a "substantial or important interest" in making sure police could trace guns. Myriad cases used similar logic and language.

Yes, state and local governments could take steps to protect public order and fight against violence. But those moves now might be limited by a right, proudly brandished by an individual, which at some level might trump the public need. Over the years, communitarian critics have argued that American culture stresses rights over responsibilities. A constitutional vision that enshrines gun rights risks becoming a parody of that individualist vision. But so far, judges have steered away from that mistake.

The most significant new cases have addressed the question of whether people can carry loaded guns outside the home. Here the NRA is pushing hardest for new changes; this is where police insist that gun rights could start to impinge on law enforcement. Does a right to have a gun in "hearth and home" include the right to carry a gun down a busy city street?

As of early 2014, nearly all courts upheld "concealed carry" laws. One of the oldest such laws is in New York, the Sullivan Act, that pioneering urban gun control passed a century before by Big Tim Sullivan. Gun rights lawyers challenged its constitutionality, in particular the requirement that New Yorkers could get a license to carry a weapon only if they show "a special need for self protection distinguishable from that of the general community or persons engaged in the same profession." The Second Circuit Court of Appeals rejected that bid in *Kachalsky v. Cacace*. Judge Richard Wesley, appointed by President George W. Bush, wrote for a unanimous panel. Robert Katzmann joined him; he was a respected former Brookings Institution scholar who was one of Bill Clinton's last judicial appointments. So did Judge Gerald Lynch, an Obama appointee. The judges explained their "assumption" that "the [Second] Amendment must have some application" outside the home. *Kachalsky* said that the law should be subject to intermediate scrutiny and ruled it to be substantially related to an "important governmental interest." The opinion cited history, too—a century's worth of judicial support for a law, as a court ruled in 1913, that "picked out one particular kind of arm, the handy, the usual and the favorite weapon of the turbulent criminal class." (History, at least, from a time that more closely resembles ours than the colonial moment invoked by *Heller*.) After the appeals court upheld the state's strict gun law, the plaintiffs appealed to the U.S. Supreme Court, which refused to take the case.

But not all courts stood aside as readily. Possibly the most unnerving decision came in Chicago. *McDonald* had nullified the city's law that barred a loaded gun to protect "hearth and home." Now a gun rights group challenged another Illinois law, which prohibits the carrying of a loaded weapon outside the home. The Seventh Circuit Court of Appeals agreed and overturned the law.

The opinion's author? None other than Richard Posner. Fresh from his flame war with Scalia, Posner had kept up his public commentary on *Heller*'s overreach. In a 2011 blog post, he lamented "the unwisdom of the Supreme Court's recent decisions that have created—on the basis of a tendentious interpretation of the drafting history of the Second Amendment and an intellectually untenable (as it seems to me) belief in 'originalist' interpretations of the Constitution—a constitutional right to possess guns for personal self-defense." Now Posner was charged with faithfully implementing the Supreme Court's doctrine, the job of a lower court judge. His opinion was a masterpiece of passive aggression. Posner cites the historians who argued against the individual right, with gusto and at length. "The Supreme Court rejected the argument. [Illinois asks] us to repudiate the Court's historical analysis. That we can't do." *Heller*'s version of history was "debatable," but it controlled.

Instead of holding back, though, Posner went further—well beyond what Scalia's and Alito's rulings required. "Twenty-first century Illinois has no hostile Indians," Posner explained. "But a Chicagoan is a good deal more likely to be attacked on a sidewalk in a rough neighborhood than in his apartment on the 35th floor of the Park Tower." It would make no sense to say that an individual has less scope to defend herself on the streets than at home. Posner edged close to refusing to apply any level of scrutiny at all. Perhaps, Posner reasoned, the law in question makes Chicago's streets less safe, though economic and crime studies cut both ways. "Anyway the Supreme Court made clear in *Heller* that it wasn't going to make the right to bear arms depend on casualty counts." Some suggested that Posner, who spent a career preaching cost-benefit analysis (casualty counts), verged on satire. He especially had argued that urban areas should be able to enact policies that fit their needs, rather than being forced to adhere to the norms of rural voters and transient national political majorities. His personal views aside, Posner chose to write an opinion that clearly extended Second Amendment rights outside the home. He and the other judges gave the Illinois legislature a deadline to revise its law. No longer would Illinois be the only state that barred citizens outright from carrying a concealed weapon.

Posner's ruling and the scramble to rewrite the statute came amid armed mayhem in Chicago. On Father's Day weekend 2013, forty-seven people were shot and nine killed. On July 4th weekend, as lawmakers finalized their plan, sixty-seven Chicagoans were shot, and twelve died from their wounds. A journalist asked one resident to explain how the sound of gunfire differs from a firecracker. Shots rang out. "That's the difference," he explained. The outcome in the state capitol at Springfield was ugly. Rural officials dominated. They crafted a bill that allowed Illinois citizens to carry concealed weapons, requiring a background check and training. Law enforcement could object. And nobody could carry a loaded weapon onto the El or other public transportation. But in a truly unnerving bit of codified machismo, rural lawmakers insisted that gun owners be able to carry their loaded weapons into a bar. Governor Pat Quinn vetoed the measure. The legislature overturned the veto on the last day before the court's deadline.

In general, though, one law professor has concluded, "The lower courts have essentially made judicial restraint their guiding principle." Given unclear instructions from the High Court and a long history of policymaking by legislators and law enforcement, that makes sense. Despite *Heller*'s historicist bluster, when it came to actually implementing the new rule, Stephen Breyer's dissent proved more influential than Antonin Scalia's majority opinion. Breyer said judges would have no choice but to weigh costs and benefits; that is just what has happened.

Those who hope courts will continue to defer to state legislatures in assessing gun laws cannot breathe easy yet, however.

One keen-eyed judge sees the trend and does not like it. Brett Ka-

vanaugh is a well-networked conservative, sitting on the D.C. Circuit
Court of Appeals. He came to national attention as an author of the
salacious report on the Monica Lewinsky scandal as a deputy to White-
water special prosecutor Kenneth Starr. (Kavanaugh's defenders insist
he urged Starr to remove the smutty passages.) Democrats delayed his
confirmation for three years: he is bruited as a possible future Republican Supreme Court nominee. Kavanaugh was one of three appeals court
judges who weighed the District of Columbia's revised gun laws. After
Heller, the District government had no choice but to rewrite its statute.
Dick Heller again challenged it in court. The appeals decision upholding the new law was crafted by a panel of judges, in an opinion written
by Douglas Ginsburg, himself a short-lived Supreme Court nominee
proposed by Ronald Reagan in 1987. Kavanaugh dissented sharply. The
two-part test constructed by judges across the country entirely misses
the point of *Heller*, he wrote. "In my view, *Heller* and *McDonald* leave
little doubt that courts are to assess gun bans and regulations based on
text, history, and tradition, not by a balancing test such as strict or intermediate scrutiny." The only proper thing to do is to scour the history of
the Founding Era for analogies to current laws. If a match can be found
to an earlier measure, then the law would be presumed constitutional.
Also, judges should look to see if the guns in question are in common
use, and have long-standing tradition. This approach travels in circles:
a law can exist because it existed before. But what if an early American
court was considering it back then? To those long ago judges, presumably, it would have been an impermissible outlier. That leaves little room
for innovation, new criminal justice approaches, or responses to new
threats. Kavanaugh insists his approach would not necessarily lead to
looser gun laws. It would certainly lead to more amateur sleuthing by
judges through the pages of history.

Kavanaugh's dissent matters. Like a Tweet from a Fox News host, it
augurs a conservative backlash against the judicial consensus about how
to interpret gun rights. No doubt the Supreme Court's conservatives
took note. It reminds that this first wave of rulings—so far undisturbed
by the justices—may not retain that status for long. When the high

court next takes up the gun issue, we can expect to hear echoes of Kavanaugh's dissent in the views of the *Heller* majority.

GUN CONTROL IN RETREAT

The determined public campaign by gun rights backers that changed constitutional doctrine continues to shift the political terrain as well.

In Congress and legislatures, gun control advocates had spent a decade in pell-mell retreat. In 1999, mass killings at a high school in Columbine, Colorado, renewed pressure on the firearms industry. A large protest urging gun safety laws gathered before the U.S. Capitol in a Million Mom March, though its energy dissipated quickly. Cities and states pressed in on the firearms industry, bringing lawsuits as they had against tobacco companies. In truth the political contest proved a mismatch. Gun control supporters were strategically scattered and organizationally weak. Key constituencies for stronger laws, such as police departments, found other priorities. More important, those who supported gun control may have had good intentions, but lacked passionate intensity. Few legislators feared losing a seat because they voted to back, not buck, the NRA. Gun rights supporters could mobilize when needed. In 1997, for example, manufacturers stood with President Bill Clinton in the White House as he praised their decision to ship trigger locks with every gun. Some firms prepared to settle lawsuits. When the venerable manufacturer Smith & Wesson reached a tentative agreement, NRA members boycotted its products. The company pulled out of talks.

Then George W. Bush took office. The assault weapons ban expired in 2004. Congress declined to renew it. The next year, Bush signed a law providing broad immunity from lawsuits for gun manufacturers and sellers. Manufacturers quietly began to provide substantial funding for the NRA. Around the country, trends were even more pronounced. In 1986, eight states had laws requiring authorities to issue permits to carry concealed weapons (called "shall issue" states); by 2013, thirty-seven did.

The number of states where it was flatly illegal to carry a gun fell from sixteen to zero. In Florida, flanked by the head lobbyist for the NRA, Governor Jeb Bush signed the Stand Your Ground law in 2005. Increasingly the gun group focused on state legislatures, which could preempt antigun ordinances or laws enacted by cities.

Pro-gun activists continued to wage a long game to pursue constitutional change. Increasingly the NRA focused on federal judicial nominations. Before 2009, the organization had never counted a vote for or against a Supreme Court nominee toward the "score" it keeps of pro-gun votes. It had little reason to oppose Sonia Sotomayor, who had never ruled on any major Second Amendment issues, when President Obama nominated her for the High Court. Senate minority leader Mitch McConnell, hoping to hold down Sotomayor's margin, asked the NRA to "score" the vote, as a favor to the Republican leadership. Lawmakers seeking a perfect NRA grade would have to vote no. The group did so again opposing the nomination of Elena Kagan the next year. As a result, each jurist received just a handful of Republican votes. Kagan recalls her private meetings with senators as they considered her nomination. Repeatedly they asked about her view of the Second Amendment. "But because you don't say anything about your views on anything, when they ask you well, they'll try to figure out what your views on the Second Amendment are likely to be and they'll say, 'Well, have you ever held a gun? Have you ever gone hunting? Do you know anybody who's gone hunting?'" (Finally, Kagan promised that if confirmed, she would join Antonin Scalia on a hunting trip. Now Justice Kagan, she later confirmed to an Aspen audience, "I shot myself a deer.")

Gun rights activists pressed for change in state constitutions and courts, as well. Forty states already had gun rights provisions mirroring the Second Amendment in their constitutions. In 2012 legislators in eight states introduced near-identical proposals to apply "strict scrutiny" to laws that might impinge on gun rights. Louisiana moved first. Voters overwhelmingly voted to change their state's charter. It now read, "The right of each citizen to keep and bear arms is fundamental and shall not be infringed. Any restriction on this right shall be subject to strict scrutiny." The key words are "fundamental" and "strict scrutiny." These legalistic phrases have a profound impact. Without them, criminal laws relating to guns were previously presumed constitutional if they rationally sought to "protect the public safety." Now Louisiana judges are allowed to uphold gun laws only if they meet the most exacting standard: the state must prove the law protected a "compelling government interest," be narrowly tailored to do only that, and be the "least restrictive" way to achieve its goal. Many otherwise sensible laws would fall. This was a boon for criminal defendants as well as gun rights advocates. The Orleans Parish public defender office, representing poor residents in the Crescent City, challenged a half dozen convictions. Twenty-year-old Glen Draughter had been convicted of burglary. Police arrested him and others driving with a loaded AK-47 and magazine clip in the trunk, a .40 caliber Smith & Wesson pistol in the backseat. A judge overturned Draughter's conviction on the grounds that his right to "keep and bear arms" had been infringed. An appeals court later reversed it. This was likely the first of many such rulings as cases swamped the courts. Constitutional claims now rang loudly. Louisiana's children accidentally are shot to death at three times the national average. A proposed law to require guns to be stored safely at home died in committee, opposed because it would infringe constitutional gun rights.

Once we realize that gun ownership is now deemed a constitutionally protected, legal right, we cannot know how it may unspool over time. Legislatures cannot deny someone their First Amendment right to speak, just because they have committed a violent crime. The clear evidence that the Framers accepted limits on gun ownership by dangerous people only goes so far. In Iowa, in 2013, disability advocates argued that legally blind people should be able to carry loaded weapons. Otherwise, their Second Amendment rights were at risk. If a right is deemed fundamental, as in Louisiana, it will prove harder to deny it when an individual has not been found guilty of a crime. A court restraining order intended to keep a man from harming his ex-wife, for example, might not be enough to overcome a "fundamental" right.

"THE WORST DAY"

In his first four years as president, Barack Obama barely mentioned gun control. He proposed no new restrictions. In fact, he signed only laws to make it easier to bring a gun into a national park or onto an Amtrak train. In the summer of 2012, in Aurora, Colorado, a gunman slipped into a midnight showing of *The Dark Knight Rises*, the new Batman movie. He set off smoke grenades and fired into the theater with guns including an assault rifle with a one-hundred-round drum magazine. Eighty-two people were shot; twelve died. Obama's press secretary insisted there would be no new gun moves from the president, referring to "existing law" three times in one media briefing. That did not stop the NRA: executive vice president Wayne LaPierre warned of a "conspiracy to ensure re-election by lulling gun owners to sleep." "All that first term lip service to gun owners," he insisted, "is just part of a massive Obama conspiracy to deceive voters and hide his true intentions to destroy the Second Amendment during his second term."

One month after the election, on a Friday morning, word came of the carnage at Newtown. By noon Obama spoke with Governor Dan Malloy of Connecticut. This was the worst day of his presidency, he said, and much would change. "It's the first time that I cried in the Oval Office," he reported to longtime aide David Axelrod. Obama spoke at the memorial service for the schoolchildren and their heroic teachers. Citizens in recent decades expect their president to reach out during tragedy. Obama had spoken at his share of funerals and disaster sites. Usually the president stuck to platitudes. This time, he vowed action. "We will be told that the causes of such violence are complex, and that is true. No single law—no set of laws can eliminate evil from the world, or prevent every senseless act of violence in our society. But that can't be an excuse for inaction. Surely, we can do better than this."

For the first time in fourteen years, a White House sought to lead national action to curb gun violence. Vice President Joseph Biden had presided over enactment of the Brady Bill and assault weapons ban in the 1990s as chair of the U.S. Senate Judiciary Committee. Obama assigned him to cull a menu of actions. One month after the shooting, Biden's task force reported its recommendations. Most of the steps it urged were constitutionally unassailable, or at least posed no problems for even the most die-hard Second Amendment adherent. Other recommendations seemed noncontroversial, though in fact they did provoke diatribes against "gun grabbers." Obama wanted to invest more money in research on gun violence, seemingly a goal without controversy. In fact, this would reverse the policy of gagging research at the Centers for Disease Control.

Some seemed gimmicky. For example, the Biden task force recommended an increase in mandatory minimum sentences for gun crimes. Tough talk: wouldn't lengthier sentences lead to fewer gun crimes? But evidence is debatable at best that putting people in prison for longer times reduces violent crime, as opposed to sure and swift punishment. And such an approach risks repeating errors made early in the "war on drugs." Criminal lawmaking is especially susceptible to good intentions marred by dangerous and unintended consequences. Unthinkingly piling up one long sentence after another has led to an explosive growth in the incarcerated population, so that the United States—with 5 percent of the world's population—now has 25 percent of its prisoners.

Other proposals required congressional action. President Obama plunged forward to urge legislation. The move suggested a new political calculus. Obama clearly felt liberated by his reelection, and perhaps a bit guilty over his previous silence. Still, it was the first time in years that national Democrats had approached the gun issue. A generation of political leaders and operatives saw gun control as a sign of cultural alienation from rural and moderate voters. It was not worth taking on, they thought, and any legislative push was destined for defeat anyway. Now the issue was joined again. For the first time in nearly two decades, Congress considered legislation to tighten, not weaken, federal gun laws. Plainly these would implicate the newly found constitutional right.

One proposal seemed constitutionally ironclad. Current law requires that gun purchasers undergo an instant computerized background check. Some two million purchases have been stopped. But weapons bought at gun shows or sold by private parties generally are not covered. Legislation brought to the floor of the U.S. Senate would have expanded the system to include gun shows. Here there was a ready historical analogy, the favored mode of argument: the Framers prohibited dangerous people from having guns. The NRA once had supported background checks, partly as an alternative to longer waiting periods or gun bans. In the spring of 2013, expanded checks were supported by upward of 90 percent of the public. When Republican Pat Toomey of Pennsylvania and Democrat Joe Manchin III of West Virginia brought a compromise to the floor, a majority backed it. This time the NRA threw its weight against it, and it was blocked by a filibuster. Arguments over red tape and practicality dominated. Foes were less eager to wield the Second Amendment as a talisman.

More controversial was the proposal to reinstate the assault weapons ban, and expand it to include high-capacity magazines. "Assault weapon" is an imprecise term. A semiautomatic weapon does not need to be reloaded each time it is fired. (As opposed to a machine gun, which allows the shooter to fire continuously just by holding down the trigger.) High-capacity magazines, holding dozens of rounds at a time, enabled mass killers to shoot without having to stop and reload. The AR-15, a military-style weapon similar to the M-4 and M-16 rifles used by the United States Army since Vietnam, has become one of the country's favorites. A previous version of the ban had expired; it had shown limited impact on gun crime. As a political and policy matter, the attention given to the assault weapons ban was a strategic blunder, since it was always utterly unlikely to pass Congress. Jurisprudential issues remained pertinent, though, since two ambitious governors—Andrew Cuomo in New York and John Hickenlooper in Colorado—were pressing forward to enact similar measures.

Would a renewed ban on these weapons pass constitutional muster? A Senate Judiciary Committee hearing boiled over.

Ted Cruz was the newly elected senator from Texas. As the state's solicitor general, he had appeared frequently before the U.S. Supreme Court. He had even argued part of *Heller* in a lower court on behalf of

Texas and other states. Now he was in his third month in the Senate. He turned to Dianne Feinstein, the longtime senator from California. In 1979, she had become mayor of San Francisco after she discovered the body of her murdered predecessor, George Moscone, along with that of Supervisor Harvey Milk.

"It seems to me that all of us should begin with our foundational document of the Constitution," Cruz began. She agreed.

He continued his interrogation in the mock formal language of the Senate. The Second Amendment used the phrase "the right of the people," as had the First and Fourth. "Would she deem it consistent with the Bill of Rights for Congress to engage in the same endeavor that we are contemplating doing with the Second Amendment in the context of the First or Fourth Amendment? Namely, would she consider it constitutional for Congress to specify that the First Amendment shall apply only to the following books and shall not apply to the books that Congress has deemed outside the protection of the Bill of Rights? Likewise, would she think that the Fourth Amendment's protection against searches and seizures could properly apply only to the following specified individuals and not to the individuals that Congress has deemed outside the protection of the Bill of Rights?" Cruz picked up a cardboard coffee cup and drank deeply.

Feinstein leaned in and glared. "I'm not a sixth grader.

"Senator, I've been on this committee for 20 years. I was a mayor for nine years. I walked in, I saw people shot. I've looked at bodies that have been shot with these weapons. I've seen the bullets that implode. In Sandy Hook, youngsters were dismembered. Look, there are other weapons. I'm not a lawyer, but after 20 years I've been up close and personal to the Constitution. I have great respect for it. This doesn't mean weapons of war, and the *Heller* decision clearly points out three exceptions, two of which are pertinent here. You know, it's fine you want to lecture me on the Constitution. I appreciate it. Just know I've been here for a long time. I've passed on a number of bills. I've studied the Constitution myself. I am reasonably well educated, and I thank you for the lecture."

The theatrical encounter crystallized the constitutional concern. Progressive pundits recoiled at Cruz's sneer, his lack of deference to an older colleague, his oversimplification. Conservatives crowed Feinstein had been hit by a "Cruz missile." But was Cruz wrong?

To be sure, he engaged in demagogy when he implied the First and Fourth Amendments have no limitations. As a constitutional litigator, he knew better. We cherish free speech but ban child pornography. No law could prohibit one book and allow another—unless the barred book was flammable and prone to explode in bookstores. The Fourth Amendment applies to all people—but there are emergency exceptions. Cruz acknowledged that *Heller* allowed limits for guns not in "common use." But assault weapons, well, they were everywhere. "I would suggest on any measure, four million weapons qualifies as in common use. And so under the terms of *Heller*, they cannot constitutionally be prohibited." Four million assault weapons are enough to equip a medium-sized army. On the other hand, they make up a tiny percentage of the hundreds of millions of American guns in circulation. The entire exercise shows the absurdity of measuring constitutionality by market share. It also displays the constitutional hall of mirrors engendered by Scalia's selective originalism. After all, an assault weapon is precisely the kind of armament a modern-day Minute Man might want to use. Now that right, rooted in military obligation, is untethered to actual military service. Does that make an assault weapon less protected, or more?

Laurence Tribe, the Harvard professor who a decade earlier had endorsed an individual rights interpretation, testified that the assault weapons bill did not come near being unconstitutional. "The central message of *Heller* and its lower-court progeny is thus to take the application of the Second Amendment seriously but also cautiously," he said in a written statement before Congress. After all, guns that were "dangerous and unusual" could be regulated or prohibited. And it should not be necessary to fire so many bullets to protect a home from a burglar. Robert Levy, the Cato Institute chair who funded and led the winning litigation team in *Heller*, agreed. He told *The Washington Post* he assumed assault weapons and high-capacity magazines could be banned.

Constitutional arguments flew fast. In one respect, debates in 2013 differed from those that came before. The NRA long had argued that gun measures were the first step toward a program of confiscation. It still did so, blaring to its members that the Obama administration was "closing in fast on your Right to Keep and Bear Arms."

But the justices now had spoken. When the Supreme Court declares something a constitutional right, it rocks not only the legal world. It enshrines an idea with legitimacy. It booms a political talking point with an august baritone and becomes a simple talking point for "low information" voters and legislators. In this way, *Heller* was a huge boon to gun rights forces. If it is unchallenged, its legitimacy will only grow with time.

And yet, it also put a trigger lock on the greatest threat feared by gun rights supporters. Does a power-mad government want to take everyone's guns away? It couldn't even if it wanted to. *Heller* would stop the "gun grabbers."

Joe Scarborough, the Florida Republican congressman turned MSNBC cable TV host, supported an assault weapons ban. He found that *Heller* made his arguments easier. Scarborough repeatedly insisted, as he did one morning, "Justice Scalia, the strongest supporter of the Second Amendment on the Supreme Court, said this amendment does not apply to assault weapons. No way! There is no constitutional issue here." Democratic politicians embraced the Second Amendment with gusto. Vice President Biden could say, "The first foundational principle is: there is a Second Amendment. The President and I support the second amendment. And it comes with the right of law abiding, responsible citizens to own guns—to use it for their protection as well as for recreation."

Some surmise that, in the long run, *Heller* and *McDonald* will make it easier for gun control advocates, by drawing a sharp line over which they cannot cross. This would hardly be the first time an adverse but limited Supreme Court ruling has helped the losing side. In recent years when justices have issued a ruling to curb affirmative action, the steam escaped from efforts to repeal it altogether. So far, though, evidence is slim that such a political benefit has accrued. Perhaps Barack Obama was able to win North Carolina (in 2008) and Virginia (both times he ran) because gun issues were less salient than a decade earlier. But the intense animosity of the NRA and its leadership, surely, seems unabated, regardless of politicians' catechism-like invocation of "belief" in the Second Amendment.

So perhaps *Heller* will leave a mark fainter than some hoped and others feared. Yet the injection of constitutional fundamentalism into gun policy comes at precisely the moment when it might do the most harm in the long run.

NINE

Flying Blind

The Supreme Court now has enshrined a right. But it did so at an odd moment: a time when there are reasons to think the push for gun rights might otherwise lose some of its potency. It entrenched a particular worldview, when the tides of politics and demographics might move away from it.

Begin with a basic fact: the number of guns in the United States has continued to climb. Firm numbers are unavailable, because unlike autos, guns are not registered. Today there are estimated to be as many as 270 million civilian firearms in the country. That is three times as many guns per person as Canada, and fifteen times as many as England.

But the ranks of gun *owners* have not swelled. In fact, they have dropped sharply. For four decades, the General Social Survey, a study regularly conducted by the National Opinion Research Center, has asked respondents whether they have a gun at home. Every decade, gun ownership rates have slid, from half of all households in the 1970s to 34 percent. Today only one in five Americans reported owning any guns at all. Gun ownership has shrunk in all regions, including the South and West, where firearms imbue the culture. Three of four city dwellers don't have a gun. Nearly half of people who live in rural areas don't, either.

In short, fewer people own more guns.

There is one more relevant trend. Gun violence is down. To be clear: murder and violence remain higher in America than in the rest of the industrialized world. A gun policy center at Johns Hopkins University concluded, "Although there is little difference in the overall crime rates between the United States and other high income countries, the homicide rate in the U.S. is seven times higher than the combined homicide rate of 22 other high-income countries." Even so, the gun homicide rate dropped by nearly half from 1993 to 2010. "The victimization rate for other violent crimes with a firearm—assaults, robberies and sex crimes—was 75 percent lower in 2011 than in 1993," according to a Pew Research Center study. The broad drop in violent crime across America is one of the most significant phenomena in recent decades. It is among the least understood. In the 1990s, experts issued dire warnings that a remorseless generation of "superpredator" teenagers would make cities unlivable. Today those cities are safer than they have been in decades. Confusing things further, crime rates are dropping all over the Western world. Criminologists and sociologists have studied, and debated, the causes of these unexpected improvements. A recent blue-ribbon panel concluded more data was needed. Such studies are inconclusive as to whether most gun control laws have a major impact.

The NRA, of course, has a theory: it heavily promoted the idea that an armed population is the reason crime is dropping. In 1998 economist John Lott published *More Guns, Less Crime*. The book became the best-selling title ever published by the University of Chicago Press. Lott looked at states that had liberalized "concealed carry" laws, and saw crime rates ease. The book's thesis proved wildly controversial, at best. When other researchers delved into Lott's findings, they found no credible evidence that the passage of right-to-carry laws decreases or increases violent crime. Lott furiously defended his research. One former student spoke up on his behalf. "I have to say that he was the best professor I ever had," effused Mary Rosh on the Internet. She enthusiastically posted on her mentor's defense on Amazon.com, as well. She turned out to be a "sock puppet"—"Mary Rosh" evidently was "John

Lott." Lott left the American Enterprise Institute, and no longer teaches at a university. He now is best known as a Fox News columnist.

This new era of gun rights will intersect with the real world of gun violence and public health in several ways.

Now that judges must weigh new and existing gun laws against the Second Amendment, law enforcement officials will face a new hurdle. Advocates of measures to curb gun violence now must prove the efficacy of their policies to a judge, to survive even intermediate scrutiny. The dearth of scholarly data will pose obstacles. In 1996, Representative Jay Dickey, Republican of Arkansas—who later described himself as the NRA's "point person in Congress"—won passage of a provision effectively eliminating funding from the Centers for Disease Control's budget for the study of gun violence. Research funding in and out of government simply dried up. According to *The New York Times*, "The centers also ask researchers it finances to give it a heads-up anytime they are publishing studies that have anything to do with firearms. The agency, in turn, relays this information to the NRA as a courtesy." In 2011, Congress extended that ban to the National Institutes of Health as well. Peer-reviewed, valid scientific evidence is in short supply, at the very moment courts will be requiring it. Taking executive action in 2013, the Obama administration ordered the CDC to go ahead and conduct research. Results will take time.

Historians will need to get busy, too. To the extent that historical analogies will need to be drawn to obscure gun policies of the early republic, pro-regulation advocates are about two decades behind. They have just begun to catalogue early American gun laws, a vital step to show that "tradition" allowed reasonable regulation. This is, putting it mildly, a bizarre quest for policymakers in the twenty-first century, but it's the formal, near-religious test hinted at in its oracular way by the Court.

More promising, some of the most effective current measures to curb gun violence seem the most impervious to constitutional challenge. Law enforcement still can keep guns from the hands of dangerous people, as *Heller* made clear. These prohibitions could be strengthened. For example, many states do not bar from gun ownership individuals with misdemeanor convictions or who were convicted of felonies in juvenile court. Yet these individuals are significantly more likely to use guns in violent crime later.

Many of the most effective steps to curb gun violence fall outside the traditional purview of gun control legislation altogether. NYU Law professor James Jacobs, skeptical about the impact of laws like the Brady Bill, concludes that the demonstrated impact on firearms violence comes from a regime of strong punishment for any crime involving a gun. Police departments assert that enforcement has played a significant role in the decline of gun use in major cities. It is not gun laws, but policing that has changed. Even there, controversy swirls around policy and efficacy. Policing practices shifted markedly since the early 1990s. Beginning in New York City and Boston, "community policing" flooded the streets, and pulled police out of their cars for direct interaction with citizens in high-crime neighborhoods. In Boston, police targeted gangs to make clear that gun use would not be tolerated. New York sharply increased the number of officers on patrol. They focused on crime "hot spots," a policy that soon morphed into the controversial "stop and frisk" tactic. But it is far from clear that the way police search for guns has actually brought down gun crime. Evidence suggests that the sheer number of police in a crime-ridden neighborhood does more to push back against firearms violence than do adjustments in policing practices. All these efforts, of course, are subject to constitutional limitations other than the Second Amendment—most notably, the Fourth Amendment and its prohibition against unreasonable search and seizure.

Still, we are early in the post-*Heller* era. Already, Second Amendment fundamentalism has grown so intense it may crimp strategies that do work. In the 1990s, the NRA and the Bureau of Alcohol, Tobacco and Firearms lauded "Project Exile" in Virginia. This sought to arrest and prosecute any felon caught with a firearm. Again, studies differ on how successful it really was—but the NRA touted it as the way to "enforce existing laws" rather than pass new ones. If the Louisiana model of "strict scrutiny" spreads, police will find it far harder to target gun possession.

It is the very focus on history, the very need to look backward at colonial practices, that suggests a genuine hurt from *Heller*. The gun control debate is stymied. Obama's most visible reform proposals, after all, differed little from measures debated and passed in Bill Clinton's first term in the early 1990s. Technology and local experimentation could leap past the sterile arguments. But Adam Samaha, Jens Ludwig, and Philip Cook—three academic experts—worry that "the possibility of constitutional litigation certainly can deter novel government responses to old or new social problems—and passages in *Heller* seem designed to have this dampening effect." They point to "technological and regulatory innovations, including microstamping shell casings for the purpose of tracing crime guns, reviewing the design of new guns before they hit the market, and requiring personalized gun technology that attempts to restrict usage to owners only." Local governments will know that costly constitutional litigation will now ensue should they try to put in place cutting-edge reforms.

Consider ballistic microstamping. California governor Arnold Schwarzenegger signed an innovative law requiring semiautomatic pistols to stamp a serial number on each bullet as it leaves the chamber. A public-spirited NRA member had invented the technology; he wanted his patent to expire so he could give it to the state. It took five years, due to legal disputes, but California finally implemented it in 2013. The NRA fought the proposal. Litigation challenges are likely.

Other possible methods to control gun violence could be frozen, too. Certain kinds of guns could be highly taxed, to pay for the unusual amount of damage they do. (That is how the 1934 law treated some weapons.) Gun manufacturers, or gun owners, could be required to purchase insurance to pay for health and property claims due to improper use of a given firearm. Thumbprint recognition could be a foolproof form of trigger lock to prevent children from accidentally shooting a playmate. We do not know if future courts will regard any or all of these as an impermissible restriction on a sacred right. But the very worry about litigation could well deter local governments from embarking on policy innovation. Criminal justice policy is rarely ever solely about what works. Gun control, as much as gun rights, can become a matter of faith, or competing fear. But to the extent possible, society gains when it is able to weigh costs, benefits, and competing claims for safety policy. That has just become much harder. And judges will be asked to do much more of the weighing.

IN THE CULTURE WARS, ONE SIDE IS ARMED

One can hope that commonsense gun regulation could evolve further. *Heller* and *McDonald* could ultimately point toward a world of limited gun rights subject to regulation, an accurate description, after all, of most of America's history. But Second Amendment fundamentalism challenges that sunny view. Increasingly, it is clear that the gun issue is not one of evidence-based public safety policy, but of culture. The rediscovery and glorification of the Second Amendment reflects that divide— but will likely only make it worse.

The desire to buy a gun for protection has raw emotional elements, and it certainly may reflect aspects of racial panic (especially when gun sales spike after the country elects an African American president). Surveys show most Americans do not believe gun violence is down—which may spur more desire for gun control among some, and to buy guns among others. On the other hand, the lived experience of people in the places where violence was most pervasive, America's cities, suggests that people there understand crime has dropped.

In parts of America, for much of its history, having a gun was a deeply rooted cultural tradition, part of what it meant to be a man. The custom of giving an adolescent boy his "first gun" has been called "the bar mitzvah of the rural WASP." We speak of America's "gun culture." But that culture is changing. Hunting is in decline, in part because suburban development has reduced the land available for it. Fewer people proclaim their need for a gun to protect themselves from crime, as well.

And there is another reason that the gun culture is shrinking, one central to the story of the Second Amendment. A well regulated militia once included all adult white men. At several other times in our history, mass mobilizations pulled millions of Americans into the military. The colonial militias were cited as precedent for the first federal draft, during World War I. Franklin Roosevelt said he was calling up a "muster" when he instituted the first peacetime draft in the uneasy days before Pearl Harbor. In 1970, the peak of the Vietnam War, over three million Americans were on active military duty. The volunteer army was introduced in 1971. Since then, the volunteer army has shrunk, grown more professional, and more lethal. Morale and training are far higher. But fewer Americans take part. The tradition of military service behind the Second Amendment—which helped create the gun culture in the post–World War II years—has faded. Relatively few of the men who wear camouflage and accessorize their assault weapons have ever served a minute in the military or heard a shot fired in anger. A clue to the cultural basis of current gun politics comes from the nature of the guns themselves. The fastest-growing gun, in terms of popularity, is precisely the AR-15—the semiautomatic rifle, designed to look like a warrior's weapon. Boys with toys.

Increasingly cultural dimensions cut deeper than a mere divide between urban and rural Americans. That we have had since the beginning. (Indeed, since the debate over the ratification of the Constitution that pitted backwoods Pennsylvanians against Quaker Philadelphians.) If it seems as though gun rights adherents and gun control backers occupy different mental universes, seeing the same facts in entirely different ways, that largely is true. The Pew Research Center presents some startling statistics: "The general profile of gun owners in America differs substantially from the general public. Roughly three-quarters (74 percent) of gun owners are men, and 82 percent are white. Taken together, 61 percent of adults who own guns are white men. Nationwide, white men make up only 32 percent of the adult U.S. population." Gun owners are nearly twice as likely to identify as Republicans as non–gun owners. For years, gun owners have been far more intense in their advocacy than broad majorities who support restrictions. That has been true for generations. Now, though, Americans have "sorted" themselves into increasingly distinct, isolated, bristling partisan camps.

One compelling study explored the split between those who oppose and back gun control. It suggests the divide goes even deeper than political ideology, religion, region, or race. What matters is what people fear: are citizens more afraid of gun violence or of being exposed to a predator without the ability to protect themselves? The way people perceive that risk flows from basic worldview. Those who are fiercely individualist, or who are especially imbued with respect for authority (including the military), are more likely to oppose gun restrictions. Those who tend to think more in terms of community, support them. "Whether one is hierarchical or egalitarian, individualistic or solidaristic . . . matters more than whether one is Republican or Democrat, conservative or liberal."

The Supreme Court's decision to enshrine the individual rights interpretation of the Second Amendment can only worsen that polarization.

Second Amendment fundamentalism rests powerfully on the idea that an empowered individual—armed to protect himself (gender definitely intended) and his family—is the morally virtuous way to live. It is not just that people cannot rely on police to protect them; it would be worse if they could.

That explains why, to many city dwellers, the reaction of gun rights leaders so often seems so bizarre, even apocalyptic. Wayne LaPierre feverishly explained that all Americans must be armed. "After Hurricane Sandy, we saw the hellish world that the gun prohibitionists see as their utopia," he wrote. "Looters ran wild in south Brooklyn. There was no food, water or electricity. And if you wanted to walk several miles to get supplies, you better get back before dark, or you might not get home at all." LaPierre's version of the hurricane mystified those who lived through it. Coney Island was unusually peaceful: there were no murders, no rapes, and no shootings that week, according to the New York City Police Department.

When LaPierre first spoke out after Sandy Hook, his approach flabbergasted many. In a nationally televised statement, many expected him to mouth words of contrition, to vow to "work together" and seek reconciliation. "The only way to stop a *monster* from killing our kids is to be personally involved and invested in a plan of absolute protection," he declared angrily. "The only thing that stops a bad guy with a gun is a good guy with a gun." He proposed an armed guard in every elementary school. To many unfamiliar with the language of gun rights, this was simply an astounding change of subject. The New York *Daily News* blared, THE CRAZIEST MAN ON EARTH. The conservative *New York Post* front page wood read: NRA LOON IN BIZARRE RANT OVER NEWTOWN. It painted what many regard as a grim and dystopian world of mutual, armed suspicion. To LaPierre and others, it was simply a logical extension of their worldview. To them the "Standard Model" of individual gun bearing, drawing on pre-colonial history, has utter, continued relevance in our interdependent, wired, densely populated world.

And it echoed the language and arguments of the majority opinion in *Heller*: its talk of individual protection, of self-defense. Gun issues already are polarized, values laden, driven by cultural notions of right and wrong rather than what works. The Supreme Court's rulings are likely to make that values-driven polarization only worse. When the Court speaks, its words echo not only in marble halls and courtrooms. Given its enormous prestige, it provides validation and momentum in the political realm, too. When an opinion is accepted and embraced, that legitimacy extends. Gun rights supporters may have enshrined their constitutional approach at their moment of peak political power. Given long-term demographic trends, their power may recede. But constitutional doctrine can prove harder to dislodge than temporary legislative majorities. As a legal matter, *Heller* may create space for reasonable gun regulation. As a matter of politics and culture, though, it can only deepen polarization. Whereas once gun debates turned on hunting or street crime, now it almost instantly reverts to evocations of hallowed constitutional rights. So while gun debates need not devolve into a tired argument over Second Amendment absolutes, there are all too many reasons to think they will.

CONCLUSION

"The Right of the People"

In the story of the Second Amendment we learn much about our country, our Constitution, and how we read it—and live it. Three major lessons emerge.

The first touches on the way we read the Constitution: simply, originalism is untenable. Antonin Scalia called *Heller* the "vindication" of the theory. In fact, it displays the limitations of trying to answer today's questions by consulting the oracles of the past.

After all, the world of the Second Amendment is unrecognizable: a world where every white American man served in the military for his entire adult life, where those citizen soldiers bought their own military weapons and stored them at home, and where the idea of a United States Army would be enough to send patriots to grab their musket. When the militias evaporated, so did the original meaning of the Second Amendment.

As for the Fourteenth Amendment, which pointed more firmly toward an individual right, that, too, comes from a strikingly different moment: a time of armed guerrilla war between the races. We can and do learn from the majestic generality of the amendment's vision of equality—but the notion of personal safety guaranteed only by a gun in every hand, drawn to fend off the marauding Klan, happily is past, too.

• • •

In all the ways that help us understand the role of guns, twenty-first-century America differs profoundly from the time of the Framers. Weapons are far more destructive (a point acknowledged by the most thoughtful gun rights adherents). Americans live in dense urban environments, where violence can cascade out of control. Murders, suicide, robbery, all are more widespread today than in 1789. Today, we rely on professionalized police departments to protect us from crime and unrest, and a United States Army to protect us from overseas threats—all institutions unknown to the Founders. The idea that we should arm the population so they could mount an insurrection against the government, just in case, seems absurd. Sadly, the sense of civic duty that impelled Americans to bear arms for their country is largely a thing of the past, too.

In this new era, Americans built an approach to guns and gun violence. Guns are more plentiful than elsewhere. But we have always had gun regulations and strong criminal laws, too. What we did not have was a regime of judicially enforced individual rights, able to trump the public good—and the encroaching decoupling of rights and responsibility. Debates about what to do, about how to strike that balance, rested above all on what was good for Americans here and now. We did not make gun policy based on half-remembered history or sentimentalized notions of personal empowerment.

These tangled threads suggest a second lesson, this one for the courts: the importance of judicial restraint.

As Americans, we take for granted the notion that a paragraph cobbled together over two centuries ago, for reasons historians debate fiercely, would constrain how society protects itself today. Alone among major democracies, we eagerly shoo political and policy questions into the courtroom. That has long been true. (Back in 1835, Alexis de Tocqueville observed, "There is almost no political question in the United States that does not sooner or later resolve itself into a judicial question.") Our system has evolved to give the Supreme Court ultimate authority over vast areas of policy and everyday life. Yet the Supreme

Court by its nature is a political institution. Appointed by partisan politicians, forced to interpret vague constitutional phrases, the justices inevitably make political choices. For all those reasons, the Court husbands its democratic legitimacy when it steps carefully into political realms.

Once it was progressives who urged judicial restraint. Then conservatives embraced it. Now they giddily slice through sheaths of statute books. *Heller, Citizens United, Shelby County* likely are just the start (unless Court personnel changes). And despite confirmation hearing bromides, judges are increasingly willing to overturn the laws enacted by generations of democratically elected politicians. A too easy recourse to rights language, the decoupling of rights from responsibilities, and the turn to the courts as the first resort all have consequences.

This seems profoundly mistaken. The Court's current five-vote majority—all chosen by Republican presidents, even as Democrats have won most recent presidential elections—have chosen to interpose the Court as a bulwark against longer and larger social trends. The rising electorate wants a stronger government; the Court increasingly insists on a smaller one. *Heller* was an outlier: its methodology was suspect, but its result was popular. But the train of other, even bolder decisions risks a backlash as potent as the one against liberal decisions after the 1960s.

Perhaps conservative overreach will remind left and right that in our constitutional system, it is far better for fundamental questions to be resolved, if at all possible, by the push-and-pull of politics.

That is especially true when it comes to gun violence. This is a remarkably dense and thorny issue. The controversy is thick with symbolic politics. It pits rural culture against urban norms. It asks us to avoid emotionalism, to rely more on research, to find policies that actually work. Efforts to enact sensible regulations of guns face many obstacles: powerful organizations, inflamed opponents, cowardly politicians, a media culture that (when not suffused with violence itself) quickly loses interest. To surmount these will require grit and wisdom. It should not have to require overcoming a hostile judiciary, misreading history, over-interpreting text, and imposing political views in the guise of judicial philosophy.

All of which suggests a third lesson, perhaps most fundamental: how the Supreme Court sees the Constitution is ultimately up to us. A full scan of American history shows that the public, fully engaged, has made constitutional law every bit as much as jurists and lawyers.

After all, the Framers added the Second Amendment to the Constitution not because they solemnly believed it necessary, but as a "tub to the whale"—a concession to popular discontent. From the beginning, American politics was marked by triangulation, compromise, tactical retreats. Fretful citizens have always been anxious about governmental overreach by Washington. (*George* Washington, not the city, not yet formed.) Even the Founders found it necessary to appease the Tea Party. Justice Roger Taney's view of gun ownership as a white man's "privilege" in *Dred Scott* was the product not of originalism but the rising Slave Power of the 1850s—and the story of the Fourteenth Amendment, in turn, is driven by the passion of the Radical Republicans and the freedmen who organized militias and governments after war's end. And at every step of the way, the way we viewed gun rights was couched and conditioned by the way we saw government.

Does the Constitution today guarantee a right to bear arms? Chances are vanishingly small that *Heller* will be overturned. Gun control advocates do not seek that. They think it unnecessary. Taking at face value the caveats and conditions built into Scalia's "I am not a nut" opinion, it ought to be possible to craft an effective regime of public safety while carefully stepping around newly erected judicial obstacles.

But the reason the Court has pronounced that limited right is not because the Framers of the Second Amendment intended it to confer it. (They didn't.) Nor is it because of a dictionary from 1730, or a state court judicial interpretation from 1830, or even a Supreme Court case from 1939. Rather, it is because the people today believe there is such a right. The country has evolved—the Constitution is living, as it were— and the widespread acceptance of some form of gun ownership is part of the way Americans think. Not then, now. *Heller* can be justified not as originalism, but as something more rooted in common sense: it reflected a popular consensus won by focused activists.

It is hardly surprising that the NRA—like myriad other social movements and pressure groups before—sought to bend the Constitution. Gun rights campaigners began with scholarship, moved on to persuading politicians and governmental bodies, began to test the law, and finally went to the High Court. By the time the case was brought before the justices, it fell like a ripe apple. This model for legal change earlier had been developed by advocates for civil rights, women's equality, worker and consumer protection, all causes traditionally identified with the left.

Today's progressives and gun control advocates have much to learn from the NRA's history, and their own. Popular constitutionalism cannot be just a theory of interpretation. It must be what they do. They will have to enlist historians and legal scholars, for example, to make the case for gun regulations under the new, history-driven regime. They will need to scrape together social science research to help new laws stand up in court. They will have to wage a far more aggressive effort than before to win elections and win over lawmakers. The rise of new groups such as Mayors Against Illegal Guns and Americans for Responsible Solutions offers a chance for greater professionalism and impact.

And just as conservatives and the NRA have focused on changing the public's opinion on gun rights, progressive advocates must focus with equal intensity on changing the public mind. Oddly, many seem reluctant to do so. Lawyers fill the ranks of progressive leadership like an overstuffed briefcase. The last two Democratic presidents were lawyers (Yale, Harvard). By contrast, the last Republican president with a law degree left office in 1977. In years past, so many of the great victories for liberalism were won in the courtroom. But persuading the public, waging a broad campaign to shift the terrain of debate, is not an alternative to a legal strategy. This approach goes to the heart of legal change, every bit as much as the most skilled legal brief. Debating slavery and an earlier Court decision, Abraham Lincoln said, "Public sentiment is everything. With public sentiment, nothing can fail; without it, nothing can succeed. Consequently he who molds public sentiment goes deeper than he who enacts statutes or pronounces decisions. He makes statutes and decisions possible or impossible to be executed."

And over the longer term, a progressive vision of the Constitution must challenge the primacy of originalism.

Some liberals, reeling from defeat, argue that originalism is right—but that modern conservatives just pick the parts of the past they want to revere. But what makes us think that the Framers wanted us to read their words, their misplaced commas, as if they were Scripture? Too often, when liberals insist that they are the real originalists, their protestations can feel too strained, too cute by half. One gets a whiff of the sense that they think originalism is a clever piece of political jujitsu rather than the way a strong nation should govern itself.

A frank acknowledgment of the power of the living Constitution has its appeal. After all, the country made itself stronger, more egalitarian, more effective in the world precisely during the mid-twentieth-century period when jurists were most willing to seek meaning in the spirit but not the letter of the Constitution. A living Constitution does not discard the spirit of the document, but seeks to apply its timeless principles to modern challenges that could not have been imagined by the Framers or their contemporaries. It reflects with frankness that our sense of human dignity has, in fact, evolved. Wide public acceptance of same sex marriage is only the latest evidence of evolution upward, one hard to square with what would have been plausible for the Founders. Some sophisticated progressives have sought to square the circle. Jack Balkin, a Yale professor and the author of an influential blog, has argued for a "living originalism," recognizing that the Framers drafted a document designed to be broadly interpreted by future generations.

But the strength of the conservative vision of originalism has never solely been in its "Eureka!" pretension that it has at long last discovered the hidden key to the Constitution. The justices did not choose conservatism because they were originalists; they chose originalism because they were conservatives. (It did not hurt that arguing for the infallibility of ancient texts appeals to a broad segment of the public in its religious and spiritual life as well as in its constitutional dogma.)

Ultimately, we must fight for a Constitution that is imbued with a powerful set of values. Justice Stephen Breyer has offered the most compelling approach. He argues that the Constitution is best understood as a charter for a vibrant, self-governing democracy. The structural integrity of our system, at times, must trump a narrow reading of any particular right. That frame, applied (as he did) to guns, would suggest strongly that the courts are the wrong branch of government to parse the costs and benefits of greater regulation.

We can draw inspiration from perhaps the least debated phrase in the Second Amendment. Least debated, but perhaps most important. "The right of the people." Put aside the tendentious dialogue over whether that conferred an individual right to own a gun. It surely also referred to the people as a political community—the militia of all the people, as we are constantly reminded. Those people today grapple with complex issues of violence and social order through the democratic process. Some may wince at the NRA's power to pass legislation, just as others may grimace at new gun laws. But those fights take place in public, in legislatures, online, in the media, in the realm of political organizing and the ballot box. When the courts intrude—to rewrite and rewire public policies in service to a particular constitutional theory or ideological approach—they can do damage to our democracy and the law. When they stand by to prudently intervene on behalf of those who need their protection, and who cannot get it through the normal political processes, courts immeasurably strengthen the country. Conservatives argued that for years; liberals are learning it again.

We can be true to the spirit of the Constitution and the animating forces behind the Second Amendment if we understand that above all else, whenever possible, the ability to make and set gun and other policies through the messy, imperfect democratic process is the ultimate "right of the people."

ACKNOWLEDGMENTS

I began this book in the months after the Newtown massacre, when gun control proposals once again became a subject for wide debate. Strikingly, gun rights now vied with public safety as powerful public arguments. I wrote this book in part to understand the meaning and history of the Second Amendment and how we read the Constitution. This is not a book about guns or gun control. Others have far more to say (and certainly say it more loudly). Rather, I was most interested in the question of how our view of the Constitution has changed over time—when and whether we should allow the past to guide our national life today. I have long supported commonsense gun laws. I also worked for a president who taught me about the passionate attachment to guns—for hunting and other purposes—shared by millions of Americans. I did not enter into this inquiry with a fixed set of views about what the framers of the Second Amendment did and did not mean. Much of what I learned surprised me, and, I hope, will inform the reader.

I am immensely grateful to my colleagues at the Brennan Center for Justice at NYU School of Law. They joined in this project enthusiastically and with skill. I am privileged to be part of such a dynamic institution.

Poy Winichakul was my close collaborator throughout the research and writing of the book. She is a gifted writer, a top-notch activist and organizer, and a stellar future lawyer and leader. She was willing to go the extra mile, as when she traveled to the National Rifle Association's headquarters in Fairfax, Virginia, to confirm that, yes, the NRA still has an edited and inaccurate version of the Second Amendment on the wall of its lobby.

She led an energetic and committed team. Rebecca Guiterman and David Berman, summer legal associates at the Brennan Center, provided top-quality factual and legal research. Andrea Adomako, a Barnard undergraduate, proved a tireless researcher. Lena Glaser and Kate Brennan proved invaluable in the final stretch. The law firm Paul, Weiss, Rifkind, Wharton and Garrison provided hugely appreciated pro bono assistance in tracing the course of the law post-*Heller*. We owe tremendous thanks to Christopher Filburn for his pro bono assistance in tracing the course of the law post-*Heller* and to Robert Atkins for his generous help.

I am especially grateful to experts who commented on the manuscript at various stages: Saul Cornell, Adam Winkler, Kate Shaw, Brina Milikowsky, Jeff Shesol, and Jonathan Alter. The views here emphatically are my own, as are any errors. I am grateful, too, to Brina's colleagues at Mayors Against Illegal Guns for setting out the legal implications of the ongoing fight over guns. Adam Samaha, David Yassky, Stephen Schulhofer, Burt Neuborne, and James Jacobs offered expertise and cautions. Professor Lilly Geismer of Claremont McKenna College provided valuable guidance on the political transformations in the 1970s.

Good friends and family read the manuscript: Stephen Bowman, Robert Caro, Steve Waldman, Martin Waldman, and Sandra Waldman. I cannot thank them enough for their time and encouragement.

Brennan Center colleagues provided astute and challenging editing. Fritz Schwarz, our chief counsel, read the manuscript closely even as he finished his own book on government secrecy. I want to especially thank Jeanine Plant-Chirlin, for her insight, edits, and encouragement, and James Lyons and Jennifer Weiss-Wolf, who provided hugely helpful edits. Inimai Chettiar, Oliver Roeder, Julia Bowling, and John Ablan were especially helpful on the intersection between criminal law, social science research, and gun policy. Wendy Weiser, John Kowal, Vivien

Watts, Tony Butler, Sidney Rosdeitcher, Larry Norden, Johanna Kalb, and others offered valuable support and insight on constitutional issues. Thank you as well to our generous supporters; to our board cochairs, Patricia Bauman and Lawrence Pedowitz, for their encouragement; and to two successive deans of the Law School, Ricky Revesz and Trevor Morrison.

The driving force behind this volume was the incomparable Alice Mayhew at Simon & Schuster. She saw the value in a concise popular explanation of the Second Amendment and where the Supreme Court's jurisprudence leaves the country. Her insights, editing, and sweeping knowledge are remarkable, and I count myself lucky to work with her again after more than a decade's time. Thanks too to Jonathan Cox for all his work on the book, as well as Jonathan Karp, Julia Prosser, Maureen Cole, Stephen Bedford, Lisa Healy, Fred Chase, Michael Accordino, Akasha Archer, and others at Simon & Schuster. Rafe Sagalyn, my agent, was enthusiastic and savvy, and his support over so many years is greatly appreciated.

As ever, my most profound thanks go to my wonderful family. Liz Fine read the manuscript and provided, as ever, wisdom and encouragement—and tolerance—and love—in equal measure. Ben Waldman embodies the spirit of patriotism and service in the idea of a "well regulated militia." In college in California, he joined the Army ROTC. I was proud to shoot with him at the shooting range on parents' weekend. Susannah Waldman was my housemate, preparing to go to college, as I brought this book to a close. I learned much from her social commitment and interest in constitutional law, even in high school. Josh Waldman has been my most unflagging cheerleader and my hardworking colleague on our mutual late night homework binges. I wrote previous books when they were young. It is a special thrill to see how they have each grown into insightful, independent, and very different men and women.

The Brennan Center was named after the late Supreme Court Justice William J. Brennan, Jr. It carries forward his humanist vision and passion for justice. What of Justice Brennan? Perhaps he might take issue with the idea of judicial restraint as a governing premise? I never met the Justice, and I cannot say what he would have thought. But when his former clerks formed the organization, they went to him to ask permission to use his name and dedicate it in his honor. He said he would agree, under one condition. It could not simply follow his views and his opinions.

"That," he told them, "would be originalism."

Brooklyn, New York
November 2013

A NOTE ON SOURCES

After many years in which the Second Amendment received little attention, in the past three decades it has been the subject of a remarkable number of articles and books. Whole forests have fallen. Here is a guide to some of the most useful works for further reading.

A few key books offer the most cogent arguments about the changing meaning of the Second Amendment. Adam Winkler's *Gun Fight: The Battle over the Right to Bear Arms in America* (New York: Norton, 2011) offers the most complete, panoramic view of the role both of guns and gun control throughout American history. Saul Cornell's groundbreaking *A Well Regulated Militia: The Founding Fathers and the Origins of Gun Control in America* (New York: Oxford University Press, 2006) and H. Richard Uviller and William G. Merkel's *The Militia and the Right to Arms, or, How the Second Amendment Fell Silent* (Durham: Duke University Press, 2002) make the most compelling case about the civic duty embodied in the original Second Amendment.

Works arguing most energetically for an individual rights interpretation are by Stephen P. Halbrook, *That Every Man Be Armed: The Evolution of a Constitutional Right* (Albuquerque: University of New Mexico Press, 1984); *Freedmen, The Fourteenth Amendment, and the Right to Bear Arms, 1866–1876* (Westport: Praeger, 1998); and *The Founders' Second Amendment: Origins of the Right to Bear Arms* (Chicago: Ivan R. Dee, 2008); and Joyce Lee Malcolm, *To Keep and Bear Arms: The Origins of an Anglo-American Right* (Cambridge: Harvard University Press, 1994).

Akhil Reed Amar's *The Bill of Rights: Creation and Reconstruction* (New Haven: Yale University Press, 1998) argues that the Second Amendment was designed to strengthen militias, but that its meaning was transformed by the Fourteenth Amendment. Of note, most of these books came before the more recent wave of research by Saul Cornell and others about the militias and early American gun laws.

Several valuable essay collections illuminate the ongoing debate over the Second Amendment. Carl Bogus, ed., *The Second Amendment in Law and History* (New York: The New Press, 2002) collects scholarly essays, generally from a pro–gun control perspective. Saul Cornell and Nathan Kozuskanich's 2013 collection, *The Second Amendment on Trial* (Amherst: University of Massachusetts Press, 2013), is a good compendium of commentary on *Heller* and other recent cases with all sides represented. Cornell also edited *Whose Right to Bear Arms Did the Second Amendment Protect?* (New York: St. Martin's, 2000), which also includes multiple points of view.

Countless law review articles have been published, many of them repetitive or pawing at narrow turf. I consulted dozens of them; when appropriate, they are cited in the notes.

When conservatives began to urge "originalism" as the one true path to understanding the Constitution, many records from the founding era were available only in research libraries. Today, more and more, these records are available online. James Madison's notes for the Constitutional Convention—available in book form in *Notes of Debates in the Federal Convention of 1787* (Athens: Ohio University Press, 1985)—are also now available on several excellent websites. The multivolume *Founders' Constitution*, published by the University of Chicago, is online (http://press-pubs.uchicago.edu/founders/). It includes transcripts of the Constitutional Convention, as well as the debate over the Bill of Rights in the first Congress. *The Documentary History of the Ratification of the Constitution* is a justly celebrated set, twenty-six volumes and counting, that includes public documents, transcripts of debates, letters, publications and other sources. (It is available online, though only to subscribers: http://rotunda.upress.virginia.edu/founders/RNCN.html.) A new

Library of Congress website hosts 123,000 documents from the papers of six key founders: www.founders.archives.gov. Key source materials are found in Herman Schwartz's two-volume *The Bill of Rights: A Documentary History* (New York: Chelsea House/McGraw-Hill, 1971).

Of course, a library's worth of history explores the American Revolution and era of Constitution-writing. Pauline Maier's authoritative *Ratification: The People Debate the Constitution* (New York: Simon & Schuster, 2011) is the essential current work on the struggle over the Constitution's ratification. Popular histories of the Constitutional Convention include David O. Stewart, *The Summer of 1787: The Men Who Invented the Constitution* (New York: Simon & Schuster, 2007), Christopher Collier and James Lincoln Collier, *Decision in Philadelphia: The Constitutional Convention of 1787* (New York: Random House, 1986), and Catherine Drinker Bowen's still compelling *Miracle in Philadelphia* (Boston: Little, Brown, 1966). A delightfully paced narrative about James Madison's role is Richard Labunski, *James Madison and the Struggle for the Bill of Rights* (Oxford: Oxford University Press, 2006), a story also well told by Kenneth R. Bowling, "'A Tub to the Whale': The Founding Fathers and the Adoption of the Federal Bill of Rights," *Journal of the Early Republic* 8 (Fall 1988). Among the many works that mull the thinking of the founding generation as it affected the Constitution, I drew heavily on the ideas in Jack N. Rakove, *Original Meanings: Politics and Ideas in the Making of the Constitution* (New York: Alfred A. Knopf, 1996). Eric Foner's *Reconstruction: America's Unfinished Revolution, 1863–1877* (New York: Harper & Row, 1988) remains the best single volume on the period that created the Civil War Amendments. Jack Rakove offers a withering assessment of mangled history in current debates over the Second Amendment in "The Second Amendment: The Highest Stage of Originalism," which first appeared in the *Chicago-Kent Law Review* in 2000 and appears in Carl Bogus's collection as well.

General well-regarded histories of gun laws and policy include Alexander DeConde, *Gun Violence in America* (Boston: Northeastern University Press, 2000) and Lee Kennett and James LaVerne Anderson, *The Gun in America: The Origins of a National Dilemma* (Westport: Greenwood, 1975). The arc of the militia is traced in John K. Mahon, *History of the Militia and the National Guard* (New York: Macmillan, 1983). NYU professor James Jacobs argues that with the ubiquity of guns, among other factors, traditional gun control laws have limited value: James B. Jacobs, *Can Gun Control Work?* (New York: Oxford University Press, 2002). Other recent books include Mark Tushnet, *Out of Range: Why the Constitution Can't End the Battle over Guns* (New York: Oxford University Press, 2007) and Craig Whitney, *Living With Guns: A Liberal's Case for the Second Amendment* (New York: Public Affairs, 2012). The changing role of the NRA is traced in Joel Achenbach, Scott Higham, and Sari Horwitz, "How NRA's True Believers Converted a Marksmanship Group into a Mighty Gun Lobby," *Washington Post*, January 12, 2013.

The surge of the conservative legal movement and the drive to *Heller* is described in many places. The most perceptive and important work about the pro-gun-rights movement's success in changing the popular view of the meaning of the Second Amendment is by Yale professor Reva B. Siegel, "Dead or Alive: Originalism as Popular Constitutionalism in *Heller*," *Harvard Law Review* 122 (2008). A good overview of originalism comes in a book celebrating the anniversary of the Federalist Society, Steven G. Calabresi, ed., *Originalism: A Quarter-Century of Debate* (Washington, D.C.: Regnery, 2007). Justice Antonin Scalia's *A Matter of Interpretation: Federal Courts and the Law* (Princeton: Princeton University Press, 1997) includes debates with critics. Stephen Teles offers a useful history, *The Rise of the Conservative Legal Movement* (Princeton: Princeton University Press, 2008). Progressive scholars have begun, at last, to fully debate conservative originalist ideas. A clear critique for a popular audience comes in David Strauss, *The Living Constitution* (New York: Oxford University Press, 2010). Jack Balkin's *Living Originalism* (Cambridge: Harvard University Press, 2011) suggests that a more flexible approach is what the Framers had in mind. Justice Stephen Breyer's two books, valuable but necessarily constrained by his role on the Court, seek to frame the Constitution as a charter for a self-governing democracy: *Active Liberty: Interpreting Our Democratic Constitution* (New York: Random House, 2005) and *Making Our Democ-*

racy Work (New York: Vintage, 2010) (which offers a bland recounting of his dissent in *Heller*). The American Constitution Society (ACS) was formed to be a liberal counterweight to the Federalist Society. A valuable collection of the works by its scholars is Goodwin Liu, Pamela S. Karlan, and Christopher H. Schroeder, *Keeping Faith with the Constitution* (Washington, D.C.: American Constitution Society for Law and Policy, 2009). The continued explication of popular constitutionalism by progressive scholars includes Larry Kramer, *The People Themselves* (New York: Oxford University Press, 2005) and Barry Friedman, *The Will of the People: How Public Opinion Has Influenced the Supreme Court and Shaped the Meaning of the Constitution* (New York: Farrar, Straus & Giroux, 2009).

The politics and personalities of the current Supreme Court are well-traced in Jeffrey Toobin's *The Nine: Inside the Secret World of the Supreme Court* (New York: Doubleday, 2007) and *The Oath: The Obama White House and the Supreme Court* (New York: Random House, 2012), and in Marcia Coyle's *The Roberts Court: The Struggle for the Constitution* (New York: Simon & Schuster, 2013). Justice Antonin Scalia's life is examined by Supreme Court reporter Joan Biskupic in *American Original: The Life and Constitution of Supreme Court Justice Antonin Scalia* (New York: Farrar, Straus & Giroux, 2009).

Finally, the fully story of the *Heller* and *McDonald* cases can be traced in the remarkable online resource at the website scotusblog. It includes all the lower court rulings, pleadings, and friend-of-the-court briefs for *Heller* (www.scotusblog.com/case-files/cases/dc-v-heller/), *McDonald* (www.scotusblog.com/case-files/cases/mcdonald-v-city-of-chicago/), and other recent cases.

NOTES

INTRODUCTION

xiii *Jefferson issued a terse announcement:* Bernard Schwartz, ed., *The Bill of Rights: A Documentary History*, Volume II (New York: Chelsea House/McGraw-Hill, 1971), 1203.

xiv *In the case: District of Columbia v. Heller*, 554 U.S. 570 (2008).

xv *An iconic photo of Dodge City:* Adam Winkler, *Gun Fight: The Battle over the Right to Bear Arms in America* (New York: Norton, 2011), 165.

xv *Chief Justice Warren Burger:* Charlayne Hunter-Gault, *The NewsHour with Jim Lehrer: Interview with Warren Burger* (Alexandria: PBS Video, 1991).

xvi *Justice Robert Jackson: Brown v. Allen*, 344 U.S. 443 (1953).

CHAPTER ONE: PATRIOTS' DAY

3 *They would seek to arrest:* For the authoritative description of Paul Revere's ride, see David Hackett Fischer, *Paul Revere's Ride* (New York: Oxford University Press, 1995). For a survey of the British troops and the town of Boston, see Robert Middlekauff, *The Glorious Cause: The American Revolution, 1763–1789* (New York: Oxford University Press, 1982), 297.

4 *"Lay down your arms":* Fischer, *Paul Revere's Ride*, 189–91.

4 *Firing a victory volley:* Arthur Bernon Tourtellot, *Lexington and Concord: The Beginning of the War of the American Revolution* (New York: W. W. Norton, 2000), 138.

4 *"The farmers gave them ball for ball":* Henry Wadsworth Longfellow, "Paul Revere's Ride," *Henry Wadsworth Longfellow: Poems and Other Writings* (New York: Library of America, 2000), 365.

5 *"The fighting on this day":* Fischer, *Paul Revere's Ride*, 202–3.

5 *four thousand militiamen:* John R. Galvin, *The Minute Men* (Dulles, VA: Potomac, 1989), 2–3.

5 *"hearing the Lexington Alarm":* A point made by Fischer, *Paul Revere's Ride*, xvi.

6 *being armed was a duty:* For a comprehensive and groundbreaking look at how Founding Era Americans saw bearing arms as a civic right, see Saul Cornell, *A Well-Regulated Militia: The Founding Fathers and the Origins of Gun Control in America* (Oxford: Oxford University Press, 2004).

7 *Machiavelli's ideas were widely influential:* See Niccolò Machiavelli, *The Art of War,* Revised and with an Introduction by Neal Wood (New York: Da Capo, 2001).

7 *a book of science fiction:* James G. Harrington, *'The Commonwealth of Oceana' and 'A System of Politics'* (Cambridge Texts in the History of Political Thought) (Cambridge: Cambridge University Press, 1992; paperback ed.), 55.

7 *the colonists believed powerfully in duty:* See Bernard Bailyn, *The Ideological Origins of the American Revolution* (Cambridge: Belknap Press, 1992; rev. ed.) and Gordon S. Wood, *The Creation of the American Republic* (New York: W. W. Norton, 1969).

7 *influenced by so-called radical British political thought:* Bailyn notes that the Anti-Federalists who later opposed the Constitution drew much inspiration from the political thought present at the beginning of the Revolution in 1776. Two important early articles spelled out the implications of this ideology for militia policy: Lawrence Delbert Cress, "An Armed Community: The Origins and Meaning of the Right to Bear Arms," *Journal of American History* 71, no. 1 (1984): 22–42. A different early approach to the same material is found in Robert E. Shalhope, "The Ideological Origins of the Second Amendment," *Journal of American History* 69, no. 3 (1982): 599–614. Shalhope argues that the Founders *did* intend an individual right to bear arms, but were influenced in this by their belief in the militias.

7 *"trained band":* Lois Schwoerer, *No Standing Armies: The Antiarmy Ideology in Seventeenth-Century England* (Baltimore: Johns Hopkins University Press, 1974), 14–15.

7 *militia service was for everyone:* Robert H. Churchill, "Gun Regulation, the Police Power, and the Right to Keep Arms in Early America: The Legal Context of the Second Amendment," *Law and History Review* 25, no. 1 (2007): 144–49.

7 *Sir Francis Bacon:* Quoted in Edmund S. Morgan, *Inventing the People: The Rise of Popular Sovereignty in England and America* (New York: W. W. Norton, 1989; paperback ed.), 155.

7 *"In a militia, the character of the labourer":* Adam Smith, *The Wealth of Nations,* Books IV–V (New York: Penguin, 1999), 287.

8 *"a species of animals":* Pamphleteers quoted in Morgan, *Inventing the People,* 162.

8 *One colonist explained:* Joel Barlow, *Advice to the Privileged Orders in the Several States of Europe* 44 (1956), quoted in David C. Williams, "Civic Republicanism and the Citizen Militia: The Terrifying Second Amendment," *Yale Law Journal* 101 (1992–93): 551, 574.

8 *"near neighbourhood of the Indians and French":* Contemporary writer quoted in Cornell, *A Well-Regulated Militia*, 13.

8 *They mustered often, drilled frequently:* Galvin, *The Minute Men*, 6–7.

8 *In New England, militias elected their commanding officers:* John Shy, *A People Numerous and Armed: Reflections on the Military Struggle for American Independence* (New York: Oxford University Press, 1976), 22–34.

9 *At times they were balky:* Gordon Wood, *The Radicalism of the American Revolution* (New York: Alfred A. Knopf, 1991), 163–64.

9 *Some paid others to do their time:* John Whiteclay Chambers II, *To Raise an Army: The Draft Comes to Modern America* (New York: Free Press, 1987), 17–18.

9 *Exemptions and excuses abounded:* For discussion of the weakness of the militia, see Garry Wills, *A Necessary Evil: A History of American Distrust of Government* (New York: Simon & Schuster, 1999), 27.

9 *"it seems never to have crossed the introspective mind of young John Adams":* Shy, *A People Numerous and Armed*, 31. Perhaps, like a future vice president, Dick Cheney, he had "other priorities . . . than military service." Katherine Q. Seelye, "Cheney's Five Draft Deferments During Vietnam Era Emerge as a Campaign Issue," *New York Times*, May 1, 2004, www.nytimes.com/2004/05/01/politics/campaign/01CHEN.html?pagewanted=print.

9 *Colonial legislatures repeatedly passed laws:* Wills, *A Necessary Evil*, 28.

9 *militia members demanded that the government provide guns:* Kevin M. Sweeny, "Firearms, Militias and the Second Amendment," in Saul Cornell and Nathan Kozuskanich, eds., *The Second Amendment on Trial: Critical Essays on* District of Columbia v. Heller (Amherst: University of Massachusetts Press, 2013), 364.

9 *The colonies had few gun factories:* When the American Revolution began, the colonists first seized British arms. Virginia and Pennsylvania opened state foundries. The colonies also signed contracts with gunmakers, and tried to buy arms in Europe. (Ultimately, France became the arsenal of our nascent democracy.) See Lee Kennett and James LaVerne Anderson, *The Gun in America: Origins of a National Dilemma* (Westport: Greenwood, 1975), 84–85.

9 *Many militiamen showed up:* Fischer, *Paul Revere's Ride*, 161.

9 *"When no danger was in the offing":* Edmund S. Morgan, *The Birth of the Republic, 1763–89* (Chicago: University of Chicago Press, 1992; 3rd ed.), 68.

9 *"But most Americans were content with the festivity":* Morgan, *Inventing the People*, 170.

10 *Britain's Stamp Act of 1765 changed that:* For a general discussion of the Stamp Act, the Townshend Acts, and the colonial response, see Middlekauff, *The Glorious Cause*, 70–173.

10 *Britain imposed an arms embargo:* Stephen Halbrook, *The Founders' Second Amendment: Origins of the Right to Bear Arms* (Chicago: Ivan R. Dee, 2008), 74.

10 *Massachusetts's Provincial Congress responded:* Fischer, *Paul Revere's Ride*, 151–53.

10 *townspeople kept the powder beneath the pulpit:* Ibid., 159.

10 *Massachusetts enacted a law:* Shy, *A People Numerous and Armed*, 24.

11 Rage Militaire: See Kevin Phillips, *1775: A Good Year for Revolution* (New York: Penguin, 2012), 3. He notes that "Virtue, the old Roman credo, clad itself in a uniquely American garb. Hunting shirts, belts, and leggings became fashionable, what a later era might term militia chic."

11 *yearning for democracy:* The militias that formed at the Revolution's outset in Pennsylvania, for example, included many men who did not appear on the tax rolls. Militias were "the first step from crowd activity to organized politics." They were a "school for political democracy." Eric Foner, *Tom Paine and Revolutionary America* (New York: Oxford University Press, 1984; paperback ed.), 64–65.

11 *Declaration of Rights passed by the Virginia legislature:* Bernard Schwartz, ed., *The Bill of Rights: A Documentary History*, Volume I (New York: Chelsea House/McGraw-Hill, 1971), 235.

12 *"every man who pays his shot":* Alexander Keyssar, *The Right to Vote: The Contested History of Democracy in the United States* (New York: Basic Books, 2009; rev. ed.), 12.

12 *Pennsylvania's charter:* Schwartz, ed., *The Bill of Rights*, I, 263.

12 *citizens could "keep" as well as "bear" arms:* For a concise description of the differences among the state constitutions, see William S. Fields and David T. Hardy, "The Militia and the Constitution: A Legal History," *Military Law Review* (1992): 27–31.

13 *The men who wrote the Constitution:* See generally Wood, *The Radicalism of the American Revolution*.

13 *the bumbling first expedition:* For Washington's sour experiences in the Virginia militia, see Ron Chernow, *Washington: A Life* (New York: Penguin, 2010), 71.

13 *"Colonel Washington appears at Congress":* John Adams to Abigail Adams, May 29, 1775, Founders Online, National Archives, http://founders.archives.gov /documents/Adams/04-01-02-0138, ver. 2013-08-02; source: Lyman H. Butterfield, ed., vol. 1 of *The Adams Papers, Adams Family Correspondence, December 1761–May 1776* (Cambridge: Harvard University Press, 1963), 207–8.

13 *"He has so much martial dignity":* Chernow, *Washington*, 183.

14 *"now the troops of the United Provinces":* Ibid., 195.

14 *as he rode through camp:* James Thomas Flexner, *Washington: The Indispensable Man* (Boston: Little, Brown, 1974), 68.

14 *He wrote his brother:* George Washington to Samuel Washington, July 20, 1775, Founders Online, National Archives, http://founders.archives.gov/documents /Washington/03-01-02-0083, ver. 2013-08-02; source: Philander D. Chase, ed., vol. 1 of *The Papers of George Washington, Revolutionary War Series, 16 June 1775–15 September 1775* (Charlottesville: University Press of Virginia, 1985), 134–36.

14 *"are nearly of the same kidney"*: Chernow, *Washington*, 196.

14 *"Whole divisions"*: Ibid., 261.

14 *"To place any dependence upon Militia"*: George Washington to the President of Congress, September 24, 1776, in John C. Fitzpatrick, ed., *The Writings of George Washington* (Washington, D.C.: Government Printing Office, 1932), 112.

15 *General Charles Lee*: The maneuverings of Washington's rival are described in Charles Royster, *A Revolutionary People at War: The Continental Army and American Character, 1775–1783* (New York: W. W. Norton, 1981), 41. Lee was court-martialed for retreating against orders during the Battle of Monmouth, convicted, and died before war's end.

15 *"zeal and alacrity of the militia"*: Ibid.

15 *"As to the Minute Men"*: Ibid.

15 *Congress drafted*: Articles of Confederation, sec. 6, par. 4, http://avalon.law.yale.edu/18th_century/artconf.asp.

15 *"remained primarily a technique"*: Royster, *A Revolutionary People at War*, 267.

15 *But only one third of the American forces*: John K. Mahon, *History of the Militia and the National Guard* (New York: Macmillan, 1983), 41.

15 *General Jeremiah Wadsworth reported*: Morgan, *Inventing the People*, 162, quoting The Debates and Proceedings of the Congress of the United States, 3rd Cong., 1st Sess. (Washington, D.C., 1855) (Annals of Congress, III), 162, January 6, 1794. Cf. ibid., II, 796.

15 *"Would any Man in his Senses"*: Royster, *A Revolutionary People at War*, 37.

16 *"I had as many sore legs"*: Thomas Jefferson to John Page, October 29, 1780, Founders Online, National Archives http://founders.archives.gov/documents /Jefferson/01-15-02-0564.

16 *Militias kept order*: Shy, *A People Numerous and Armed*, 45.

16 *In parts of the country*: Mark V. Kwasny, "Militia Guerilla Warfare, Tactics, and Weaponry," in Jack P. Greene and J. R. Pole, eds., *A Companion to the American Revolution* (Malden: Blackwell, 2000), 314–15.

16 *In the South, militias were beefed up*: A. Leon Higgenbotham, *In the Matter of Color: Race and the American Legal Process* (New York: Oxford University Press, 1979), 259–61.

16 *"In the early stages of this war"*: George Washington to John Sullivan, December 17, 1780, Founders Online, National Archives, http://founders.archives.gov /documents/Washington/99-01-02-04257, ver. 2013-08-02.

16 *Communities celebrated with giant feasts*: Royster, *A Revolutionary People at War*, 360–63.

17 *By March 1783*: Washington's performance at Newburgh is underappreciated as a key moment in American history. See Flexner, *Washington*, 168. ("Almost every revolution in the history of the world, however idealistically begun, had ended in tyranny. The American Revolution had now reached its moment of major political crisis.") For compelling retellings, see Richard Brookhiser,

Founding Father (New York: Free Press, 1996), 41–45; Garry Wills, *Cincinnatus: George Washington and the Enlightenment* (Garden City: Doubleday, 1984), 6–9.

17 *"open the flood Gates"*: George Washington address to Officers of the Army, March 15, 1783, www.gilderlehrman.org/sites/default/files/inline-pdfs /t-2437.09443.pdf.

17 *When news finally arrived from Paris:* H. Richard Uviller and William C. Merkel, *The Militia and the Right to Arms, or How the Second Amendment Fell Silent* (Durham: Duke University Press, 2002), 117.

17 *Society of the Cincinnati:* The society drew its name from the Roman general Cincinnatus, who was returned to civilian life after military service. For a discussion of the impact of classical history on eighteenth-century American leaders, see Garry Wills, *Cincinnatus: George Washington and the Enlightenment.*

17 *Mercy Warren:* Catherine Drinker Bowen, *Miracle in Philadelphia* (Boston: Little, Brown, 1966), 188.

18 *he sketched out a plan:* Marcus Cunliffe, *Soldiers and Civilians* (New York: Free Press, 1973), 181.

18 *Washington persuaded the state's governor:* Morgan, *Inventing the People,* 172.

18 *"critical period":* Adams's address is quoted in Wood, *The Creation of the American Republic,* 379; see also John Fiske, *The Critical Period of American History, 1783–1789* (Boston: Houghton Mifflin, 1888).

18 *"Notwithstanding the most pressing orders":* David P. Szatmary, *Shays' Rebellion: The Making of An Agrarian Insurrection* (Amherst: University of Massachusetts Press, 1980), 80.

18 *ordered militiamen to march into Great Barrington:* Leonard L. Richards, *Shays' Rebellion: The Revolution's Final Battle* (Philadelphia: University of Pennsylvania Press, 2002), 12.

18 *agrarian army:* Szatmary, *Shays' Rebellion,* 85–86, 104–5.

19 *Properly rattled:* Washington's friends did all they could to alarm him about the rebellion. David O. Stewart, *The Summer of 1787: The Men Who Invented the Constitution* (New York: Simon & Schuster, 2007), 14–16.

19 *Virginian James Madison arrived early:* For Madison's outsized role and biography, see Irving Brant, *James Madison: Father of the Constitution* (New York: Bobbs Merrill, 1950); Ralph Ketchum, *James Madison* (Charlottesville: University of Virginia Press, 1971). For a brisk description of Madison's eagerness and his influence at the convention, see Richard Brookhiser, *James Madison* (New York: Basic Books, 2011), 50–54.

20 *he confessed to Washington:* Letter from James Madison to George Washington, April 16, 1787, in *The Founders' Constitution,* vol. 1, chap. 8, doc. 6, http://press-pubs.uchicago.edu/founders/documents/v1ch8s6.html, University of Chicago Press; *The Papers of James Madison,* ed. William T. Hutchinson et al. (Chicago: University of Chicago Press, 1962–77, vols. 1–10; Charlottesville: University Press of Virginia, 1977– vols. 11–).

20 *"enlarge the sphere": Notes of Debates in the Federal Convention of 1787,* Reported by James Madison (Athens: Ohio University Press, 1985) (first published in vols. 2–3 of *The Papers of James Madison,* Washington, 1840) (June 6, 1787), 76.

20 *"control the centrifugal tendency":* Ibid. (June 8, 1787), 89.

21 *Fully one third had served as officers in the Continental Army:* Christopher Collier and James Lincoln Collier, *Decision in Philadelphia: The Constitutional Convention of 1787,* 317.

21 *many of the most influential backers of the Constitution:* Stanley Elkins and Eric McKitrick, "The Founding Fathers: Young Men of the Revolution," *Political Science Quarterly* 76, no. 2 (1961): 181–216. David Hackett Fischer argues this thesis was considerably overstated, and that there was little statistically significant difference in the ages of Federalists and Anti-Federalists. David Hackett Fischer, *Historians' Fallacies* (New York: Harper & Row, 1970), 105–6. Pauline Maier notes that the leading voices of the pro-Constitution forces—especially Madison, John Jay, and Hamilton—were born decades after Patrick Henry, Richard Henry Lee, and Samuel Adams. See Pauline Maier, "On Faith and Generations in Revolutionary Politics," *The Old Revolutionaries: Political Lives in the Age of Samuel Adams* (New York: Random House, 1980), 269–94; see also Pauline Maier, *Ratification: The People Debate the Constitution, 1787–1788* (New York: Simon & Schuster, 2010), 238.

21 *Many who laud him as "Father of the Constitution":* A point made by Brant, *James Madison,* 155.

22 *the Constitution gives Congress the power:* U.S. Constitution, art. 2, § 8, cl. 12–16.

23 *A division of military authority:* See Uviller and Merkel, *The Militia and the Right to Arms,* 78.

23 *"The particular two-year cutoff meshed perfectly":* Akhil Reed Amar, *The Bill of Rights: Creation and Reconstruction* (New Haven: Yale University Press, 1998), 51.

23 *"two or three thousand" men: Notes of Debates* (August 18, 1787), 482.

24 *"no foreign enemy should invade the United States":* George Washington's stage whisper is recounted in David Robertson, *The Original Compromise: What the Constitution's Framers Were Really Thinking* (New York: Oxford University Press, 2013), 207. See also Charles Warren, *The Making of the Constitution* (Boston: Little, Brown, 1928), quoted in Collier and Collier, *Decision in Philadelphia,* 323.

24 *"A standing army is like a standing member":* Gerry's blue humor is found, among other places, in Samuel Eliot Morison, *The Oxford History of the American People* (New York: Oxford University Press, 1972; rev. ed.), 398–99.

24 *"subdue a rebellion in any state": Notes of Debates* (August 6, 1787), 389.

24 *"One senses the excitement":* Bowen, *Miracle in Philadelphia,* 218.

24 *"letting loose the myrmidons": Notes of Debates* (August 17, 1785), 475.

24 *"We first form a strong man to protect us":* Ibid.

24 *"call forth the aid of the militia": Notes of Debates* (August 6, 1787), 389.

24 *"Thirteen states will never concur in any one system":* Ibid., (August 18, 1787), 478.

25 *Madison made clear:* Ibid., 484.

25 *John Dickinson of Pennsylvania proposed:* Ibid., 483.

25 *"The states will never submit to the same militia laws":* Ibid., 484.

25 *"make laws for organizing, arming":* Ibid., (August 23, 1787), 512.

25 *"is making the states drill-seargents":* Ibid., 513.

25 *"The primary object":* Ibid., 514–15.

25 *"Let us at once destroy the State Govts":* Ibid., 516.

26 *Even the militias:* For a good analysis of how war scrambled traditional thinking, see Williams, "Civic Republicanism and the Citizen Militia," 574.

26 *"sooner chop off his right hand":* Notes of Debates (August 31, 1787), 566.

26 *"would give great quiet":* Ibid. (September 12, 1787), 630.

26 *"parchment barriers":* In a letter to Thomas Jefferson, October 17, 1788, Founders Online, National Archives, http://founders.archives.gov/documents/Madison /01-11-02-0218, ver. 2013-08-02; source: *The Papers of James Madison*, vol. 11, *7 March 1788–1 March 1789*, ed. Robert A. Rutland and Charles F. Hobson (Charlottesville: University Press of Virginia, 1977), 295–300.

26 *James Wilson of Pennsylvania offered the most influential explanation:* Wilson spoke to a crowd gathered during election for delegates to the state ratification convention on October 6, 1787. Ralph Ketcham, ed., *The Anti-Federalist Papers and the Constitutional Convention Debates* (New York: New American Library, 2003), 181–87. Also available at www.constitution.org/afp/jwilsono.htm.

CHAPTER TWO: RATIFICATION

29 *"We hear that the Convention propose to adjourn":* Bowen, *Miracle in Philadelphia*, 243.

30 *gave the public a mistaken impression:* Maier, *Ratification*, 58.

30 *"In reading through this immensity":* Bernard Bailyn, *Faces of Revolution: Personalities and Themes in the Struggle for American Independence* (New York: Vintage, 1992), 229–30.

30 *"This is a new event in the history of mankind":* Governor Samuel Huntington quoted in Jack N. Rakove, *Original Meanings: Politics and Ideas in the Making of the Constitution* (New York: Alfred A. Knopf, 1996), 131–32. Huntington spoke to a crowd at the ratification convention in the state.

31 *Amid this contention:* Bernard Bailyn believes the fear of the Constitution's military provisions matched concerns over representation. "There is simply no way to measure the volume and fervor of the antifederalists' denunciation of this provision, which revived for them not simply a general fear of military power but the specific danger of 'standing armies,' a peculiar and distinctive threat to liberty that had been formulated for all time, they believed, in England in the 1690s, and had been carried forward intact to the colonies. There the danger had been fully realized in 1768, when the first British troops were stationed in

peaceful Boston, and the predictable 'massacre' occurred." Bailyn, *The Ideological Origins of the American Revolution*, 338–39.

31 *Congress could "march the whole militia":* Luther Martin, Genuine Information VII, *Baltimore Maryland Gazette*, January 18, 1788, DHRC XV. The full text can also be found at http://teachingamericanhistory.org/library/document /luther-martin-genuine-information-vii/.

31 *"Who can deny":* "Essays of Philadelphiensis IX," in Herbert Storing, ed., *The Complete Anti-Federalist*, vol. 3 (1981), 127–28 (originally published in the *Independent Gazetteer*, February 7, 1788). Also available at Teaching American History, http://teachingamericanhistory.org/library/document/philadelphien-sis-ix/.

31 *In Boston a pamphleteer:* Letter from John De Witt to the Free Citizens of the Commonwealth of Massachusetts (December 3, 1787), in Storing, ed., *The Complete Anti-Federalist*, vol. 4 (1981), 36. Also available at *The Founders' Constitution*, vol. 3, art. 1, sec. 8, cl. 16, doc. 5, http://press-pubs.uchicago.edu /founders/documents/a1_8_16s5.html, The University of Chicago Press.

32 *Seven state constitutions:* At the time of the Constitutional Convention, the states with a bills of rights or a declarations of rights were: Virginia (1776): "That a well-regulated militia, composed of the body of the people, trained to arms, is the proper, natural, and safe defense of a free state; that standing armies, in time of peace, should be avoided as dangerous to liberty; and that in all cases the military should be under strict subordination to, and governed by, the civil power." North Carolina (1776): "XVII: That the people have a right to bear arms, for the defence of the State; and, as standing armies, in time of peace, are dangerous to liberty, they ought not to be kept up; and that the military should be kept under strict subordination to, and governed by, the civil power." Maryland (1776): "XXV. That a well-regulated militia is the proper and natural defence of a free government. XXVI. That standing armies are dangerous to liberty, and ought not to be raised or kept up, without consent of the Legislature. XXVII. That in all cases, and at all times, the military ought to be under strict subordination to and control of the civil power." Pennsylvania (1776): "XIII. That the people have a right to bear arms for the defence of themselves and the state; and as standing armies in the time of peace are dangerous to liberty, they ought not to be kept up; And that the military should be kept under strict subordination to, and governed by, the civil power." Delaware (1776): "Sect. 10. That every member of society hath a right to be protected in the enjoyment of life, liberty and property, and therefore is bound to contribute his proportion towards the expense of that protection, and yield his personal service when necessary, or an equivalent thereto; but no part of a man's property can be justly taken from him or applied to public uses without his own consent or that of his legal Representatives: Nor can any man that is conscientiously scrupulous of bearing arms in any case be justly compelled thereto if he will pay such equiva-

lent." Massachusetts (1780) "XVII. The people have a right to keep and to bear arms for the common defence. And as in time of peace armies are dangerous to liberty, they ought not to be maintained without the consent of the legislature; and the military power shall always be held in an exact subordination to the civil authority, and be governed by it." New Hampshire (1783): "XIII. No person who is conscientiously scrupulous about the lawfulness of bearing arms, shall be compelled thereto, provided he will pay an equivalent." These declarations are available in Schwartz, ed. *The Bill of Rights*, I, 179–382.

32 *gun regulations were common:* The best compendium of early gun regulations is Saul Cornell and Nathan Dedino, "A Well Regulated Right: The Early American Origins of Gun Control," *Fordham Law Review* 73 (2004): 506.

32 *Other states imposed restrictions less defensible to modern eyes:* For a survey of gun laws in the colonial era, see Robert H. Churchill, "Gun Regulation, the Police Power, and the Right to Keep Arms in Early America: The Legal Context of the Second Amendment," *Law and History Review* 25, no. 1 (2007): 162.

32 *Rhode Island conducted a house-to-house census:* Ibid., 147.

32 *In the middle of the ratification fight:* Kevin M. Sweeney, "Firearms, Militias, and the Second Amendment," in Cornell and Kozuskanich, eds., *The Second Amendment on Trial*, 355.

33 *"the natural right of resistance":* William Blackstone, *Commentaries on the Laws of England: A Facsimile of the First Edition of 1765–1769* (Chicago: University of Chicago Press, 1979), 105.

33 affrighting: Justice Antonin Scalia cites this tort as an example of the kinds of limits on the right to bear arms he envisioned after *Heller.* He told PBS's NewsHour, "[*Heller*] didn't purport to say everybody can carry whatever weapons he wants. In fact, it mentioned that there was a misdemeanor in ancient times caled affrighting. Affrighting consisted of carrying a frightening weapon, a head axe or something like that, to scare people." Margaret Warner, PBS NewsHour, "Justice Scalia Writes How-to Interpret Guide for Interpreting the Law," August 9, 2012, www.pbs.org/newshour/bb/law/july-dec12/scalia_08-09.html.

33 *"It ought to be left to the state governments":* Brutus, No. 7 (January 3, 1788), in Storing, ed., *The Complete Anti-Federalist*, 7 vols. (Chicago: University of Chicago Press, 1981). Also available at *The Founders' Constitution*, vol. 1, chap. 8, doc. 26, http://press-pubs.uchicago.edu/founders/documents/v1ch8s26.html.

33 *"The states will regulate and administer the criminal law":* Tench Coxe, "A Freeman," Essays: I–III, in Colleen A. Sheehan, *Friends of the Constitution: Writings of the "Other" Federalists, 1787–1788,* ed. Colleen A. Sheehan and Gary L. McDowell (Indianapolis: Liberty Fund, 1988), http://oll.libertyfund.org/title/2069/156158on2013-07-31.

33 *"Technological advances have created a sharp distinction":* Nelson Lund, "The Past and Future of the Individual's Right to Bear Arms," *Georgia Law Re-*

view 31 (1996): 1–76. Lund has acknowledged the mismatch between the intense focus of the time of the Framers and debates today: "The central purpose of the Second Amendment—discouraging political oppression—offers little justification for a right to possess or carry handguns." Nelson Lund, "The Second Amendment, Political Liberty, and the Right to Self-Preservation," *Alabama Law Review* 29 (1987): 103–30. Lund nonetheless believes the Second Amendment was also intended to protect private gun ownership for personal protection.

34 *In the decade before the Revolution:* Cornell, *A Well-Regulated Militia,* 22.

34 *Some patterns start early:* Senator Obama's controversial musings were revealed by a blogger, Mayhill Fowler, "No Surprise That Hard-Pressed Pennsylvanians Turn Bitter," *Huffington Post,* April 11, 2008.

35 *Opponents tried to block the bid:* The effort to dragoon legislators to achieve a quorum in Pennsylvania is recounted in Maier, *Ratification,* 62–64.

35 *Anti-Federalists presented a list of proposed amendments:* "Report of the Minority of the Convention," in John P. Kaminski, Gaspare J. Saladino, Richard Leffler, Charles H. Schoenleber, and Margaret A. Hogan, eds., *The Documentary History of the Ratification of the Constitution X Digital Edition* (Charlottesville: University of Virginia Press, 2009) (hereinafter *DHRC*), 623.

35 *This may have been a response:* For a discussion of the English Game Act of 1671, see Joyce Lee Malcolm, *To Keep and Bear Arms: The Origins of an Anglo-American Right* (Cambridge: Harvard University Press, 1994), 69–76.

35 *Pennsylvania was convulsed:* Maier, *Ratification,* 121.

35 *The dissidents printed their own unofficial minority report:* "The Address and Reasons of Dissent of the Minority of the Convention of Pennsylvania to their Constituents," in Ketchum, ed., *The Anti-Federalist Papers and the Constitutional Convention Debates,* 243–65. This pamphlet has been the source of much controversy among later disputants. Anti-gun-control lawyers insist that it illuminates the meaning of the Second Amendment, which they contend protected gun ownership for self-defense as well as for militia service. Some writers and historians, notably Garry Wills, have insisted that the minority report merely reflects the last-minute cavils of the losing side in one state. Garry Wills, "To Keep and Bear Arms," *New York Review of Books* (September 21, 1995), www.nybooks.com/articles/archives/1995/sep/21/to-keep-and-bear-arms/?pagination=false. Pauline Maier, in her authoritative *Ratification,* concludes it was, in fact, widely circulated.

35 *Noah Webster:* Bowen, *Miracle in Philadelphia,* 246.

36 *Hancock's theatricality proved decisive:* Maier, *Ratification,* 192.

36 *Hancock's triangulation seemed to recoil:* Ibid., 198.

36 *The delegates recommended that Congress enact nine amendments:* Massachusetts ratifying convention, January 31, 1788, in Schwartz, ed., *Bill of Rights,* II, 677–78.

36 *Adams proposed additional changes:* The amendments forwarded by the vote of the Massachusetts convention did not much mirror state bills of rights. Samuel Adams proposed additional amendments, including one that declared, "the said Constitution be never construed to authorize Congress . . . to prevent the people of the United States, who are peaceable citizens, from keeping their own arms; or to raise standing armies, unless when necessary for the defence of the United States, or of some one or more of them . . ." The journal of the convention notes broadly that Adams's proposals were "debated a considerable time," but were opposed by the convention; he withdrew them. Schwartz, ed., *The Bill of Rights*, II, 707. In fact, they were not withdrawn—they were defeated. Ibid., 675. We have no transcript from the convention to suggest whether the "bearing arms" provisions were specifically among those debated.

37 *New Hampshire ratified:* New Hampshire ratifying convention proposed amendments, ibid., 761, also available at http://avalon.law.yale.edu/18th_century/ratnh.asp.

37 *dominated its politics:* See generally Harlow Giles Unger, *Lion of Liberty: Patrick Henry and the Call to a New Nation* (New York: Da Capo, 2010).

37 *issues of slavery:* Carl Bogus argues that the Southerners on both sides of the Constitution followed a euphemistic code in discussing the peculiar institution during the convention. See Carl T. Bogus, "The Hidden History of the Second Amendment," *University of California at Davis Law Review* 31 (1998): 309. Others dispute that slave revolt was in mind: the manumission societies just forming in the North were dominated by pacifist Quakers. See Uviller and Merkel, *The Militia and the Right to Arms*, 189–90.

37 *"They'll take":* Henry Mayer, *Son of Thunder: Patrick Henry and the American Republic* (New York: Grove, 2001), 434. Mayer cites Hugh Blair Grigsby, a nineteenth-century historian, who interviewed attendees at the convention in his book *The History of the Virginia Federal Convention of 1788* (Virginia Historical Society, 1890). Grigsby quotes Henry as warning, "They'll free your niggers!" ("The audience passed instantly from fear to wayward laughter; and my informant said that it was most ludicrous to see men who a moment before were half frightened to death, with a broad grin on their faces.")

38 *George Mason focused with vehemence:* Here Mason was being disingenuous. In the Constitutional Convention, he had proposed that the federal government be given much more power over state militias than it was ultimately granted. Those records were still secret, though. Once Mason decided he was against the Constitution, as Madison had worried in a letter to Washington, he would throw all consistency aside to seek to block it. James Madison to George Washington, October 18, 1787.

38 *"from their situation":* Statement of delegate George Nicholas, Virginia Ratification Convention, June 14, 1788, *DHRC*, X, 1280. Also available at www .constitution.org/rc/rat_va_12.htm.

38 *prepared for a duel:* Unger, *Lion of Liberty*, 227.

38 *"The militia may be here destroyed"*: DHRC, X, 1276. Also available at http://press-pubs.uchicago.edu/founders/print_documents/a1_8_15s13.html.

38 *"The militia, Sir"*: Ibid. Henry's speech would be flagrantly misquoted in later debates over gun rights. See Part Two of this book.

39 *"Slavery is detested"*: DHRC, X, 1476–77.

39 *Its proposed Seventeenth Amendment proclaimed:* Schwartz, ed., *Bill of Rights*, II, 842.

40 *"shall have the power to provide"*: Ibid., 843.

40 *Madison was aghast:* To Alexander Hamilton from James Madison, June 27 [1788], Founders Online, National Archives, http://founders.archives.gov/documents/Hamilton/01-05-02-0012-0032, ver. 2013-08-02; source: *The Papers of Alexander Hamilton*, vol. 5, *June 1788–November 1789*, ed. Harold C. Syrett (New York: Columbia University Press, 1962), 91–92; James Madison to George Washington, June 27 [1788].

40 *Without revenue, government would grow so weak:* Conservative activist Grover Norquist articulated this strategy in an interview with NPR's Mara Liasson on May 25, 2001. "I don't want to abolish government. I simply want to reduce it to the size where I can drag it into the bathroom and drown it in the bathtub."

41 *The state's ambitious governor:* George Clinton was another archetype: a scheming New York political boss who mixed business with politics. For a pithy description, see Brookhiser, *James Madison*, 63.

41 *"If a well-regulated militia"*: Federalist 29, in Alexander Hamilton, James Madison, and John Jay, *The Federalist Papers*, ed. Lawrence Goldman (New York: Oxford University Press, 2008), 139.

41 *"The Letters of Brutus"*: Robert Yates, a state judge who had walked out in alarm from the Constitutional Convention, presumably wrote as Brutus, though some scholars now favor the merchant Melancton Smith.

41 *Two mighty nations:* Brutus's reply is in Ketchum, *The Anti-Federalist Papers and the Constitutional Convention Debates*, 303.

41 *"Let a regular army"*: Federalist 46, in Hamilton, Madison, and Jay, *The Federalist Papers*, 237.

42 *Madison resisted*: http://founders.archives.gov/documents/Jefferson/01-13-02-0023.

42 *The states had proposed:* For a comprehensive look at the amendments proposed by the various state conventions, see Donald S. Lutz, "The State Constitutional Pedigree of the U.S. Bill of Rights," *Publius: The Journal of Federalism* 22, no. 2 (1992): 19–45. Lutz shows how Madison exercised an editor's prerogative in ignoring some, combining others.

42 *If they were ever debated:* Kenneth R. Bowling, "A Tub to the Whale: The Founding Fathers and the Adoption of the Federal Bill of Rights," *Journal of the Early Republic* 8 (1988): 228.

43 *"I will now add"*: Thomas Jefferson letter to James Madison, December 20, 1787, www.loc.gov/exhibits/jefferson/jefffed.html.

CHAPTER THREE: THE TUB TO THE WHALE

45 *"The edicts of Mr. Henry":* George Washington to James Madison, November 17, 1788, Founders Online, National Archives, http://founders.archives.gov/documents /Washington/05-01-02-0090, ver. 2013-08-02; source: *The Papers of George Washington,* Presidential Series, vol. 1, *24 September 1788–31 March 1789,* ed. Dorothy Twohig (Charlottesville: University of Virginia Press, 1987), 112–16.

45 *"rivulets of blood":* Brant, *James Madison,* 237.

46 *"Henry did not arrange":* Richard Labunski, *James Madison and the Struggle for the Bill of Rights* (Oxford: Oxford University Press, 2006), 142.

46 *Monroe nursed a grudge:* Ibid., 153.

46 *"dogmatically attached":* Bowling, "'A Tub to the Whale,'" 231.

47 *Patrick Henry bitterly suspected:* Unger, *Lion of Liberty,* 233.

47 *"At the same time":* Madison wrote to Jefferson on October 17, 1788: "Repeated violations of these parchment barriers have been committed by overbearing majorities in every State. In Virginia I have seen the bill of rights violated in every instance where it has been opposed to a popular current." From James Madison to Thomas Jefferson, October 17, 1788. Founders Online, National Archives, http://founders.archives.gov/documents/Madison/01-11-02-0218, ver. 2013-08-02; source: *The Papers of James Madison,* vol. 11, *7 March 1788–1 March 1789,* ed. Robert A. Rutland and Charles F. Hobson (Charlottesville: University of Virginia Press, 1977), 295–300.

47 *"give to the Government":* From James Madison to Thomas Jefferson, December 8, 1788. Founders Online, National Archives, http://founders.archives .gov/documents/Jefferson/01-14-02-0119, ver. 2013-09-28; source: *The Papers of Thomas Jefferson,* vol. 14, *8 October 1788–26 March 1789,* ed. Julian P. Boyd (Princeton: Princeton University Press, 1958), 339–42.

47 *White Southern Baptists:* For a full discussion of the Virginia Baptists and their role as pioneering religious dissidents, see Steven Waldman, *Founding Faith: Providence, Politics and the Birth of Religious Freedom in America* (New York: Random House, 2008), 100–106. Before the Revolution, the Episcopalians were known as Anglicans.

48 *Madison wrote a missive:* James Madison to George Eve, January 2, 1789, Founders Online, National Archives, http://founders.archives.gov/documents/ Madison/01-11-02-0297, ver. 2013-08-02; source: *The Papers of James Madison,* vol. 11, *7 March 1788–1 March 1789,* ed. Robert A. Rutland and Charles F. Hobson (Charlottesville: University of Virginia Press, 1977), 404–6.

48 *"read-my-lips pledge":* Waldman, *Founding Faith,* 143.

48 *he won by 336 votes:* Chris DeRose, *Founding Rivals: Madison vs. Monroe, the Bill of Rights, and the Election That Saved a Nation* (Washington, D.C.: Regnery, 2011), 246.

49 *George Washington's de facto prime minister:* Stuart Leibiger, *Founding Friendship: George Washington, James Madison, and the Creation of the American Republic* (Charlottesville: University of Virginia Press, 1999), 97–123.

49 *"the nauseous project":* James Madison letter to Richard Peters, August 19, 1789, in *Papers of James Madison,* 346–47. Richard Labunski argues that the gastric metaphor responds to a letter from Peters, which described the process as one with many cooks adding ingredients. Peters called Madison's foes the "Anti-Soupites." Perhaps. The metaphor is strikingly queasy nonetheless.

49 *"if we must have amendments":* Bowling, "'A Tub to the Whale,'" 233.

49 *"Like a barrel thrown to the whale":* [Samuel Bryan], "Centinel NO. 19," (Philadelphia) *Independent Gazetteer,* October 7, 1788, quoted in ibid.

50 *easy way to get under Madison's skin:* Charlene Bangs Bickford and Kenneth R. Bowling, *Birth of the Nation: The First Federal Congress, 1789–1791* (Washington, D.C.: First Federal Congress Project/George Washington University, 1989), 53.

50 *"The storm has abated":* Representative John Vining's speech is in Schwartz, ed., *The Bill of Rights,* II, 1022.

50 *Madison rose to speak again:* Ibid., 1016–34.

50 *"It strikes me":* Ibid.

50 *His lengthy, clotted speech:* Ibid.

51 *"it may occasion suspicions":* Ibid., 1019.

51 *"to quiet that anxiety":* Ibid., 1021.

51 *Faced with strenuous calls:* This point is well made by Paul Finkelman, "It Really Was About a Well Regulated Militia," *Syracuse Law Review* 59 (2008): 267.

51 *"There have been objections":* Schwartz, ed., *The Bill of Rights,* II, 1021.

52 *"The right of the people":* Ibid., 1026.

52 *His notes for his talk:* A photograph of Madison's original notes is available at www.loc.gov/exhibits/madison/images/vc11.jpg.

52 *"No state":* Schwartz, ed., *The Bill of Rights,* II., 1027.

52 *"the most valuable amendment":* Madison's statement was made during the debate of August 17, 1788. Ibid., 1113.

53 *"Mr. Madison has introduced":* Ames added, "Upon the whole, it may do good towards quieting men who attend to sounds only, and may get the mover some popularity—which he wishes." Fisher Ames to Theodore Dwight (June 11, 1789), in Helen E. Veit, Kenneth R. Bowling, and Chalene Bangs Bickford, eds., *Creating the Bill of Rights: The Documentary Record from the First Federal Congress* (Baltimore: Johns Hopkins University Press, 1991), 247. Veit et al. translate the Latin to read "could you forbear the laughter of a friend."

53 *"As civil rulers":* *Federal Gazette,* June 18, 1789, at 2, col. 1. Some attribute significant influence to Coxe's views. See Stephen Halbrook and David Kopel,

"Tench Coxe and the Right to Keep and Bear Arms," *William and Mary Bill of Rights Journal* 7 (1999): 347–400. Coxe was indeed a well-known Federalist. Madison replied to him, "it is much to be wished that the discontented part of our fellow Citizens could be reconciled to the Government they have opposed, and by means as little as possible unacceptable to those who approve the Constitution in its present form. The amendments proposed in the House of Representatives had this twofold object in view." Madison's note reads like the polite reply of a busy man who has been sent a newspaper clipping by an ardent supporter. Letter from James Madison to Tench Coxe, 24 June 1789, Founders Online, National Archives, http://founders.archives.gov/documents/Madison /01-12-02-0158, ver. 2013-08-02; source: *The Papers of James Madison*, vol. 12, *2 March 1789–20 January 1790 and supplement 24 October 1775–24 January 1789*, ed. Charles F. Hobson and Robert A. Rutland (Charlottesville: University of Virginia Press, 1979), 257–58. Glenn Harlan Reynolds asserts that "Madison endorsed" Coxe's view of the Second Amendment. Madison's vague response hardly supports that idea. More, as Garry Wills points out, Madison's bland reply "does not mean that he agreed with Coxe's un-Madisonian reduction of the First Amendment to restrain only 'self-righteous' and 'impious' religions. Madison no more endorsed Coxe's construction of the Second Amendment than he did this view of the First." Sanford Levinson, David C. Williams, Glenn Harlan Reynolds, and John K. Lattimer, reply by Garry Wills, "To Keep and Bear Arms: An Exchange," *New York Review of Books*, November 16, 1995, www.nybooks.com/articles/archives/1995/nov/16/to-keep-and-bear-arms-an-exchange/.

53 *The panel subtly altered the militia amendment:* Veit, Bowling, and Bickford, eds., *Creating the Bill of Rights*, 38.

54 *Elbridge Gerry was quick to his feet:* Schwartz, ed., *The Bill of Rights*, II, 1107–8.

54 *the language should be confined to people:* House of Representatives, Amendments to the Constitution 17, 20 August 1789, Annals 1: 749–52, 766–67 (Amendment 2).

54 *requiring a conscientious objector to hire someone:* Schwartz, ed., *The Bill of Rights*, II, 1108.

55 *Roger Sherman of Connecticut cut this down:* Ibid.

55 *"the benevolence of the legislature":* Ibid., 1109.

55 *The House narrowly voted to retain:* Ibid.

55 *"the uncertainty with which it is expressed":* Ibid.

55 *He "could not help himself":* Ibid.

55 *"a militia can never be depended upon":* Ibid., 1126.

55 *Twelve congressmen joined the debate:* This point is made in Uviller and Merkel, *The Militia and the Right to Arms*, 102–3.

56 *The president had written a letter:* George Washington to James Madison (circa May 31, 1789), *The Papers of George Washington Digital Edition,* ed. Theodore J. Crackel (Charlottesville: University of Virginia Press, Rotunda, 2008), http://rotunda.upress.virginia.edu/founders/GEWN-05-02-02-0305. Madison's use of the letter is described in Bowling, "'A Tub to the Whale,'" 223–42.

56 *Tantalizing reports leaked:* John Randolph. "Letter to St. George Tucker," September 11, 1789, in Veit, Bowling, and Bickford, eds., *Creating the Bill of Rights,* 293. Also available at http://consource.org/document/john-randolph-to-st-george-tucker-1789-9-11/20130122080032/.

56 *"for the common defence":* Schwartz, ed., *The Bill of Rights,* II, 1154.

57 *"It is amazing":* Ibid., 1171.

57 *none concern the amendment:* Ibid., 1171–1204.

57 *Jefferson made his laconic announcement:* Ibid.,1203.

58 *"Understanding this aspect of the politics":* Jack N. Rakove, "The Second Amendment: The Highest Stage of Originalism," in Carl T. Bogus, ed., *The Second Amendment in Law and History: Historians and Constitutional Scholars on the Right to Bear Arms* (New York: New Press, 2001), 96.

58 *"The right of individuals to be armed":* Malcolm, *To Keep and Bear Arms,* 134.

59 *Some background is in order:* For an interpretation that differs starkly from Malcolm's, see Lois G. Schwoerer, "To Hold and Bear Arms: The English Perspective," *Chicago-Kent Law Review* 76 (259): 30–48; "Brief for English/Early American Historians as Amicus Curiae in Support of Respondents," *McDonald v. City of Chicago,* www.americanbar.org/content/dam/aba/publishing/preview/publiced_preview_briefs_pdfs_09_10_08_1521_RespondentAmCuEnglish Historiansnew.authcheckdam.pdf.

59 *"That the subjects which are Protestants":* The English Bill of Rights is available at http://avalon.law.yale.edu/17th_century/england.asp.

59 *"savours of the politics to arm the mob":* Schwoerer, "To Hold and Bear Arms," 51.

60 *James Madison's notes:* Madison's handwritten notes for his June 8 speech are displayed, in digital form, at www.loc.gov/exhibits/madison/images/vc11.jpg.

60 *Law professor David Yassky:* Amicus brief filed on behalf of fifty-two historians in *United States v. Emerson,* U.S. Court of Appeals, Fifth Circuit, September 3, 1999, available at www.potowmack.org/yass.html#amici. A polymath, Yassky would later serve as an elected official in New York City, as well as its ubiquitous taxi and limousine commissioner.

60 *the opening clause:* For a discussion of the significance of explanatory clauses in eighteenth-century law, and its relevance to "popular constitutionalism," see Thomas Konig, "Why the Second Amendment Has a Preamble: Original Public Meaning and the Political Culture of Written Constitutions in Revo-

lutionary America," *U.C.L.A. Law Review* 56 (2009): 1295. Konig notes that in the eighteenth century, preambles were considered legally binding, and controlled the narrower language that followed. For example, as Vice President Thomas Jefferson compiled the *Manual of Parliamentary Practice*, he urged legislators to draft and vote on the preambles last, since they controlled the meaning of the rest. Ibid., 1130. Another scholar, Paul Finkelman, argues that a compelling preamble was especially necessary for this amendment, given the Anti-Federalists' fear of a standing army. Finkelman, "It Really Was About a Well Regulated Militia," 267. But see Eugene Volokh, "The Commonplace Second Amendment," *N.Y.U. Law Review* 73 (1998): 793. Volokh, a libertarian supporter of gun rights, concedes that the Second Amendment is the only one in the U.S. Constitution to have a statement of purpose. In his research, he found numerous provisions in state constitutions with preambles. It stood out in the Bill of Rights, but was an everyday method of drafting, he argues. So the preamble's presence here does not connote an intent to modify or limit the right-recognizing clauses.

61 *John Jay wrote: Jones v. Walker*, 13 F. Cas. 1059, 1065 (C.C.D. Va. n.d.) (no. 7507), reprinted in Maeva Marcus, *The Documentary History of the Supreme Court of the United States 1789–1800* (New York: Columbia University Press, 2004), 301.

61 *the Framers' familiarity with Latin:* See "The Second Amendment: Our Latinate Constitution," Linguistics Research Center, University of Texas at Austin, December 26, 2012, http://blogs.utexas.edu/lrc/2012/12/26/the-second-amendment-our-latinate-constitution/; Mark Liberman, "The *New Yorker* Finds the U.S. Constitution Ungrammatical," "Language Log" (blog), December 18, 2012, http://langugelog.ldc.upenn.edu/nll/?p=4378. For Second Amendment legal advocates and scholars on the same topic, see Volokh, "The Commonplace Second Amendment," 793.

61 *the only one of the ten in the Bill of Rights that has an explanatory clause:* Richard Epstein, "A Structural Interpretation of the Second Amendment: Why *Heller* is (Probably) Wrong on Originalist Grounds," *Syracuse Law Review* 59 (2008–2009): 171. Epstein, a prominent libertarian, writes:

> *Let us start with the introductory clause. Does its choice of words make any difference? Thus, suppose it said, "A healthy wildlife population, being necessary to the security of homes and farms, the right of the people to keep and bear arms shall not be infringed." The evident disjunction is that the two clauses have no relationship between them. But the Second Amendment coheres in part because there does seem to be a logical connection between the end stated in the first clause and the means chosen in the second.*

61 *Many modern readers:* Entries in the *Oxford English Dictionary* from the 1700s for "regulation" include usage such as "If a liberal Education has formed in us well-regulated Appetites and worthy Inclinations," from 1709.

61 *In the Articles of Confederation:* "No vessel of war shall be kept up in time of peace by any State, except such number only, as shall be deemed necessary by the United States in Congress assembled, for the defense of such State, or its trade; nor shall any body of forces be kept up by any State in time of peace, except such number only, as in the judgement of the United States in Congress assembled, shall be deemed requisite to garrison the forts necessary for the defense of such State; but every State shall always keep up a well-regulated and disciplined militia, sufficiently armed and accoutered, and shall provide and constantly have ready for use, in public stores, a due number of filed pieces and tents, and a proper quantity of arms, ammunition and camp equipage." Articles of Confederation, sec. 6, par. 4.

62 *In that contentious session: DHRC X,* June 14, 1788; also available at www .constitution.org/rc/rat_va_12.htm.

62 *Some find this:* Those arguing that the Second Amendment recognizes an individual right produced a massive array of articles. (See the full discussion of this in Chapter Five.) For a sample of this perspective, see Stephen Halbrook, "The Jurisprudence of the Second and Fourteenth Amendments," *George Mason Law Review* 4 (1981): 1; Stephen Halbrook, "To Keep and Bear Their Private Arms: The Adoption of the Second Amendment, 1787–1791" *Northern Kentucky Law Review* 10 (1982): 13; Don Kates, "The Second Amendments and the Ideology of Self-Protection," *Constitutional Commentary* 9 (1992): 87; David T. Hardy, "Armed Citizens, Citizen Armies: Toward a Jurisprudence of the Second Amendment" *Harvard Journal of Law and Public Policy* 9 (1986): 559; Nelson Lund, "The Second Amendment, Political Liberty and the Right to Self-Preservation," *Alabama Law Review* 39 (1987): 103; and Stephen Halbrook, "Personal Security, Personal Liberty, and 'the Constitutional Right to Bear Arms': Visions of the Framers for the Fourteenth Amendment" *Seton Hall Constitutional Law Journal* 5 (1995): 341.

62 *The official records of the time:* David Yassky, "The Second Amendment: Structure, History, and Constitutional Change," *Michigan Law Review* 99 (2000): 618.

63 *Another scholar looked at databases:* See Nathan Kozuskanich, "Originalism in a Digital Age: An Inquiry into the Right to Bear Arms," *Journal of the Early Republic* 29 (2009): 586–88.

63 *A search for the phrase "bear arms":* http://founders.archives.gov/.

63 *a last vestige of "civic republicanism":* David C. Williams notes, "[The] Anti-Federalist framers of the Second Amendment may not have thought consciously about whether they were relying on liberal or republican rights of revolution. Indeed, they may have relied on both rights without worrying

about inconsistency. But in context, their primary loyalty seems clear. They self-consciously cast themselves as defenders of the War for Independence, a revolution made for republican principles. They gave the right to bear arms to a militia—a sacred concept in the republican tradition but one that [John] Locke does not even mention." Williams, "Civic Republicanism and the Citizen Militia," 584. Williams believes that the militias were designed with an insurrectionist purpose—to provide a military check on central power. Uviller and Merkel, too, argue that the militia amendment was "too wedded to the ancient, mixed, and balanced Constitution, too steeped in English political history to make an easy transition into a universal 'rights' framework. . . . The right to arms differs from its now individualistic companions . . . because it never escaped its heritage as a corporate entitlement belonging to individuals only because they were members of a group." Uviller and Merkel, *The Militia and the Right to Arms*, 164.

CHAPTER FOUR: ARKANSAS TOOTHPICKS, BEECHER'S BIBLES, AND THE FOURTEENTH AMENDMENT

65 *began to crumble:* See generally Cunliffe, *Soldiers and Civilians*, 205–12. John Mahon, on the other hand, argues that the militia was strong—if decentralized—before the War of 1812. See Mahon, *History of the Militia and the National Guard*, 54–55.

65 *George Washington convened his cabinet:* The first president's reaction to congressional investigations into the St. Clair episode is described in Louis Fisher, "Congressional Access to Executive Branch Information: Legislative Tools," Congressional Research Service, May 17, 2001, www.fas.org/sgp/crs/secrecy /RL30966.pdf. See also Emily Berman, *Executive Privilege: A Legislative Remedy* (New York: Brennan Center for Justice, 2009), 63, n. 44.

65 *The new federal law: Militia Act:* 1 stat. 271 (Uniform Militia Act of 1792). Its full title was An Act more effectually to provide for the National Defense by establishing an Uniform Militia throughout the United States. That same month, Congress passed another act, delegating "to the president some of Congress' power to call the militia into federal service." Mahon, *History of the Militia and the National Guard*, 52–53.

65 *"each and every free able-bodied white male citizen":* This law introduced a racial element into the militia. In the late 1700s, in most of the country free African Americans could vote and serve in the militia. The codification of a whites-only militia likely had to do with their potential use to enforce slavery. For a challenging perspective on the racial politics behind the Second Amendment, see Robert Cottrol and Raymond Diamond, "The Second Amendment: Toward an Afro-Americanist Reconsideration," *The Georgetown Law Journal* 80 (1991): 309–61.

66 *a profound degree of governmental intrusion:* The Militia Act of 1792 resurfaced as an ironic constitutional footnote. Long forgotten, it assumed sudden

prominence in 2012, when President Barack Obama's Affordable Care Act faced legal challenge. Litigants opposed the requirement that citizens purchase private health insurance. Where before had the federal government ordered Americans to buy something in private commerce? Here was an example, one signed into law by George Washington himself. In truth the fit was incomplete. The Militia Act implemented a provision of the Constitution specifically designed to preserve state military forces. The health law, by contrast, relied on the more elastic clause letting Congress regulate "interstate commerce." In both instances, Congress could have provided the public good by buying guns or insurance itself. (In the end the law was deemed to rest on a different authority: Congress's power to tax.) See *National Federation of Independent Business v. Sebelius*, 567 U.S. ___ (2012), (fn. 3).

66 *"compulsory military service":* Uviller and Merkel, *The Militia and the Right to Arms*, 119.

66 *nationwide registry:* See, e.g., "return" for 1804: March 22, 1804, Library of Congress. "A Century of Lawmaking for a New Nation: U.S. Congressional Documents and Debates," 1774–1875, American State Papers, 8th Cong., 1st Sess., Military Affairs: Vol. 1, http://lcweb2.loc.gov/cgi-bin/ampage?collId=llsp&fileName=016/llspo16.db&recNum=173. Jefferson's efforts to learn the readiness of the militias is described in Mahon, *History of the Militia and the National Guard*, 64.

66 *Most of the federal militiamen:* Alexander DeConde, *Gun Violence in America* (Boston: Northeastern University Press, 2000), 41.

67 *government established its authority:* See William Hogeland, *The Whiskey Rebellion: George Washington, Alexander Hamilton, and the Frontier Rebels Who Challenged America's Newfound Sovereignty* (New York: Simon & Schuster, 2006). Many of the rebels thought they were merely organizing militias as had been done against British tyranny. They were surprised to learn there was a new federalized militia in town.

67 *Hamilton took effective command:* See Ron Chernow, *Alexander Hamilton* (New York: Penguin, 2004), 553–54.

67 *Northeastern states refused:* A. J. Langguth, *Union 1812: The Americans Who Fought the Second War of Independence* (New York: Simon & Schuster, 2006), 197; J.C.A. Stagg, *The War of 1812: Conflict for a Continent* (Cambridge: Cambridge University Press, 2012), 73.

67 *British soldiers landed:* The failure of the Maryland militia is described in Langguth, *Union 1812*, 297–312. "Even as their troops proceeded toward the capital . . . the Americans were not firing on them," Langguth writes. "One British soldier compared their progress to strolling through open fields on a summer picnic."

67 *Two historians dryly wondered:* Uviller and Merkel, *The Militia and the Right to Arms*, 121.

67 *the duty-bound concept of militia service withered:* A window on the phenomenon is found in the writings of Joseph Story. A Supreme Court justice and
devotee of Blackstone, Story wrote a highly influential treatise on the U.S.
Constitution, published in 1833. He wrote of the Second Amendment:

> *The importance of this article will scarcely be doubted by any persons,
> who have duly reflected upon the subject. The militia is the natural
> defence of a free country against sudden foreign invasions, domestic
> insurrections, and domestic usurpations of power by rulers. It is against
> sound policy for a free people to keep up large military establishments
> and standing armies in time of peace, both from the enormous expenses,
> with which they are attended, and the facile means, which they af-
> ford to ambitious and unprincipled rulers, to subvert the government,
> or trample upon the rights of the people. The right of the citizens to
> keep and bear arms has justly been considered, as the palladium of the
> liberties of a republic; since it offers a strong moral check against the
> usurpation and arbitrary power of rulers; and will generally, even if
> these are successful in the first instance, enable the people to resist and
> triumph over them. And yet, though this truth would seem so clear, and
> the importance of a well regulated militia would seem so undeniable, it
> cannot be disguised, that among the American people there is a grow-
> ing indifference to any system of militia discipline, and a strong dispo-
> sition, from a sense of its burthens, to be rid of all regulations. How it
> is practicable to keep the people duly armed without some organization,
> it is difficult to see. There is certainly no small danger, that indiffer-
> ence may lead to disgust, and disgust to contempt; and thus gradually
> undermine all the protection intended by this clause of our national bill
> of rights.*

Joseph Story, *Commentaries on the Constitution of the United States,* 3: § 1890,
Boston, 1833; *The Founders' Constitution,* vol. 5, amend. II, doc. 10, University of Chicago Press. http://press-pubs.uchicago.edu/founders/documents/
amendIIs10.html. Story's patriotic lament for the militia has taken on a new
light in recent years. Revisionists have focused on one line—"The right of the
citizens to keep and bear arms has justly been considered, as the palladium
of the liberties of a republic"—to prove that Story embraced a twenty-first-
century individual rights view. Stephen Halbrook, for example, writes that
Story "interpreted the Second Amendment as providing for an individual right
to bear arms that would be sufficient to overcome even the standing army of an
oppressive government." He cuts off Story's full quote, omitting the last three
sentences—the ones where the jurist frets that it is hard "to keep the people
duly armed without some organization." Stephen P. Halbrook, *That Every Man
Be Armed: The Evolution of a Constitutional Right* (Albuquerque: University of
New Mexico Press, 1984), 92–93.

67 *Popular illustrations:* Compare the drawing, "President Washington reviews the well-regulated militia used by the government to put down the Whiskey Rebels in 1994," Cornell, *A Well-Regulated Militia*, 72, with the depiction of a militia muster from 1841, ibid., 136.

67 *gun violence rose sharply:* Walter Russell Mead has identified an affinity for being armed—and a quickness to affront—as central to the Jacksonian tendency in American life. Mead, *Special Providence: American Foreign Policy and How It Changed the World* (New York: Routledge, 2009), 223–33. "Jacksonians are armed for defense: of the home and person against robbers; against usurpations of the federal government; and of the United States against its enemies."

67 *Andrew Jackson himself fought numerous duels:* See Jon Meacham, *American Lion: Andrew Jackson in the White House* (New York: Random House, 2008), 25–26. In one duel, Jackson let the other man shoot first. Despite being hit, he carefully took aim, and fired a fatal shot. He told a friend, "If he had shot me through the brain, sir, I should still have killed him."

68 *new state provisions had an individualist cast:* Saul Cornell, "*Heller*, New Originalism, and Law Office History: 'Meet the New Boss, Same as the Old Boss,'" *UCLA Law Review* 56 (2009): 1112.

68 *Arkansas's court ruled: State v. Buzzard*, described in Cornell, *A Well-Regulated Militia*, 147.

68 *In 1820, a Kentucky state court: Bliss v. Commonwealth of Kentucky*, 12 Littell 90 Ky. 1822.

68 *Kentucky stood apart:* There are other cases as well. For example, *Heller* cites a Virginia state case in 1820 in which a judge noted that free blacks in Virginia do not have the constitutional rights extended to whites, including the right to enter the state and to bear arms. *Aldridge v. Commonwealth*, 2 Va. Cas. 447, 449 (1824), cited in *Heller*, 554 U.S. 510 (2008) (fn. 21).

68 *Two models emerged:* The dominant "Arkansas doctrine" was spelled out in the 1870s by the prominent legal scholar John Forrest Dillon. He found a strong judicial consensus that the constitutional protection extended only to militia arms; there was a common law right of self-defense, but subject to restrictions such as a ban on carrying a concealed weapon. See Cornell, *A Well-Regulated Militia*, 186–89. On the other hand, for a survey of state constitutions, commentaries, and rulings in the 1800s that support an individualist interpretation, see David B. Kopel, "The Second Amendment in the 19th Century," *Brigham Young Law Review* 1360 (1998), http://lawreview.byu.edu/archives/1998/4/kop.pdf.

68 *It was pungently expressed by the Supreme Court: Aymette v. State*, 21 Tenn. 154 (1840) at 148, 161.

69 *"It would give to persons of the negro race": Dred Scott v. Sanford*, 60 U.S. 417 (1857).

70 *Abraham Lincoln's speech:* See Harold Holzer, *Lincoln at Cooper Union: The Speech That Made Abraham Lincoln President* (New York: Simon & Schuster, 2006), 123–31.

70 *Many laws:* Cottrol and Diamond, "Toward an Afro-Americanist Reconsideration, 340–42."

70 *"Beecher's Bibles":* Debby Applegate, *The Most Famous Man in America: The Biography of Henry Ward Beecher* (New York: Doubleday, 2006), 281–82.

70 *Brown had even drafted a proposed new U.S. Constitution:* The abolitionist's attorney used the proposed constitution at his trial to try to prove he was of "unsound mind." Tony Horwitz, *Midnight Rising: John Brown and the Raid That Started the Civil War* (New York: Henry Holt, 2011), 80–82.

71 *President Lincoln called for 75,000 militiamen:* James M. McPherson, *Battle Cry of Freedom: The Civil War Era* (Oxford: Oxford University Press, 1988), 274–75.

71 *the U.S. Army comprised sixteen thousand men:* Ibid., 348. The states sent troops, especially during the first two years of the war, but the numbers fell far short of what was needed. By 1863, the Union resorted to a draft. Chambers, *History of the Militia and the National Guard,* 97–107.

71 *On April 9, 1865:* The surrender and the contrast between the two generals is described in Jay Winik, *April 1865: The Month That Saved America* (New York: HarperCollins, 2001), 174–91.

72 *"In Mississippi houses have been burned":* Congressional Globe, 39th Cong., 1st Sess., 1866, Freedmen's Bureau Bill, Representative Thomas D. Eliot.

72 *South Carolina's black citizens sent a petition:* Stephen P. Halbrook, *Freedmen, The Fourteenth Amendment, and the Right to Bear Arms, 1866–1876* (Westport: Praeger, 1998), 9–10.

72 *An army general issued a proclamation:* Congressional Globe , 39th Cong., 1st Sess. 908–9 (1866), quoted in Saul Cornell and Justin Florence, "The Right to Bear Arms in the Era of the Fourteenth Amendment: Gun Rights or Gun Regulation," *Santa Clara Law Review* 50 (2010): 1043, http://digitalcommons .law.scu.edu/lawreview/vol50/iss4/1.

73 *Freedman's Bureau:* The agency was formally called the Bureau of Refugees, Freemen, and Abandoned Lands. Lincoln signed it into law the month before he died. Section 14 of the legislation to strengthen the bureau, enacted July 16, 1866, stated, "The right . . . to have full and equal benefit of all laws and proceedings concerning personal liberty personal security, and the acquisition, enjoyment, and disposition of estate, real and personal, including the constitutional right to bear arms, shall be secured to and enjoyed by all the citizens . . . without respect to race or color, or previous condition of slavery."

73 *These sweeping guarantees:* The Fourteenth Amendment is the subject of massive amounts of scholarship. A good recent narrative history of its enactment is Garrett Epps, *Democracy Reborn: The Fourteenth Amendment and the Fight for*

Equal Rights in Post–Civil War America (New York: Henry Holt, 2006). For a good survey of the issues pertaining to the Fourteenth Amendment and its impact on state laws affecting guns, see Lawrence Rosenthal, "Second Amendment Plumbing After *Heller*: Of Standards of Scrutiny, Incorporation, Well-Regulated Militias and Criminal Street Gangs," *Urban Lawyer* 41 (2009): 1.

73 *"The problem of establishing the Amendment's 'original intent'"*: Eric Foner, *Reconstruction: America's Unfinished Revolution, 1863–1877* (New York: Harper & Row, 1988), 256–58.

74 *There is some evidence in these debates*: *Congressional Globe*, 39th Cong., 1st Sess., March 8, 1866, Civil Rights Act 1866, Representative Henry J. Raymond.

74 *"the personal rights guaranteed"*: Senator Jacob M. Howard, *Congressional Globe*, 39th Cong., 1st Sess., 2764–65 (May 23, 1866), quoted in Stephen Halbrook, "Personal Security, Personal Liberty, and 'the Constitutional Right to Bear Arms': Visions of the Framers for the Fourteenth Amendment," *Seton Hall Constitutional Law Journal* 5 (1995): 341–434.

74 *"In Mississippi"*: *Congressional Globe*, 39th Cong., 1st Sess., December 13, 1865, 14th Amendment debates, Senator Henry Wilson.

74 *"Of whom will that militia consist?"*: *Congressional Globe*, 40th Cong., 2nd Sess., 2198 (Representative Michael C. Kerr) (1868), quoted in Stephen Halbrook, "The Jurisprudence of the Second and Fourteenth Amendments," *George Mason Law Review* 4 (1981): 1, 25.

74 *The amendment's supporters did not sell the controversial measure*: For a forceful articulation of the view that the Republicans were not of one mind on the question of whether the Fourteenth Amendment intended to apply the Second Amendment right to states, see Carole Emberton, "The Limits of Incorporation: Violence, Gun Rights, and Gun Regulation in the Reconstruction South," *Stanford Law and Policy Review* 17, no. 3 (2006): 615–34.

75 *"Between 1775 and 1866"*: Amar, *The Bill of Rights*, 266.

75 *"Whatever its appeal might be"*: Uviller and Merkel, *The Militia and the Right to Arms*, 267.

75 *In Texas, armed conflict raged*: James E. Bond, *No Easy Walk to Freedom: Reconstruction and the Ratification of the Fourteenth Amendment* (Westport: Praeger, 1997), 222–23.

75 *"barbarous practice"*: Ibid., 45.

76 *And the Supreme Court led the judiciary*: *Slaughter-House Cases*, 83 U.S. 36 (1873).

76 *An even more troubling case*: The Colfax massacre is described in detail in Charles Lane, *The Day Freedom Died: The Colfax Massacre, the Supreme Court, and the Betrayal of Reconstruction* (New York: Henry Holt, 2008), 9–22.

76 *The U.S. Supreme Court heard the case in 1876*: *United States v. Cruikshank*, 92 U.S. 542, 553 (1876).

77 The Day Freedom Died: The justices in their conferences wanted to free the

three white defendants, invalidating the indictments on technical grounds. It then shifted, and decided on broad constitutional grounds. Lane, *The Day Freedom Died*, 244.

77 *The ruling hindered federal enforcement:* The U.S. Supreme Court continues to cite the case. For example, it cited *Cruikshank* in striking down a rape victim's lawsuit under the federal Violence Against Women Act. *United States v. Morrison*, 529 U.S. 598 (2000). See Nathan Newman and J. J. Gass, *A New Birth of Freedom: The Forgotten History of the 13th, 14th, and 15th Amendments* (New York: Brennan Center for Justice, 2004).

77 *"The increase of crimes of blood":* James O'Meara, "Concealed Weapons and Crimes," *Overland Monthly* 2 (1890), 11–15, cited in DeConde, *Gun Violence in America*, 71.

77 *Dodge City, Kansas:* Winkler, *Gun Fight: The Battle over the Right to Bear Arms in America*, 165.

78 *It had vanished:* The Civil War required a draft. In the decades that followed, the United States had little need for an army. But when it went to war against Spain in 1898, the strictures of the militia system proved inadequate. For a full discussion, see Mahon, *History of the Militia and the National Guard*, 138–53.

78 *By the end of the nineteenth century, many state constitutions:* A typical example is Montana's constitution of 1889: "The right of any person to keep or bear arms in defense of his own home, person, and property, or in aid of the civil power when thereto legally summoned, shall not be called in question, but nothing herein contained shall be held to permit the carrying of concealed weapons." Mont. Const. of 1889, art. III, § 13. State constitutional provisions on the right "to keep and bear arms" are compiled in Eugene Volokh, "State Constitutional Rights to Keep and Bear Arms," *Texas Review of Law and Politics* 11 (2006): 191–217. Adam Winkler argues the forty-two state constitutional provisions point toward a "reasonable right to bear arms," subject to limitations. See Adam Winkler, "The Reasonable Right to Bear Arms," *Stanford Law & Policy Review* 17 (2006): 597–613. There is a surprising paucity of research on gun regulations in the nineteenth century. One extremely useful compilation is Mark Anthony Frassetto, "Firearms and Weapons Legislation up to the Early 20th Century" (January 15, 2013). Available at SSRN: http://ssrn.com/abstract=2200991 or http://dx.doi.org/10.2139/ssrn.2200991.

78 *easily concealed knives and clubs:* See Herbert Asbury, *Gangs of New York: An Informal History of the Underworld* (New York: Alfred A. Knopf, 1928).

78 *Municipal police departments:* A concise history of the development of police departments in the United States is Craig G. Uchida, "The Development of American Police: An Historical Overview," in Roger G. Dunham and Jeffrey P. Alpert, eds., *Critical Issues in Policing: Contemporary Readings* (Long Grove, IL: Waveland, 2010), 17–36.

78 *"I don't know whether you fully understand":* H. W. Brands, *T.R.: The Last Romantic* (New York: Basic Books, 1997), 721.

79 *an unlikely champion:* Sullivan's story is told in Dan Czitrom, "Underworld and Underdogs: Big Tim Sullivan and Metropolitan Politics in New York, 1889–1913," *Journal of American History* 78, no. 2 (1991); Robert F. Welch, *King of the Bowery: Big Tim Sullivan, Tammany Hall, and New York City from the Gilded Age to the Progressive Era* (Madison, NJ: Farleigh Dickinson University Press, 2008), 143–46. Welch concludes, "all available evidence is that Tim [Sullivan's] fight to bring firearms under control sprang from heartfelt conviction."

79 *The measure required a license:* The Sullivan Law is described in James B. Jacobs, *Can Gun Control Work?* (New York: Oxford University Press, 2002), 33; Lee Kennett and James LaVerne Anderson, *The Gun in America: The Origins of a National Dilemma* (Westport: Greenwood, 1975), 174–86.

79 *"Your bill won't stop murders":* "Bar Hidden Weapons on Sullivan's Plea," *New York Times*, May 12, 1911, http://graphics8.nytimes.com/packages/pdf/nyregion/2011/bar-hidden-weapons.pdf.

80 *"Revolver Act":* Winkler, *Gunfight*, 207–8.

80 *At this time, courts had ruled:* That began to change in 1925, when the Supreme Court first applied part of the First Amendment to states. See *Gitlow v. New York*, 268 U.S. 652 (1925).

80 *armed parade of German immigrants: Presser v. Illinois,* 116 U.S. 252 (1886).

80 *"We have examined the record in vain": Miller v. Texas,* 153 U.S. 585 (1894).

81 *The "constitutional revolution" of the New Deal:* See Bruce Ackerman, *We the People, Volume I: Foundations* (Cambridge: Belknap Press of Harvard University, 1991).

81 *National Firearms Act of 1934:* Act of June 26, 1934, c. 757, 48 Stat. 1236–40, 26 U.S.C.A. s 1132 et seq.

81 *the National Rifle Association—then a sportsmen's group—backed the plan:* Winkler, *Gun Fight,* 64.

82 *Hoover used the crackdown on armed gangsters:* Curt Gentry, *J. Edgar Hoover: The Man and the Secrets* (New York: W. W. Norton, 1991), 178–79.

82 *By 1938, the administration sought another gun bill:* Federal Firearms Act of 1938, described in DeConde, *Gun Violence in America,* 145–47.

82 *Supreme Court upheld the 1934 law: United States v. Miller,* 307 U.S. 174 (1939).

82 *The case boasted a picturesque background:* For a detailed history of the case, including the colorful story of Depression-era bank robbers, see Brian L. Frye, "The Peculiar Story of *United States v. Miller*," *NYU Journal of Law and Liberty* 3 (2008): 48–82. This history of the case, written by a law firm associate who did double duty as a documentary filmmaker, had the distinction of being cited by Justice Scalia in *Heller*.

83 *Gun Control Act of 1968:* Franklin E. Zimring, "Firearms and Federal Law: The Gun Control Act of 1968," *Journal of Legal Studies* 4 (1975): 133.

83 *It also prohibited certain classes of people deemed dangerous:* 18 U.S.C. sec. 922 (d).

84 *"This has been the subject":* Charlayne Hunter-Gault, "The NewsHour with Jim Lehrer: Interview with Warren Burger."

CHAPTER FIVE: REVOLT AT CINCINNATI

87 *"the nation's longest standing":* http://home.nra.org/history.

87 *target practice a waste of time:* Osha Gray Davidson, *Under Fire: The NRA and the Battle for Gun Control* (New York: Henry Holt, 1993), 21.

87 *"There will be no war":* Ibid., 26.

87 *the NRA began to shift its focus:* Ibid., 20–29.

88 *it did not object to the first federal gun control measure:* U.S. Congress, Hearings Before the Committee on Ways and Means of the House of Representatives, 73rd Cong., 2nd Sess. (1934), 38.

88 *"I have never believed":* Ibid., 52.

88 *an advertisement appeared:* Josh Sugarmann, *The National Rifle Association: Money, Firepower and Fear* (Washington, D.C.: National Press Books, 1992), 35.

88 *Hidell was Lee Harvey Oswald:* Gerald Posner, *Case Closed: Lee Harvey Oswald and the Assassination of JFK* (New York: Random House, 1993), 102–3.

88 *"We do not think that any sane American":* Davidson, *Under Fire*, 30.

89 American Rifleman *started a new column:* Rick Perlstein, *Nixonland* (New York: Scribner, 2008), 199.

89 *"criminal-coddling do-gooders":* DeConde, *Gun Violence in America*, 180.

89 *"The most gun-addicted sections of the United States":* Richard Hofstadter, "America as a Gun Culture," *American Heritage* 21, no. 6 (October 1970), http://somd .com/news/headlines/2013/16749.shtml.

89 *For years after, politicians would whisper:* See Jeremy Barr, "45 Years Later, Tydings' Gun Control Bill Remains a Cautionary Tale," *Southern Maryland Online* newspapers, April 11, 2013.

89 *"The measure as a whole":* The story of the transformation of the NRA into a feared militant organization is told in gripping fashion in Joel Achenbach, Scott Higham, and Sari Horwitz, "How NRA's True Believers Converted a Marksmanship Group into a Mighty Gun Lobby," *Washington Post*, January 12, 2013, http://articles.washingtonpost.com/2013-01-12/politics/36311919 _1_nra-leaders-nra-officers-mighty-gun-lobby/3.

90 *"does not necessarily approve":* *American Rifleman*, March 1968, 16.

90 *"Revolt at Cincinnati":* Achenbach, Higham, and Horwitz, "How NRA's True Believers Converted a Marksmanship Group into a Mighty Gun Lobby."

90 *"Is it possible that some of these incidents":* Ibid.

90 *"What the NRA Is":* Scott Melzer, *Gun Crusaders: The NRA's Culture War* (New York: NYU Press, 2009), 89.

91 *the response from the right:* A prescient and perceptive look at the phenomenon is Thomas Byrne Edsall and Mary Edsall, *Chain Reaction: The Impact of Race, Rights and Taxes on American Politics* (New York: W. W. Norton, 1991). Grip-

ping narrative histories of the immediate backlash—and its cultural roots—include Rick Perlstein, *Before the Storm: Barry Goldwater and the Unmaking of the American Consensus* (New York: Hill & Wang, 2001), and Matthew Dallek, *The Right Moment: Ronald Reagan's First Victory and the Decisive Turning Point in American Politics* (New York: Free Press, 2000).

91 *Evangelical Christian churches underwent a similar change:* On the rise and politicization of the Religious Right at the same time the NRA was becoming more militant, see Darren Dochuk, *From Bible Belt to Sunbelt: Plain Folk Religion, Grassroots Politics, and the Rise of Evangelical Conservatism* (New York: W. W. Norton, 2010); Daniel K. Williams *God's Own Party: The Making of the Christian Right* (Oxford: Oxford University Press, 2010).

91 *Proposition 13:* See Robert Kuttner, *Revolt of the Haves: Tax Rebellions and Hard Times* (New York: Simon & Schuster, 1980).

91 *landowners opposed the Interior Department:* "Sagebrush Rebellion," *U.S. News & World Report*, December 1, 1980.

91 *Organized business shifted:* Jacob S. Hacker and Paul Pierson, *Winner Take All Politics: How Washington Made the Rich Richer, and Turned Its Back on the Middle Class* (New York: Simon & Schuster, 2010), 95–135; Thomas Byrne Edsall, *The New Politics of Inequality* (New York: W. W. Norton, 1984), 76–78. See generally David Vogel, *Fluctuating Fortunes: The Political Power of Business in America* (New York: Basic Books, 1989).

92 *measured by polls:* Polls are compiled in "Public Trust in Government: 1958–2013" by the Pew Research Center, January 31, 2013, www.people-press.org /2013/01/31/trust-in-government-interactive/. The 1958 poll was conducted by the American National Election Study; the 1980 study by CBS/*New York Times*.

92 *an overtly political coalition:* The Olin Foundation was one of the major sources of funds for various streams of conservative thought and activism. Olin is a major manufacturer of ammunition and guns. For an excellent overview, see Alice O'Connor, "Financing the Counterrevolution," in Bruce J. Schulman and Julian E. Zelizer, eds., *Rightward Bound* (Cambridge: Harvard University Press, 2008), 148–68.

92 *"Over the past forty years":* Thomas Byrne Edsall, *Building Red America: The New Conservative Coalition and the Drive for Permanent Power* (New York: Basic Books, 2007), 5.

92 *From the time of the first urban rioting:* David Frum, *How We Got Here: The 70s, The Decade That Brought You Modern Life—For Better or Worse* (New York: Basic Books, 2000), 19.

92 *Reagan gave the new constitutional thrust rhetorical support:* The former governor argued against gun control in his radio broadcasts. For a discussion of the shift rightward by the NRA, and the embrace of gun rights language by the Republican Party, see Rick Perlstein, "How the NRA Became an Organization

for Aspiring Vigilantes," TheNation.com, January 9 and 10, 2013, www.the-nation.com/blog/172100/how-nra-became-organization-aspiring-vigilantes-part-1#axzz2dBPH6Zpv, and at www.thenation.com/blog/172125/how-nra-became-organization-aspiring-vigilantes-part-2#axzz2dBPH6Zpv. See also Jill Lepore, "Battleground America: One Nation, Under the Gun," *The New Yorker*, April 23, 2012, www.newyorker.com/reporting/2012/04/23/120423fa_fact_lepore.

92 *The 1972 Republican platform:* Republican Party Platform, August 21, 1972, www.presidency.ucsb.edu/ws/index.php?pid=25842.

93 *Reagan wrote:* Ronald Reagan, "Ronald Reagan Champions Gun Ownership," *Guns & Ammo*, September 1975, 34, cited in Reva B. Siegel, "Dead or Alive: Originalism as Popular Constitutionalism in *Heller*," *Harvard Law Review*, no.122 (2008): 209.

93 *"We believe the right of citizens":* Republican Party Platform of 1980, July 21, 1980, www.presidency.ucsb.edu/ws/index.php?pid=25844.

93 *the NRA gave Reagan its first-ever presidential endorsement:* Dudley Clendenin, "Campaign Report," *New York Times*, October 30, 1980. The same article reported that *TV Guide* had also backed Reagan in its first-ever presidential endorsement.

93 *"What if there had been a Brady Bill 150 years ago?":* Achenbach, Higham, and Horwitz, "How NRA's True Believers Converted a Marksmanship Group into a Mighty Gun Lobby."

94 *"But he would say":* President William J. Clinton, "Remarks to the Convocation of the Church of God in Christ," Memphis, Tennessee," November 13, 1993, http://millercenter.org/president/speeches/detail/3436. I have written about the speech and its gestation in *My Fellow Americans: The Most Important Speeches of America's Presidents, from Washington to Obama* (Naperville, IL: Sourcebooks, 2011; 2nd ed.), 285–90.

94 *"Not a single hunter in America has lost a weapon":* Bill Clinton, *Between Hope and History* (New York: Times Books, 1996), 81.

94 *gun measures cost Democrats dearly:* Jeffrey Birnbaum, "Under the Gun," *Fortune*, December 6, 1999. Birnbaum describes the organization's state-of-the-art political and lobbying operation, including a staff of thirty telemarketers. In addition to Foley, the NRA was credited with the defeat of Representative Jack Brooks (D-TX), the chair of the House Judiciary Committee, which was responsible for the Brady Bill.

94 *"The NRA is the reason the Republicans control the House":* Evelyn Theiss, "Clinton Blames Losses on NRA," Cleveland *Plain Dealer*, January 14, 1995. Clinton estimated the fight over the assault weapons ban cost twenty Democrats their seats.

94 *Conventional wisdom echoed Clinton's plaint:* The assault weapons ban was only one controversy dogging Democrats that year. In addition, the party had raised

taxes and had sought, but failed, to pass national health insurance. In addition, it had failed to enact campaign finance or other political reforms, helping spur support for term limits. For an analysis of the 1994 elections that puts the gun issue in context, see Gary C. Jacobson, "The 1994 House Elections in Perspective," *Political Science Quarterly* 111, no. 2 (1996): 203.

94 *An organizational resolution declared:* Charles M. Sennott, "NRA Becomes Militias' Beacon," *Boston Globe*, August 13, 1995 (quoting NRA's Civilian Militia Statement of November 10, 1994).

94 *Wayne LaPierre:* Greg Zoroya, "On the Defensive: Amid Both Political and Public Turmoil, NRA Chief Wayne LaPierre Has Stood Fast. But the Strains of Combat—from Within as Well as Without—Are Showing," *Los Angeles Times*, June 29, 1995.

94 *fund-raising letter:* Richard Kell, "NRA Apologizes for 'Jack Boot' Letter," Associated Press, May 18, 1995, http://community.seattletimes.nwsource.com /archive/?date=19950518&slug=2121718.

95 *Timothy McVeigh:* For an exploration of Timothy McVeigh's views, including his opposition to the Brady Bill as one reason for the bombing, see John Kifner, "McVeigh's Mind: A Special Report; Oklahoma Bombing Suspect: Unraveling of a Frayed Life," *New York Times*, December 31, 1995, www.nytimes.com /1995/12/31/us/mcveigh-s-mind-special-report-oklahoma-bombing-suspect-unraveling-frayed-life.html?pagewanted=all&src=pm.

95 *founder of* Soldier of Fortune *magazine:* The board member was Robert K. Brown, still on the NRA board in 2013. See Dave Gilson, "Meet the NRA's Board of Directors," *Mother Jones*, January 16, 2013, www.motherjones.com /politics/2013/01/nra-board-members-selleck-nugent.

95 *George H. W. Bush resigned:* "Letter of Resignation Sent by Bush to Rifle Association," *New York Times*, May 11, 1995, www.nytimes.com/1995/05/11/us /letter-of-resignation-sent-by-bush-to-rifle-association.html.

95 *"I am not really here":* Charlton Heston, Speech at Free Congress Foundation's 20th Anniversary Gala, December 7, 1997, www.vpc.org/nrainfo/speech .html.

96 *"sacred stuff resides":* Charlton Heston, NRA Members' Meeting, Charlotte, North Carolina, July 29, 2000; video available at http://home.nra.org/events /video/charlton-heston-2000-meetings/list/2000-nra-annual-meetings.

96 *the wall of the building's lobby:* See "The Second's Missing Half," *Mother Jones*, January/February 1994, www.motherjones.com/politics/1994/01/seconds-missing-half. The lobby of the NRA headquarters building still contains the edited, incomplete version of the Second Amendment. Personal visit by researcher for this volume, July 2013.

97 *The first to argue otherwise:* Stuart Hays, "The Right to Bear Arms, A Study in Judicial Misinterpretation," *William and Mary Law Review* 2 (1960): 381–406.

97 *"From 1970 to 1989":* Carl Bogus, "The History and Politics of Second Amend-

ment Scholarship: A Primer," in Carl Bogus, ed., *The Second Amendment in Law and History: Historians and Constitutional Scholars on the Right to Bear Arms* (New York: New Press, 2002), 4.

98 *He served as a lawyer in the NRA's general counsel's office:* See ibid., 284, fn. 24: "Although in these [six] articles Halbrook identifies himself only as an attorney in Fairfax, Virginia, in 1986 he told a federal district court that he was a lawyer in the Office of General Counsel of the NRA. *See Oefinger v. D.L.O. Manufacturing and Importing*, 1986 U.S. Dist. LEXIS 18370 (D.D.C. 1986)."

98 *three strikingly prolific writers:* Saul Cornell and Nathan Kozuskanich, "Introduction: The D.C. Gun Case," *The Second Amendment on Trial: Critical Essays on District of Columbia v. Heller*, eds. Saul Cornell and Nathan Kozuskanich (Amherst: University of Massachusetts Press, 2013), 9.

98 *One lawyer:* David Kopel, "Books and Journal Articles," davekopel.com.

98 *Patrick Henry professorship:* "NRA Endows Chair at George Mason U. Law School," *Chronicle of Higher Education* 49, no. 27 (March 14, 2003): A25, http://chronicle.com/article/NRA-Endows-Chair-at-George/19835.

98 *"Stand Up for the Second Amendment":* Robert J. Spitzer, *The Politics of Gun Control*, 5th edition (Washington, D.C.: CQ Press, 2008), 171; Robert J. Herz, "Gun Crazy: Constitutional False Consciousness and Dereliction of Dialogic Responsibility," *Boston University Law Review* 75 (1995): 57.

98 *Academics for the Second Amendment:* A private meeting of the group is described in Wendy Kaminer, "Second Thoughts About the Second Amendment," *The Atlantic*, March 1, 1996, www.theatlantic.com/magazine/archive/1996/03/second-thoughts-on-the-second-amendment/306747/.

98 *The NRA paid one lawyer $15,000:* According to the website of the NRA Civil Rights Legal Defense Fund, "At September 14, 2007, meeting an educational grant of $15,500 was provided to David T. Hardy analysis of book on right to bear arms and response thereto in William & Mary Bill of Rights Journal, for an analysis of case law on standing and an article on standing in the Thomas Jefferson Law Review, and research of U.S. Supreme Court papers." See NRA Civil Rights Legal Defense Fund, "Supported Research/Previous Years," www.nradefensefund.org/previous-years-research.aspx. Hardy published a review of Cornell's book. David T. Hardy, "A Well-Regulated Militia: The Founding Fathers and the Origin of Gun Control in America," *William & Mary Bill of Rights Journal* 15 (2007): 1237, http://scholarship.law.wm.edu/wmborj/vol15/iss4/6. The article did not mention the funding from the NRA.

98 *Joyce Lee Malcolm bragged:* Daniel Lazare "Your Constitution Is Killing You," *Harper's*, October 1999, 59.

98 *"Standard Model":* Glenn Harlan Reynolds, "A Critical Guide to the Second Amendment," *Tennessee Law Review* 62 (1995): 461–51.

98 *One law review article changed all that:* Sanford Levinson, "The Embarrassing Second Amendment," *Yale Law Journal* 99 (1999): 637–59.

99 *Laurence Tribe tentatively endorsed:* Tribe's previous edition had relegated the Second Amendment to a footnote. By the third edition, he acknowledged that the amendment had a political purpose related to militia service, which had vanished. "This is not to say, however, that the Second Amendment can properly be deemed wholly irrelevant today or that it may plausibly be construed to do no more than protect state defense forces against outright abolition by Congress." Laurence Tribe, *American Constitutional Law*, Vol. 1 (St. Paul: Foundation Press, 1999; 3rd. ed.), 900.

99 *What mattered was their political provenance:* See Adam Liptak, "A Liberal Case for Gun Rights Sways Judiciary," *New York Times*, May 6, 2007, www.nytimes .com/2007/05/06/us/06firearms.html?pagewanted=all.

99 *Tribe and Amar later penned an op-ed:* Laurence H. Tribe and Akhil Reed Amar, "Well Regulated Militias and More," *New York Times*, October 28, 1999. "The fact is, almost none of the proposed state or Federal weapons regulations appears to come close to offending the Second Amendment's core right to self-protection." After Newtown, Tribe engaged in a heated email exchange with a critical blogger, defending his views. "It badly distorts the meaning of everything I have written on the subject to treat me as remotely hostile to the comprehensive national regulation of firearms and ammunition possession, transfer, and use." Laurence Tribe, "A Response from Laurence Tribe in the Wake of Newtown," *Reader Supported News*, December 18, 2012, http://readersupportednews.org/opinion2/265-34 /15098-a-response-from-laurence-tribe-in-the-wake-of-newtown.

99 *"It is one thing to ransack the sources":* Jack Rakove, "The Second Amendment: The Highest Stage of Originalism," *Chicago-Kent Law Review*, no. 76 (2000): 103.

100 *"she is not a member":* Antonin Scalia, *A Matter of Interpretation: Federal Courts and the Law* (Princeton: Princeton University Press, 1997), 137, fn. 13.

101 *Carl Bogus fact-checked the justice:* Bogus, "The History and Politics of Second Amendment Scholarship," 5. Malcolm is now the Patrick Henry Professor of the Constitution and the Second Amendment at George Mason University Law School.

101 *"Mr. Halbrook does not recognize":* Wills, "To Keep and Bear Arms," citing Stephen P. Halbrook, *A Right to Bear Arms* (Westport: Greenwood, 1989), 101. Wills adds: "The author had published this argument five years earlier in his book *That Every Man Be Armed: The Evolution of a Constitutional Right* (University of New Mexico Press, 1984), 219, and no scholar of the movement had the heart (or perhaps the head) to correct him in the interval." www.nybooks.com/articles/archives/1995/sep/21 /to-keep-and-bear-arms/?pagination=false.

101 *declaration from Patrick Henry:* Reynolds, "A Critical Guide to the Second Amendment," 469.

101 *A $10,000 gift*: www.nraam.org/downloads/COAV_2013BenefitsTable.pdf.

101 *"Historical research demonstrates"*: Don B. Kates, "Gun Control: Separating Reality from Symbolism," *Journal of Contemporary Law* 20 (1984): 362. Others citing the same Jefferson quote include Scott A. Henderson, "*U.S. v. Emerson*: The Second Amendment as an Individual Right—Time to Settle the Issue," *West Virginia Law Review* 102 (1999): 201; L. A. Powe, Jr., "Guns, Words, and Constitutional Interpretation," *William and Mary Law Review* 38 (1997): 1358; Randy E. Barnett and Don B. Kates, "Under Fire: The New Consensus on the Second Amendment," *Emory Law Journal* 45 (1996): 1216; Anthony J. Dennis, "Clearing the Smoke From the Right to Bear Arms and the Second Amendment," *Akron Law Review* 29 (1995): 57; David Kopel, "Lawyers, Guns, and Burglars," *Arizona Law Review* 47 (2001): 356.

101 *Jefferson was not talking about guns:* The error is gleefully pointed out by David Thomas Konig, "Thomas Jefferson's Armed Citizenry and the Republican Militia," *Albany Government Law Review* 1 (2008): 261. Jefferson's letter to Washington is available at "Thomas Jefferson to George Washington, 19 June 1796," Founders Online, National Archives, http://founders.archives. gov/documents/Washington/99-01-02-00633. "While on the subject of papers permit me to ask one from you," Jefferson asked Washington, explaining that he had given handwritten letters about a disagreement among administration officials to political foes. "I have often thought of asking this one or a copy of it back from you, but have not before written on subjects of this kind to you. Tho' I do not know that it will ever be of the least importance to me yet one loves to possess arms tho' they hope never to have occasion for them. They possess my paper in my own handwriting. It is just I should possess theirs."

101 *NRA website still included the quote:* NRA-Institute for Legislative Action, "Thomas Jefferson on the Right to Bear Arms," www.nraila.org/legal/articles /2003/thomas-jefferson-on-the-right-to-bear-a.aspx.

101 *T-shirt emblazoned:* Zazzle.com, www.zazzle.com/thomas_jefferson_one_loves _to_possess_arms_though_tshirt-235716198687802382.

102 *"Time after time"*: Wills, "To Keep and Bear Arms."

102 *Charlton Heston called the thesis "ludicrous"*: Charlton Heston, "Arming America," Letter to the Editor, *New York Times*, October 1, 2000, www.nytimes.com /2000/10/01/books/l-arming-america-266906.html.

102 *notes had been lost in a flood:* James Lindgren, "Fall from Grace: Arming America and the Bellesiles Scandal," *Yale Law Journal* 111 (2002): 2195. Lindgren was a researcher who did much to expose flaws in Bellesiles's work. A summary of the controversy is: Robert F. Worth, "Historian's Prizewinning Book on Guns Is Embroiled in a Scandal," *New York Times*, December 8, 2001, www.nytimes.com/2001/12/08/books/08GUNS.html?scp=3&sq=belles iles&st=cse; Robert F. Worth, "Prize for Book is Taken Back from Historian,"

New York Times, December 14, 2002, www.nytimes.com/2002/12/14/business
/media/14BOOK.html. See also Stanley N. Katz, Hannah H. Gray and Lau-
rel Thatcher Ulrich, "Report of the Investigative Committee in the Matter of
Michael Bellesiles," Emory University, July 10, 2002, www.emory.edu/news
/Releases//Final_Report.

102 *Bellesiles turned up in Connecticut:* Jen Matteis, "Michael Bellesiles: Bartender, Writer, History Buff," *Valley Courier*, September 7, 2012, www.
theday.com/article/20120917/NWS10/309209649/-1/zip06details&town=
Valley-courier&template=zip06art.

CHAPTER SIX: CONTEST FOR THE CONSTITUTION

103 *tradition of judicial review:* Popular acceptance of judicial review, though,
has waxed and waned throughout American history. See generally Larry D.
Kramer, *The People Themselves: Popular Constitutionalism and Judicial Review*
(New York: Oxford University Press, 2004), especially 207–26.

104 Marbury v. Madison: The history and import of the case are described in Cliff
Sloan and David McKean, *The Great Decision: Jefferson, Adams, Marshall and the
Battle for the Supreme Court* (New York: PublicAffairs, 2009).

104 *the Lochner Era: Lochner v. New York*, 198 U.S. 405 (1905).

104 *"Brandeis brief"*: Melvin Urofsky, *Louis D. Brandeis: A Life* (New York: Random
House, 2009), 216.

104 *"we must ever be on our guard": New State Ice Co. v. Liebmann*, 285 U.S. 262, 311
(1932) (Brandeis, J., dissenting).

105 *"If my fellow citizens"*: Oliver Wendell Holmes to Harold J. Laski, March 4,
1920, in Mark de Wolfe Howe, ed., *Holmes-Laski Letters*, vol. 1, abridged by
Alger Hiss (New York: Atheneum, 1963), 194.

105 *Conservative judges' impulse to intervene:* The definitive recent history of the Supreme Court's fight with the New Deal is Jeff Shesol, *Supreme Power: Franklin
Roosevelt vs. the Supreme Court* (New York: W. W. Norton, 2010).

105 *"With the decisive triumph"*: Bruce A. Ackerman, "Beyond *Carolene Products*,"
Harvard Law Review 98 (1984–85): 714.

105 *Justice Harlan Fiske Stone made clear: United States v. Carolene Products Co.*, 304
U.S. 144, fn. 4 (1938).

105 *It set the Court off:* Robert M. Cover, "The Origins of Judicial Activism in the
Protections of Minorities," *Yale Law Journal* 91, no. 7 (1981–82): 1287; David
A. Strauss, "Is *Carolene Products* Obsolete," *University of Illinois Law Review*
2010, no. 4 (2010): 1251. "The *Carolene Products* footnote," Strauss wrote, "was
the Court's first—and maybe only—attempt to say, systematically, when the
courts should declare laws unconstitutional."

105 *the era of the Warren Court: Gideon v. Wainwright*, 372 U.S. 335 (1963); *New
York Times v. Sullivan*, 376 U.S. 254 (1964); *Reynolds v. Sims*, 377 U.S. 533
(1964); *Griswold v. Connecticut*, 381 U.S. 479 (1965); *Miranda v. Arizona*, 384

U.S. 436 (1966). The key abortion decision came after Earl Warren retired and was replaced by the more conservative Warren Burger: *Roe v. Wade*, 410 U.S. 113 (1973).

106 *constitutional common law:* See David A. Strauss, *The Living Constitution* (New York: Oxford University Press, 2010).

106 *"[When] we are dealing with words":* Missouri v. Holland, 252 U.S. 416, 433–34 (1920).

107 Roe *was mistakenly decided:* Ruth Bader Ginsburg, "Some Thoughts on Autonomy and Equality in Relation to *Roe v. Wade*," *North Carolina Law Review* 63 (1984–85): 375.

107 *Barack Obama, as a young law lecturer:* The interview is available at www .youtube.com/watch?v=OkpdNtTgQNM. A partial transcript is available at Michael Dobbs, "Obama's Redistribution 'Bombshell,'" washingtonpost.com, October 27, 2008. In the heat of the presidential race, Senator John McCain's campaign had charged the interview proved then Senator Obama wanted to use the courts to redistribute wealth. The transcript showed Obama was actually making the opposite point.

107 *He wrote a strategy memo for the U.S. Chamber of Commerce:* Memorandum from Lewis F. Powell Jr. to Eugene B. Snydor Jr., "Attack on American Free Enterprise System," August 23, 1971. Available at Lewis B. Powell Archives, Washington and Lee University School of Law, http://law.wlu.edu/deptimages /Powell%20Archives/PowellMemorandumTypescript.pdf.

108 *numerous arguments:* For an explication of ways conservatives could have argued constitutionally other than originalism, see Cass R. Sunstein, *Radicals in Robes: Why Extreme Right-Wing Courts Are Wrong for America* (New York: Basic Books, 2005), 53–80. Also see "Debate on *Radicals in Robes*," in Steven G. Calabresi, ed., *Originalism: A Quarter-Century of Debate* (Washington, D.C.: Regnery, 2007), 287–96.

108 *One can read a constitutional provision:* See Laurence Tribe, *American Constitutional Law*, 3rd ed. (NY: Foundation Press, 2000).

109 *the conservative voice in the "troika":* See Lou Cannon, *President Reagan: The Role of a Lifetime* (New York: Simon & Schuster, 1991), 130–31.

109 *delayed his confirmation:* Ronald J. Ostrow, "Senate Confirms Meese, 63 to 31: New Attorney General 'Not Bitter at All' at Delay and 'Very Grateful,'" *Los Angeles Times*, February 24, 1985.

109 *address to the American Bar Association:* Attorney General Edwin Meese, III, "Speech Before the American Bar Association," Washington, D.C., July 19, 1985, in Calabresi, ed., *Originalism*, 52–53. Meese's speech (and the debate it caused) has had a lasting impact. See Lynette Clemetson, "Meese's Influence Looms in Today's Judicial Wars," *New York Times*, August 17, 2005, www.ny times.com/2005/08/17/politics/17meese.html?pagewanted=all.

110 *Brennan had accepted an invitation:* Seth Stern and Stephen Wermiel, *Justice Brennan: Liberal Champion* (Boston: Houghton Mifflin Harcourt, 2010), 504–5.

110 *"arrogance cloaked as humility":* Justice William J. Brennan Jr., "The Constitution of the United States: Contemporary Ratification," Speech to the Text and Teaching Symposium, Georgetown University, Washington, D.C., October 12, 1985, reprinted in *South Texas Law Review* 27 (1985): 433.

110 *"original understanding":* Robert H. Bork, *The Tempting of America: The Political Seduction of the Law* (New York: Simon & Schuster, 1990), 143.

111 *WWJMD?:* Josh Gerstein, "SCOTUS Candidate Karlan Wants 'Bold' Choice from Obama," *Politico,* May 1, 2009. Karlan's pithy gibe summarized her book critiquing originalism. See Goodwin Liu, Pamela S. Karlan, and Christopher H. Schroeder, *Keeping Faith with the Constitution* (Washington, D.C.: American Constitution Society for Law and Policy, 2009).

111 *unthinkingly bind later generations:* Critics deemed this the "dead hand" problem: why should the decisions of the dead bind the living? For a discussion of the rationales proffered, see Reva Siegel, "*Heller* and Originalism's Dead Hand—In Theory and Practice," *UCLA Law Review* 56 (2009): 1399.

111 *James Madison, after all, kept his journals secret:* Leonard W. Levy, *Original Intent and the Framers' Constitution* (New York: Macmillan, 1988), 1.

111 *"the fairest and most rational method":* William Blackstone, "Of the Nature of Laws in General," *Commentaries on the Laws of England: A Facsimile of the First Edition of 1765–1769,* Introduction, part two, page 59.

111 *"Mr. Dooley":* Levy, *Original Intent,* 322.

112 *We revere our founding documents:* Pauline Maier, *American Scripture: Making the Declaration of Independence* (New York: Alfred A. Knopf, 1997).

112 *Originalism became yet another mobilizing principle:* The power of originalism as an instrument of political mobilization is traced in Robert Post and Reva Siegel, "Originalism as a Political Practice: The Right's Living Constitution," *Fordham Law Review* 75 (2006–2007): 553. "Originalism is so powerfully appealing because conservatives have succeeded in fusing contemporary political concerns with authoritative constitutional narrative. This fusion of political concern and constitutional narrative is driven by a politics of restoration, which encourages citizens to preserve traditional forms of life they fear are threatened—threatened by modern mores and by a Court that has (mis)construed the Constitution to require social change."

113 *Its first gathering at Yale:* Associated Press, "Federal Judge Assails Supreme Court Rulings," *New York Times,* April 27, 1982.

113 *The Federalist Society did not bring:* An excellent history is Steven M. Teles, *The Rise of the Conservative Legal Movement* (Princeton: Princeton University Press, 2008).

113 *Antonin Scalia:* Joan Biskupic, *American Original: The Life and Constitution of Supreme Court Justice Antonin Scalia* (New York: Farrar, Straus & Giroux, 2009), 21.

114 *second highest court in America:* Thus it was all the more astonishing that President Barack Obama failed to successfully nominate a single judge for the D.C. Circuit in the first four and a half years of his presidency.

114 *"faint hearted originalist":* Antonin Scalia, "Originalism: The Lesser Evil," *University of Cincinnati Law Review* 56 (1989): 855.

114 *"If the law is to make":* Ibid.

115 *"If it is good, it is so":* Scalia, *A Matter of Interpretation*, 39.

115 *"the evolving standards of decency":* Ibid., 40.

115 *"As I have explained":* Ibid., 140.

115 *Asked to explain his pragmatism:* Dan Slater, "Justice Scalia Justifies His Jurisprudence: I Am Not a Nut," *Wall Street Journal*, April 8, 2008, http://blogs.wsj.com/law/2008/04/08/scalia-justifies-his-jurisprudence-i-am-not-a-nut/.

115 *"That way of putting it":* Strauss, *The Living Constitution*, 17.

116 *When O'Connor refused to cast the deciding vote:* Webster v. Reproductive Health Services, 492 U.S. 490, 532 (1989) (Scalia, J., dissenting in part, concurring in part).

116 *his episodic thrashing of colleagues:* Linda Greenhouse, "Justice Scalia Objects," "Opinionator" (blog), *New York Times*, March 9, 2011, http://opinionator.blogs.nytimes.com/2011/03/09/justice-scalia-objects/.

116 *"realized soon enough":* Biskupic, *American Original*, 131.

CHAPTER SEVEN: THE ROAD TO *HELLER*

117 *"The Right to Keep and Bear Arms":* United States Senate, Committee on the Judiciary, Subcommittee on the Constitution, *The Right to Keep and Bear Arms*, 97th Congress, February 1982, http://constitution.org/mil/rkba82.pdf.

117 *"the individual rights claim":* Siegel, "Dead or Alive," 224.

118 *commissioned a comprehensive strategy:* Office of Legal Policy, United States Department of Justice, The Constitution in the Year 2000: Choices Ahead in Constitutional Interpretation, October 11, 1988 (Washington, D.C.: Government Printing Office), www.scribd.com/doc/7888685/The-Constitution-in-the-year-2000-choices-ahead-in-constitutional-interpretation.

118 *Timothy Emerson:* The Emerson divorce saga is described by a supporter of his, Eugene Volokh, "Guns and the Constitution," *Wall Street Journal* (1999): A23, www2.law.ucla.edu/volokh/gunconst.htm.

118 *He insisted his Second Amendment right had been violated:* United States v. Timothy Joe Emerson, 46 F. Supp. 2d 598 (1999).

118 *Justice Department official confirmed:* Solicitor General Seth Waxman, August 22, 2000, www.nraila.org/Waxman.pdf.

118 *Ashcroft announced a major policy pivot:* Letter from Attorney General John Ashcroft to James Jay Baker, Executive Director, National Rifle Associa-

tion, Institute for Legislative Action, May 17, 2001, www.nraila.org/images
/Ashcroft.pdf.

119 *"broadly protects the rights of individuals":* Timothy Joe Emerson, Petition for
Certiorari, Brief for the United States in Opposition, May 2002, p. 20, n.
3, www.justice.gov/osg/briefs/2001/oresponses/2001-8780.resp.pdf. The significance of the brief is explained by Linda Greenhouse, "Justice Department
Reverses Policy on Meaning of Second Amendment," *New York Times,* May 7,
2002.

119 *73 percent of Americans:* Jeffrey M. Jones, "Public Believes Americans Have
Right to Own Guns: Nearly Three in Four Say Second Amendment Guarantees This Right," Gallup Organization, March 27, 2008, www.gallup.com/poll
/105721/public-believes-americans-right-own-guns.aspx.

119 *In 1959:* Jeffrey M. Jones, "Americans in Agreement with Supreme Court
on Gun Rights," Gallup Poll, June 26, 2008, conducted February 8–10, 2008,
www.gallup.com/poll/108394/americans-agreement-supreme-court-gun-
rights.aspx.

119 *Second Amendment right began to become synonymous with opposition to gun control:* According to a Lexis-Nexis search conducted for this book:

Mentioned in News Articles: *New York Times*

YEAR	GUN CONTROL	SECOND AMENDMENT
1986	25	6
1993	388	16
1999	680	54
2002	307	50
2008	160	59

Mentioned in News Articles: *Washington Post*

YEAR	GUN CONTROL	SECOND AMENDMENT
1986	109	4
1993	440	24
1999	674	50
2002	468	61
2008	304	154

July 31, 2013, Lexis-Nexis.

119 *gun law passed by the local government in Washington, D.C.:* The law required residents to keep lawfully owned firearms "unloaded and disassembled or bound
by trigger lock or similar device." D.C. Code, sec. 7-2507.02 (2001).

119 *Robert Levy was a technology entrepreneur:* Paul Duggan, "Lawyer Who Wiped Out D.C. Ban Says It's About Liberties, Not Guns," *Washington Post*, March 18, 2007.

119 *The NRA tried to sideswipe the effort:* Tony Mauro, "Both Sides Fear Firing Blanks if D.C. Gun Case Reaches High Court," *Legal Times*, July 30, 2007, www.law.com/jsp/article.jsp?id=1185527215310&slreturn=20130613111444.

119 *tried to persuade Congress:* The District of Columbia also was hobbled by odd squabbles among its lawyers. Just weeks before the argument, city officials pushed aside Alan Morrison, the highly capable lawyer preparing to present its case, and brought in former acting solicitor general Walter Dellinger. A top constitutional lawyer, Dellinger had little time to prepare his argument. The story of the case, and the fratricide on both sides, is skillfully told in Marcia Coyle, *The Roberts Court: The Struggle for the Constitution* (New York: Simon & Schuster, 2013), 123–96. See also Winkler, *Gun Fight*. A summary of the litigation is in Brian Doherty, *Gun Control on Trial: Inside the Supreme Court Battle over the Second Amendment* (Washington, D.C.: Cato Institute, 2009), a partisan but useful account published by the group now chaired by one of Dick Heller's lawyers.

120 *Solicitor General Paul Clement equivocated: United States v. Dick Anthony Heller*, Brief of United States as Amicus Curiae, 07-290, www.scotusblog.com /wp-content/uploads/2008/01/us-heller-brief-1-11-08.pdf.

120 *Conservatives pounced:* Robert Barnes, "Administration Rankles Some with Stance in Handgun Case," *Washington Post*, January 20, 2008, www.washington post.com/wp-dyn/content/article/2008/01/19/AR2008011902231.html; Robert Novak, "Gun Battle at the White House?," *Washington Post*, March 13, 2008, www.washingtonpost.com/wp-dyn/content/article/2008/03/12/ AR2008031203396.html?hpid%3Dopinionsbox1&sub=AR. The intramural controversy was ably covered in Dahlia Lithwick, "Paul Clement Becomes the Target in the Legal Showdown over Guns," *Slate*, March 18, 2008, www.slate.com/articles/news_and_politics/jurisprudence/2008/03/moving _targets.html.

120 *Vice President Dick Cheney filed his own far more adamant brief:* www.gura possessky.com/news/parker/documents/07-290bsacMembersUSSenate.pdf. The Cheney-congressional brief was authored by Stephen Halbrook, who quotes his own scholarship four times as authority.

120 *At the argument before the justices:* Quotes are from transcript of argument, *District of Columbia v. Heller*, United States Supreme Court, March 18, 2008. 2008 U.S. Trans. LEXIS 22.

121 *Supreme Court issued its ruling: District of Columbia v. Heller*, 554 U.S. 570 (2008).

121 *It remains Scalia's most important majority opinion:* Jeffrey Toobin, *The Nine: Inside the Secret World of the Supreme Court* (New York: Anchor; rev. ed., 2008), 409.

121 *"is naturally divided": Heller*, 554 U.S. at 577.

121 *a surprising way to deal with that prefatory clause: Heller*, 554 U.S. at 578.

122 *"We start therefore": Heller*, 554 U.S. at 581.

122 *"At the time of the founding": Heller*, 554 U.S. at 584.

122 "The phrase 'bear arms'": *Heller*, 554 U.S. at 586. Internal citation omitted.

122 *"Giving 'bear Arms'":* Ibid.

123 *"It would be rather like saying": Heller*, 554 U.S at 587.

123 *"Putting all of these textual elements together": Heller*, 554 U.S. at 592.

123 "There seems to be no doubt": *Heller*, 554 U.S. at 595 (internal citation omitted).

123 *precisely one page: Heller*, 554 U.S. at 596. It cites a thoughtful essay by UCLA's, Eugene Volokh, "Necessary to the Security of a Free State," *Notre Dame Law Review* 83, no. 1 (2007). Volokh quotes Montesquieu, David Hume, and other Enlightenment thinkers who use "state" or "free state" to mean government. But the Framers of the Constitution referred to themselves as the United States: they jealously were guarding the sovereignty of those very governments.

123 *the word "state": Heller*, 554 U.S. at 597.

124 *It strolls through contemporary state constitutions:* Scalia also includes Vermont. That state's charter mirrored the Pennsylvania version that included the right of personal defense. But Vermont was a separate republic at the time the Bill of Rights was drafted. It did not join the United States until 1791. *Heller*, 554 U.S. at 601.

125 *"type of weapon at issue": Heller*, 554 U.S. at 622.

125 *"unsurprising that such a significant matter": Heller*, 554 U.S. at 625.

125 "Like most rights": *Heller*, 554 U.S. at 626.

126 *"it may be true": Heller*, 554 U.S. at 628.

126 *an outlier: Heller*, 554 U.S. at 629.

127 *"Scalia translated a right":* Jeffrey Toobin, *The Oath: The Obama White House and the Supreme Court* (New York: Random House, 2012), 114.

127 *"The Sceond Amendment was adopted": Heller*, 554 U.S. at 637 (Stevens, J., dissenting).

128 *Stevens made a consequential strategic choice:* Judge Richard Posner writes, "By delving into the eighteenth-century historical materials [Stevens] implicitly conceded the legitimacy of the conservative Justices' 'originalist' approach. He threw in the theoretical towel. He may well have the better of the historical case, but who will notice?" Richard A. Posner, "The Rise and Fall of Judicial Self- Restraint," *California Law Review* 100, no. 3 (2012): 549. Posner's article is adapted from his Brennan Center Jorde Lecture of October 2010.

128 *"the* beginning *rather than the* end*": Heller*, 554 U.S. 687 (Breyer, J., dissenting).

128 *hundreds of state Supreme Court decisions:* Breyer cites Adam Winkler, "Scrutinizing the Second Amendment," *Michigan Law Review* 105 (2007): 683.

128 *the overarching theme of the Constitution:* Breyer calls "originalism" (in interpret-
    ing the Constitution) and "textualism" (in interpreting statutes) both "literalism."
    He writes, "Literalism has a tendency to undermine the Constitution's efforts
    to create a framework for democratic government—a government that, while
    protecting basic individual liberties, permits citizens to govern themselves, and
    to govern themselves effectively. Insofar as a more literal interpretive approach
    undermines this basic objective, it is inconsistent with the most fundamental
    original intention of the Framers themselves." Stephen Breyer, *Active Liberty:
    Interpreting Our Democratic Constitution* (New York: Random House, 2005),
    131–32.

128 *The New York Times gave it one sentence:* The *Times*'s long-standing and es-
    teemed Supreme Court correspondent later offered a "mea culpa." See Linda
    Greenhouse, "Weighing Needs and Burdens: Justice Breyer's *Heller* Dissent,"
    Syracuse Law Review 59 (2008): 300.

129 *misquoting Patrick Henry:* A photo of Dick Heller after the decision can be
    found at www.nytimes.com/imagepages/2009/03/17/us/17bar_ready.html.

129 *"vindication of originalism":* Coyle, *The Roberts Court*, 163.

129 *Reva Siegel argued in a brilliant article:* Siegel, "Dead or Alive," 191.

129 *even if "hundreds of judges":* Heller, 554 U.S. 570, 624, n. 24 (2008).

129 *it can be appropriate for a court to recognize a right:* Cass R. Sunstein, "Second
    Amendment Minimalism: *Heller* as *Griswold*," *Harvard Law Review* 122
    (2008): 261–62.

130 *Certainly it would have prompted an uproar:* A point made by Sunstein, ibid., 208.

130 *This new school of liberal scholars:* See, for example, Barry Friedman, *The Will of
    the People: How Public Opinion Has Influenced the Supreme Court and Shaped the
    Meaning of the Constitution* (New York: Farrar, Straus & Giroux, 2009); Robert
    Post and Reva Siegel, *"Roe* Rage: Democratic Constitutionalism and Backlash,"
    Harvard Civil Rights-Civil Liberties Law Review 42 (2007): 373–433; Reva
    Siegel, "2005–06 Brennan Center Symposium Lecture, Constitutional Culture,
    Social Movement Conflict and Constitutional Change: The Case of the de
    facto ERA," *California Law Review* 94 (2006): 1323–1419; Kramer, *The People
    Themselves.*

131 *President George W. Bush had interviewed:* Elisabeth Bumiller, "An Interview by,
    Not with, the President," *New York Times,* July 21, 2005.

131 *"After decades of criticizing":* J. Harvie Wilkinson III, "Of Guns, Abortions,
    and the Unraveling Rule of Law," *Virginia Law Review* 95, no. 2 (2009): 253,
    264–65.

131 *Posner is one of America's leading public intellectuals:* See Richard A. Posner,
    Public Intellectuals: A Study of Decline (Cambridge: Harvard University Press,
    2002). Posner's list of leading public intellectuals is on page 209. He made
    number 70.

131 *"It is questionable":* Richard A. Posner, "In Defense of Looseness," *The New Republic*, August 27, 2008, www.newrepublic.com/article/books /defense-looseness.

132 *Posner's review:* Richard A. Posner, "The Incoherence of Antonin Scalia," *The New Republic*, September 13, 2012, www.tnr.com/article/magazine/books-and -arts/106441/scalia-garner-reading-the-law-textual-originalism.

132 *"simply, to put it bluntly, a lie":* Richard A. Posner, "Richard Posner Responds to Antonin Scalia's Accusation of Lying," "The Plank" (blog), *The New Republic*, September 20, 2012, www.newrepublic.com/blog/plank/107549 /richard-posner-responds-antonin-scalias-accusation-lying.

132 *"Words don't have intrinsic meanings":* Frank J. Easterbrook, foreword to *Reading Law: The Interpretation of Legal Texts* by Antonin Scalia and Bryan A. Garner (Minneapolis: West Publishing, 2012), xxv.

132 *"living political community":* Posner, "The Incoherence of Antonin Scalia."

133 *same five justices: Citizens United v. Federal Election Commission,* 558 U.S. 310 (2010). The case is analyzed in Monica Youn, ed., *Money, Politics and the Constitution: Beyond* Citizens United (New York: Century Foundation, 2011).

133 *"Sooner or later":* Edmund Morris, *Theodore Rex* (New York: Random House, 2001), 360.

133 *Roberts joined the majority: National Federation of Independent Business v. Sebelius,* 567 U.S. ___ (2012).

133 *"Lost Constitution":* Randy Barnett, *Restoring the Lost Constitution: The Presumption of Liberty* (Princeton: Princeton University Press, 2004).

134 *overturned the key provision of the Voting Rights Act: Shelby County v. Holder,* 570 U.S. ___ (2013).

134 *It poses severe challenges:* For a powerful early analysis, see Joseph Fishkin, *The Dignity of the South,* 123 *Yale Law Journal Online* 175 (2013), http://yalelaw journal.org/2013/06/08/fishkin.html.

134 *made clear their itch: Northwest Austin Municipal Utility District No. 1 v. Holder,* 557 U.S. 193 (2009).

134 *Roberts first sought a narrower ruling:* Toobin, *The Oath,* 167–68.

134 *The Court sprang multiple leaks:* Ibid., 287–91.

135 *"[We] have no power": United States v. Windsor,* 570 U.S. ___ (2013) (Scalia, J., dissenting).

135 *rare public rebuke:* Adam Liptak, "Court Is 'One of Most Activist,' Ginsburg Says, Vowing to Stay," *New York Times,* August 24, 2013.

135 *no more prone to strike down:* Lee Epstein and Andrew D. Martin, "Is the Roberts Court Especially Activist? A Study of Invalidating (and Upholding) Federal, State and Local Laws," *Emory Law Journal* 61 (2011): 737–58. They were responding to Posner, "The Rise and Fall of Judicial Self-Restraint," which

argued that in an earlier era both liberal and conservative judges were less likely to invalidate statutes.

136 *Its other public events:* James Madison Program in American Ideals and Institutions, Spring 2013 Calendar of Events, http://web.princeton.edu/sites/jmadison/calendar/current%202.html.

136 *"I don't apologize":* The speech and audience reaction are described in Ushma Patel, "Scalia Favors 'Enduring,' Not Living, Constitution," Princeton University Office of Information, posted December 11, 2012.

CHAPTER EIGHT: FROM *HELLER* TO SANDY HOOK

141 *noisy shooting late at night and early in the morning:* Summary of Newtown Police Department Gunshot Complaints, www.newtown-ct.gov/Public_Documents/NewtownCT_LegCouncilMin/ordinance/gunshot.pdf.

141 *hunters and gun activists crowded monthly meetings:* Nanci G. Hutson, "Town Ponders Target Shooting Limits," *Danbury News-Times*, www.newstimes.com/local/article/Town-ponders-target-shooting-limits-3794087.php#photo-3336959; Fred Musante, "Proposed Firearms Ordinance Scrapped by Committee," *Newtown Patch*, September 13, 2012, http://newtown.patch.com/groups/editors-picks/p/opponents-convince-committee-to-scrap-proposed-fireara04e81cf38.

141 *"This is a freedom that should never be taken away":* The unnerving saga of the gun fight in Newtown before the massacre is described in Michael Moss and Ray Riviera, "In Town at Ease with Its Firearms, Tightening Gun Rules Was Resisted," *New York Times*, December 16, 2012, www.nytimes.com/2012/12/17/nyregion/in-newtown-conn-a-stiff-resistance-to-gun-restrictions.html?pagewanted=all&_r=0.

142 *National Shooting Sports Foundation website seemed frozen in place:* "National Shooting Sports Foundation," accessed July 19, 2013, http://web.archive.org/web/20130115194748/http://nssf.org/Industry/.

142 *thirty thousand Americans die from guns:* "Firearm Injury in the U.S.," University of Pennsylvania Firearm and Injury Center, 2011, www.uphs.upenn.edu/ficap/resourcebook/pdf/monograph.pdf.

144 *Justice Samuel Alito wrote for the majority: McDonald v. Chicago*, 561 U.S. 3025 (2010).

144 *a slightly queasy argument:* Historian Eric Foner noted that Supreme Court jurisprudence is beholden to older, more racist accounts of Reconstruction, even as historians have thoroughly revised our understanding of what was intended by the framers of the Civil War amendments. The Court's conservatives rarely cite the new history, he notes, when it comes to civil rights laws. In *McDonald*, though, the majority embraced the expansive interpretation of the Fourteenth—while the liberals asserted *Cruikshank* was still good law. See Eric

Foner, "The Supreme Court and the History of Reconstruction—And Vice Versa," *Columbia Law Review* 112 (2011): 1603–4.

144 *"This is good for lawyers.":* "After Supreme Court Ruling, Cities Face Restructuring of Gun Laws," *PBS NewHour,* June 28, 2010, www.pbs.org/newshour /bb/law/jan-june10/guns2_06-28.html.

145 *Gun laws were upheld in all but two:* Only the two bans on loaded handguns at home, in Washington, D.C., and Chicago, were struck down. A third law was struck down on procedural due process grounds. See Tina Mehr and Adam Winkler, *The Standardless Second Amendment,* Issue Brief, American Constitution Society, October 2010.

145 *According to one tally:* See "Post *Heller* Litigation Summary," Law Center to Prevent Violence, updated May 20, 2013, http://smartgunlaws.org/post-heller-litigation-summary/; Brian Doherty, "The Second Amendment Cases the Supreme Court Doesn't Want to Hear," Reason.com, February 9, 2012, http:// reason.com/blog/2012/02/09/the-second-amendment-cases-the-supreme-c.

145 *As Justice Holmes wrote: Schenck v. United States* 249 U.S. 47 (1919) (Holmes, J., dissenting). The popular paraphrase often neglects the key modifier: one cannot *falsely* shout fire in a crowded theater. Shouting fire in a theater that is actually in flames is another matter.

146 *multiple justifications for gun regulations:* Eugene Volokh, "Implementing the Right To Keep and Bear Arms for Self-Defense: An Analytical Framework and a Research Agenda", *U.C.L.A. Law Review* 56 (2009): 1443.

146 *Another professor:* Mark Tushnet, "Permissible Gun Regulations After *Heller*: Speculation About Methods and Outcomes," *U.C.L.A. Law Review* 56 (2009): 1425.

146 *That is just what most courts have done:* Cases applying this two-pronged approach are collected in *Woolard v. Galagher,* 712 F.3d 865, fn. 23 (4th Cir. 2013).

146 *"need not establish a close fit":* U.S. v. Staten, 578 F.3d 803 (2010).

146 *the case of a Meadville, Pennsylvania, man: U.S. v. Marzzarella,* 614 F.3d 85 (2010).

146 *Myriad cases used similar logic and language:* For some examples of how the circuit courts have handled cases challenging state and federal gun control statutes post-*Heller,* see *United States v. Carpio-Leon,* 701 F.3d 974 (4th Cir. 2012) (upholding federal law barring possession of firearms by persons illegally or unlawfully in the United States); *Moore v. Madigan,* 702 F.3d 933 (7th Cir. 2012) (striking down Illinois's complete prohibition on carrying firearms in public); *NRA v. ATF,* 700 F.3d 185 (5th Cir. 2012) (upholding federal law banning the sale of handguns to persons under twenty-one); *Hightower v. City of Boston,* 693 F.3d 61 (1st Cir. 2012) (upholding Boston law limiting the right to carry a concealed weapon in public to certain licensed individuals);

Georgiacarry.org v. Georgia, 687 F.3d 1244 (11th Cir. 2012) (upholding Georgia law prohibiting possession of firearms in specific sensitive locations, such as bars and churches, without management's permission); *United States v. Decastro*, 682 F.3d 160 (2d Cir. 2012) (upholding federal law banning transportation of firearms across state lines); *United States v. Masciandaro*, 638 F.3d 458 (4th Cir. 2011) (upholding law banning firearms in vehicles in national parks); *Ezell v. City of Chicago*, 651 F.3d 684 (7th Cir. 2011) (striking down a Chicago law banning firing ranges in the city); *United States v. Reese*, 627 F.3d 792 (10th Cir. 2010) (upholding ban on firearm possession by a person subject to a domestic order of protection); *United States v. Williams*, 616 F.3d 685 (7th Cir. 2010) (upholding law banning firearm possession by felons); *United States v. Skoen*, 614 F.3d 636 (7th Cir. 2010) (upholding the federal prohibition on firearm possession by persons convicted of domestic violence misdemeanors).

147 *But those moves now might be limited by a right:* The idea of "rights as trumps" has been advanced by Ronald Dworkin, *Taking Rights Seriously* (Cambridge: Harvard University Press, 1978). It has been criticized as elevating the individual over the needs of society in myriad contexts. See Mary Ann Glendon, *Rights Talk: The Impoverishment of Political Discourse* (New York: Free Press, 1991).

147 *the Sullivan Act: Kachalsky v. Cacace*, 701 F.3d 81 (2d Cir. 2012).

147 *"a special need for self protection": Kachalsky*, 701 F.3d at 86 (internal quotes and citations omitted).

147 *The Second Circuit Court of Appeals rejected that bid:* Unlike the Supreme Court, the Second Circuit Court of Appeals is known for rulings across partisan or ideological lines. See Monica Youn, *Judge Sotomayor's Record in Constitutional Cases* (New York: Brennan Center for Justice, 2009).

147 *"important governmental interest'": Kachalsky*, 701 F.3d at 100.

147 *"picked out one particular kind of arm": People ex. Rel. Darling v. Warden of City Prisons*, 154 A.D. 413, 422 (1st Dep't 1913).

148 *"the unwisdom of the Supreme Court's recent decisions":* Richard Posner, "Gun Control—Posner's Comment," *The Becker-Posner Blog*, February 20, 2011, accessed July 17, 2013, www.becker-posner-blog.com/2011/02/gun-control-posners-comment.html. He gathered his critique in his 2013 volume, Richard A. Posner, *Reflections on Judging* (Cambridge: Harvard University Press, 2013), 185–86.

148 *"The Supreme Court rejected the argument": Moore v. Madigan*, 702 F.3d 933, 935 (2012).

148 *"Twenty-first century Illinois":* Ibid., 937.

149 *verged on satire:* Writing on the *Atlantic* website, Garrett Epps scolded Posner. The opinion was "unforgivably flippant in its treatment of what is

literally a life-and-death issue in every city and state in the nation." Epps pointed to this line from the ruling: "[The Second Amendment right] is not a property right—a right to kill a house-guest who in a fit of aesthetic fury tries to slash your copy of Norman Rockwell's painting *Santa with Elves*." He says Posner's friends suggested he was being ironic, given his well-publicized criticisms of *Heller*. "Posner may be having us on. If so, however, his satiric intentions do not render the opinion defensible." Garrett Epps, "Seventh Circuit's Big Chance to Redeem Itself on Gun Control," TheAtlantic.com, January 15, 2013, www.theatlantic.com/national /archive/2013/01/the-seventh-circuits-big-chance-to-redeem-itself-on-gun-control/267206/.

149 *On Father's Day weekend 2013:* Peter Nickeas, David Jackson, Mitch Smith, and Jennifer Delgado, "Weekend Violence Leaves 9 Dead, 47 Shot," *Chicago Tribune*, June 17, 2013, http://articles.chicagotribune.com/2013-06-17/news/chi-chicago-crime-shooting-gun-violence-marquette-park_1 _weekend-violence-little-village-neighborhood-day-sunday.

149 *"That's the difference":* Staff report, "8 Shot in Single West Side Attack Among 67 Shot over Long Weekend," Chicagotribune.com, July 7, 2013, http:// articles.chicagotribune.com/2013-07-07/news/chi-chicago-violence-july-6july-7-20130706_1_west-flournoy-street-drive-by-shooting-west-side.

149 *They crafted a bill that allowed Illinois citizens:* Ray Long, Monique Garcia, and Rick Pearson, "General Assembly Overrides Governor's Veto of Concealed Carry Bill," *Chicago Tribune*, July 9, 2013, http://articles. chicagotribune.com/2013-07-09/news/chi-illinois-concealed-carry_1 _harrisburg-democrat-gun-bill-quinn.

149 *"The lower courts have essentially made judicial restraint their guiding principle":* Allen Rostron, "Justice Breyer's Triumph in the Third Battle over the Second Amendment," *George Washington Law Review* 80, no.3 (2011–2012): 703.

150 *"In my view": Heller v. District of Columbia*, 670 F.3rd 1244 (2011) (Kavanaugh, J., dissenting).

151 *NRA members boycotted its products:* Paul M. Barrett, "Why Gun Makers Fear the NRA," *Bloomberg Businessweek*, March 14, 2013, www.businessweek.com /articles/2013-03-14/why-gun-makers-fear-the-nra.

151 *law providing broad immunity from lawsuits:* Protection of Lawful Commerce in Arms Act (PLCAA). Public Law 109–92.

151 *Manufacturers quietly began to provide substantial funding:* Barrett, "Why Gun Makers Fear the NRA."

151 *Around the country, trends were even more pronounced:* Eugene Volokh, "Chicago: From a Handgun Ban to a Right to Carry Concealed Handguns," *The Volokh Conspiracy*, July 10, 2013, www.volokh.com/2013/07/10/chicago-from-a-handgun-ban-to-a-right-to-carry-concealed-handguns/.

152 *Stand Your Ground:* Abby Goodnough, "Florida Expands Right to Use Deadly Force in Self-Defense," *New York Times,* April 27, 2005; Florida Statutes §776.013, Justifiable Use of Force, www.leg.state.fl.us/statutes/index.cfm?App _mode=Display_Statute&URL=0700-0799/0776/Sections/0776.013.html.

152 *NRA focused on judicial nominations:* Linda Greenhouse, "The NRA at the Bench," "The Opinionator" (blog), *New York Times,* December 26, 2012, http:// opinionator.blogs.nytimes.com/2012/12/26/the-n-r-a-at-the-bench/.

152 *Elena Kagan:* Garance Franke-Rutka, "Justice Kagan and Justice Scalia Are Hunting Buddies—Really," TheAtlantic.com, June 30, 2013.

152 *Voters overwhelmingly voted to change their state's charter:* Louisiana Constitution, Article One, Sec. 11, Acts 2012, No. 874, §1, approved November 6, 2012, eff. December 10, 2012.

153 *A judge overturned Draughter's conviction:* Claire Galofaro, "New Orleans Judge Rules Statute Forbidding Felons from Having Firearms Unconstitutional After 'Fundamental Right' Amendment," *New Orleans Times-Picayune,* March 20, 2013, www.nola.com/crime/index.ssf/2013/03/new_orleans_judge _rules_statut.html. See also Claire Galofaro, "Gun Rights Amendment Helping Felons Charged with Illegal Gun Possession," *New Orleans Times-Picayune,* March 8, 2013, www.nola.com/crime/index.ssf/2013/03/guns_rights _amendment_helping.html; *State v. Draughter,* Criminal Court for the Parish of Orleans, March 21, 2013, Case No. 512-135. The State Supreme Court will likely rule on an appeal by prosecutors.

153 *cases swamped the courts:* Rick Jervis, "Louisiana Law Floods Courts with Pro Gun Cases," *USA Today,* March 20, 2013, http://m.usatoday.com/article /news/2035561. Of course, courts may rule that there must be a tighter link between the previous felonious conduct and the risk of violence. Someone who has been convicted of a nonviolent crime (e.g., possession of marijuana) may pose less risk of violence than someone who has been convicted of assault, for example.

153 *A proposed law to require guns to be stored safely:* Claire Galofaro, "Child Gun Deaths Shake Louisiana Communities," Associated Press, July 14, 2013, www.sfgate.com/news/crime/article/Child-gun-deaths-shake-Louisiana- communities-4664566.php#page-1.

154 *referring to "existing law" three times:* The White House, "Press Gaggle by Press Secretary Jay Carney en route Aurora CO," July 22, 2012, www.whitehouse.gov/the-press- office/2012/07/22/press-gaggle-press-secretary-jay-carney-en-route-aurora- co-72212.

154 *"conspiracy to ensure re-election":* Sean Lengell, "NRA Official: Obama Wants to Outlaw Guns in 2nd Term," *Washington Times,* February 10, 2012. For a video and transcript of LaPierre's speech to the Conservative Political Action Conference (CPAC), see NRA News, www.nranews.com/resources/video /wayne-lapierre-at-cpac-2012/list/lapierre-speeches.

154 *the worst day of his presidency:* Jonathan Alter, *The Center Holds: Obama and His Enemies* (New York: Simon & Schuster, 2013), 37–3.

154 *"It's the first time":* James Warren, "The Worst Day: Newtown Massacre Made Obama Cry Twice," New York *Daily News*, April 30, 2013. David Axelrod described the email in a public talk.

154 *"We will be told":* Remarks by the president at Sandy Hook Interfaith Prayer Vigil, Newtown High School, Newtown, Connecticut. December 16, 2012.

155 *Biden's task force reported its recommendations:* Remarks by the president and the vice president on Gun Violence, the White House, January 16, 2013, www.whitehouse .gov/the-press-office/2013/01/16/remarks-president-and-vice-president-gun -violence.

155 *But evidence is debatable at best:* Colin Loftin et al., "Mandatory Sentencing and Firearms Violence: Evaluating an Alternative to Gun Control," *Law & Society Review* 17 (1983): 287; Paul G. Cassell, "Too Severe?: A Defense of the Federal Sentencing Guidelines (and a Critique of Federal Mandatory Mini-mums)," *Stanford Law Review* 56 (2004): 1017.

155 *risks repeating errors:* Inimai Chettiar, "In the War on Guns, Let's Not Repeat History," *The Nation*, January 30, 2013.

155 *25 percent of its prisoners:* Roy Walmsley, *World Prison Population List*, International Centre for Prison Studies (2013).

156 *it was blocked by a filibuster:* Brad Plumer,"Senate Bill to Extend Background Checks Killed by Filibuster," "Wonkblog," *Washington Post*, April 17, 2013, www.washingtonpost.com/blogs/wonkblog/wp/2013/04/17/senate-bill-to -extend-gun-background-checks-killed-by-filibuster/.

156 *The AR-15:* Natasha Singer, "The Most Wanted Gun in America," *New York Times*, February 2, 2013, www.nytimes.com/2013/02/03/business/the-ar -15-the-most-wanted-gun-in-america.html.

156 *it had shown limited impact:* See, e.g., Christopher S. Koper, "An Updated Assess-ment of the Federal Assault Weapons Ban: Impacts on Gun Markets and Gun Violence, 1994–2003," Report to the National Institute of Justice, United States Department of Justice, Jerry Lee Center of Criminology, University of Pennsyl-vania, June 2004; Michael Luo and Michael Cooper, "Lessons in Politics and Fine Print in Assault Weapons Ban of '90s," *New York Times*, December 20, 2012, A1.

157 *"It seems to me":* The confrontation between Senators Cruz and Feinstein is available in David Frum, "Dianne Feinstein Won't Abide Ted Cruz," *Daily Beast*, March 14, 2013, www.thedailybeast.com/articles/2013/03/14/dianne -feinstein-won-t-abide-ted-cruz.html.

158 *The Fourth Amendment applies:* For a discussion of the Fourth Amendment, see Stephen J. Schulhofer, *More Essential Than Ever: The Fourth Amendment in the Twenty-First Century* (New York: Oxford University Press, 2012).

158 *"The central message of Heller":* Laurence H. Tribe, "Protecting Communities

While Respecting the Second Amendment," Prepared testimony before the Committee on the Judiciary, Subcommittee on the Constitution, Civil Rights and Human Rights, United States Senate, February 12, 2013, 4, www.judiciary .senate.gov/pdf/2-12-13TribeTestimony.pdf.

158 *Robert Levy, the Cato Institute chair:* "Robert A. Levy on Gun Rights After Newtown Shooting," *Washington Post,* January 10, 2013, http:// articles.washingtonpost.com/2013-01-10/lifestyle/36272630_1 _assault-weapons-high-capacity-magazines-military-style-guns.

159 *"closing in fast on your Right to Keep and Bear Arms":* Eric Lach, "NRA Warns Members That Confiscation Could Be Next," Talking Points Memo, January 17, 2013.

159 *"Justice Scalia": Morning Joe,* MSNBC, transcript, January 9, 2013.

159 *"The first foundational principle":* Vice President Joseph R. Biden Jr., Remarks to the U.S. Conference of Mayors, January 17, 2013.

159 *when justices have issued a ruling to limit affirmative action:* An example: in 1995, the Supreme Court applied "strict scrutiny" to racial classifications used by the federal government, in that case as they applied to government contractors owned by "socially and economically disadvantaged individuals." *Adarand Constructors, Inc. v. Pena,* 515 U.S. 200 (1995). This came at a time of fierce pressure on the Clinton administration to end minority business preferences altogether, and amid a government-wide review of affirmative action. Clinton keyed off the ruling, announcing his goal on affirmative action was "mend it, don't end it." George Stephanopoulos wrote, "We finally came to see our decision had been made by the Court." George Stephanopoulos, *All Too Human* (New York: Little, Brown, 1999), 369. See also Christopher Edley, *Not All Black and White: Affirmative Action and American Values* (New York: Hill & Wang, 2008).

CHAPTER NINE: FLYING BLIND

161 *270 million civilian firearms:* Aaron Karp, "Estimating Civilian Owned Firearms," Small Arms Survey Research Notes, no. 9, September 2011, 2, www .smallarmssurvey.org.

161 *Every decade, gun ownership rates have slid:* Sabrina Tavernese and Robert Gebeloff, "Share of Homes with Guns Shows 4-Decade Decline," *New York Times,* March 20, 2013, www.nytimes.com/2013/03/10/us/rate-of-gun -ownership-is-down-survey-shows.html?ref=todayspaper&_r=0. *The New York Times* report relies on the General Social Survey, a biennial survey that asks about gun ownership. The Gallup Organization estimates a higher number of gun owners, but shows a similar drop. See also Philip J. Cook and Jens Ludwig, *Guns in America: Results of a National Comprehensive Survey on Firearms Ownership and Use,* National Institute of Justice Research Brief, 12, table 2.3 (1996), www.ncjrs.gov/pdffiles/165476.pdf.

162 *"Although there is little difference":* Daniel Webster et al., *The Case for Gun Policy Reforms in America,* Johns Hopkins Center for Gun Policy and Research, Johns Hopkins Bloomberg School of Public Health (October 2012), 2; Erin Richardson and David Hemenway, "Homicide, suicide, and unintentional firearm mortality: comparing the United States with other high-income countries, 2003," *Journal of Trauma* 70 (2011): 238–243.

162 *gun violence is declining:* D'Vera Cohn, Paul Taylor, Mark Hugo Lopez, Catherine A. Gallagher, Kim Parker, and Kevin T. Maas, "Gun Homicide Rate Down 49% Since 1993 Peak; Public Unaware," Pew Research Center, May 7, 2013, www.pewsocialtrends.org/2013/05/07/gun-homicide-rate-down-49-since-1993-peak-public-unaware/; Bureau of Justice Statistics, National Crime Victim Survey, National Institute of Justice, April 4, 2013, www.nij.gov/topics /crime/gun-violence/.

162 *crime rates are dropping all over the Western world:* "Falling Crime: Where Have All the Burglars Gone," *The Economist,* July 20, 2013, www.economist.com /news/briefing/21582041-rich-world-seeing-less-and-less-crime-even-face-high-unemployment-and-economic.

162 *Criminologists and sociologists have studied, and debated:* See, e.g., Steven Levitt, "Understanding Why Crime Fell in the 1990s: Four Factors That Explain the Decline and Six That Do Not," *Journal of Economic Perspectives* 18 (Winter 2004). Levitt finds that gun control laws have minimal impact on crime rates. The factors that contributed are more police, the rising prison population, the receding crack epidemic, and (controversially) the availability of legal abortion.

162 *A recent blue-ribbon panel:* Charles F. Wellford, John V. Pepper, and Carol V. Petrie, eds., *Firearms and Violence: A Critical Review* (Washington, D.C.: National Academies Press, 2005).

162 *Such studies are inconclusive:* To give a flavor of the debates: One study, conducted as an analysis of Washington, D.C.'s, restrictive handgun licensing, concluded it caused a prompt decline in homicides and suicides in the capital. Colin Loftin, David McDowall, Brian Wiersma, and Talbert Cottey, "Effects of Restrictive Licensing of Handguns on Homicide and Suicide in the District of Columbia," *New England Journal of Medicine* 325 (1991): 1615. Another study refuted that, noting that it had compared D.C. to neighboring states, rather than Baltimore, a city with similar economics and demography. That city's homicide rate had dropped even more dramatically. Chester Britt, David J. Bordua, and Gary Kleck, "A Reassessment of the D.C. Gun Law: Some Cautionary Notes on the Use of Interrupted Time Series Designs for Policy Impact Assignment," *Law & Society Review* 30 (1995): 361. One of the authors of the first study replied: in both cities, crime dropped, but in D.C. gun violence dropped further. David McDowall, Colin Loftin, and Brian Wiersema, "Using Quasi-Experiments to Evaluate Firearms Laws: Comment on Britt et al.'s Reassessment of the D.C. Gun Law," *Law & Society Review* 30 (1996): 381.

162 *The NRA, of course, has a theory:* See John R. Lott, Jr., *More Guns, Less Crime* (Chicago: University of Chicago Press, 1998).

162 *The book's thesis proved wildly controversial:* The tumult over John Lott's work is thoroughly discussed in Mark Tushnet, *Out of Range: Why the Constitution Can't End the Battle over Guns* (New York: Oxford University Press, 2007), 85–99. See also Chris Mooney, "Double Barreled Double Standards," *Mother Jones,* October 12, 2003, www.motherjones.com/politics/2003/10 /double-barreled-double-standards.

162 *found no credible evidence:* A National Research Council panel was convened to examine the data. Fifteen of the sixteen panel members concluded it was not possible to draw the conclusions from the data that Lott drew. See Committee to Improve Research Information and Data on Firearms, *Firearms and Violence: A Critical Review,* Charles F. Wellford, John V. Pepper, and Carol V. Petrie, eds. (Washington, D.C.: National Academies Press, 2004), 2. A later reexamination of the data and the NRC analysis concluded that, if anything, the evidence shows an increase in aggravated assault when concealed carry laws are loosened. Abhay Aneja, John Donohue, and Alexandria Zhang, "The Impact of Right-to-Carry Laws and the NRC Report: Lessons for the Empirical Evaluation of Law and Policy" (June 29, 2010), 5th Annual Conference on Empirical Legal Studies Paper. Available at SSRN, http://ssrn.com/abstract=1632599. A general critique of Lott's work is found in Ian Ayres and John Donahue III, "Shooting Down the More Guns, Less Crime Hypothesis," *Stanford Law Review* 55 (2003): 1193.

162 *Mary Rosh:* Richard Morin, "Scholar Invents Fan to Answer His Critics," *Washington Post,* February 1, 2003.

163 *best known as a Fox News columnist:* Lott's prolific writings are available at his website, http://johnrlott.blogspot.com/, and at www.foxnews.com/archive /author/john-lott/index.html.

163 *"point person in Congress":* The provision was included in the Omnibus Appropriations Bill of 1996, Public Law 104-208, 104th Congress; Jay Dickey and Mark Rosenberg, "We Won't Know the Cause of Gun Violence Until We Look for It," *Washington Post,* July 27, 2012, http://articles.washingtonpost.com/2012-07-27/opinions/35486709_1 _gun-violence-traffic-fatalities-firearm-deaths.

163 *Research funding:* The shameful history of the funding freeze is described by one of the scientists whose work was targeted in Arthur L. Kellerman and Frederick Rivara, "Silencing the Science on Gun Research," *Journal of the American Medical Association* 309, no. 6 (2013): 549–50.

163 *"The centers also ask researchers":* Michael Luo, "N.R.A. Stymies Firearms Research, Scientists Say," *New York Times,* January 25, 2011.

164 *strong punishment for any crime involving a gun:* James B. Jacobs, *Can Gun Control Work* (New York: Oxford University Press, 2002), 219–20.

164 *Policing practices changed markedly:* See Franklin E. Zimring, *The City That Became Safe* (New York: Oxford University Press, 2012), 100–150.

164 *"community policing":* See "Community Policing Defined," Office of Community Oriented Policing Services, U.S. Department of Justice, www.cops .usdoj.gov/Publications/e030917193-CP-Defined.pdf; Anthony A. Braga, "Police Enforcement Strategies to Prevent Crime in Hot Spot Areas," Office of Community Oriented Policing Services, U.S. Department of Justice, www.cops.usdoj.gov/Publications/e040825133-web.pdf; Michael Powell, "Former Skeptic Now Embraces Divisive Tactic," *New York Times,* April 9, 2012, www.nytimes.com/2012/04/10/nyregion/reducing-crime-squandering-good-will.html. There is some controversy over this definition of "community policing." The Justice Department provides this definition: "Community policing, recognizing that police rarely can solve public safety problems alone, encourages interactive partnerships with relevant stakeholders." The definition can be extended to include "hot spot" policing, which can include "stop and frisk" and "zero tolerance" policing. However, advocates and citizens sometimes see those tactics in direct opposition to community policing principles.

164 *controversial "stop and frisk" tactic:* Some scholars believe Second Amendment concerns could curb stop and frisk. Lawrence Rosenthal, "Second Amendment Plumbing After *Heller*," 34–78; Lawrence Rosenthal, "Second Amendment Plumbing After *McDonald*: Exploring the Contradiction in the Second Amendment," *Northwestern Law Review* 105 (2011): 439; Philip J. Cook, Jens Ludwig, and Adam M. Samaha, "Gun Control After *Heller*: Threats and Sideshows from a Social Welfare Perspective," *U.C.L.A. Law Review* 56 (2009): 1080.

164 *Evidence suggests:* Steven Levitt "Using Electoral Cycles in Police Hiring to Estimate the Effect of Police on Crime," *American Economic Review* 87 (1997): 270; Tomislav V. Kovandzic and John J. Sloan, "Police Levels and Crime Rates Revisited: A County-Level Analysis from Florida (1980–1998)," *Journal of Criminal Justice* 30 (2002): 65–76; Thomas B. Marvell et al., "Specification Problems, Police Levels, and Crime Rates," *Criminology* 34 (1996): 609–46.

165 *"the possibility of constitutional litigation":* Cook et. al., "Gun Control After *Heller*," 1089.

165 *ballistic microstamping:* Cal. Penal Code Sec. 12126(b)(7). See Bob Egelko, "California to Enforce 'Micro-Stamping' Gun Law," *San Francisco Chronicle,* May 18, 2013.

166 *"the bar mitzvah of the rural WASP":* B. Bruce-Briggs, "The Great American Gun War," *Public Interest* (Fall 1976): 41, www.nationalaffairs.com/doclib /20080527_197604503thegreatamericangunwarbbrucebriggs.pdf.

167 *Franklin Roosevelt said he was calling up a "muster":* His speechwriter recounts that Roosevelt did not campaign for a "draft" in 1940, preferring a term that

evoked Lexington and Concord. Samuel I. Rosenman, *Working with Roosevelt* (New York: Harper & Brothers, 1952), 241–42; Carol Gelderman, *All the Presidents' Words: The Bully Pulpit and the Creation of the Virtual Presidency* (New York: Walker and Company, 1997), 28.

167 *three million Americans were on active military duty:* In 1970, 3,064,760 Americans were on active duty. In 2011, that number had dropped to 1,468,364 (even as the country grew over 50 percent in population during that time). U.S. Department of Defense; Information Please Database, www.infoplease.com/ipa/A0004598.html.

167 *"The general profile of gun owners":* "Why Own a Gun? Protection Is Now Top Reason," Pew Research Center, March 12, 2013, www.people-press.org/files/legacy-pdf/03-12-13%20Gun%20Ownership%20Release.pdf.

168 *What matters is what people fear:* Dan M. Kahan, "More Statistics, Less Persuasion: A Cultural Theory of Gun-Risk Perceptions," Yale Faculty Scholarship Series, Paper 106 (2003).

168 *"Whether one is hierarchical":* Ibid., 18.

168 *"After Hurricane Sandy":* Wayne LaPierre, "Stand and Fight," *Daily Caller*, February 13, 2013, http://dailycaller.com/2013/02/13/stand-and-fight/?print=1.

168 *Coney Island was unusually peaceful:* Mark Morales, Erin Durkin, and Corky Siemaszko, "NRA Chief LaPierre Claims 'Looters Ran Wild in South Brooklyn' After Sandy, but Coney Island Residents Say He is Full of It," New York *Daily News*, February 14, 2013, www.nydailynews.com/new-york/nra-boss-defames-brooklyn-sandy-screed-article-1.1264387. LaPierre might have gotten confused by the dustup between the Brooklyn borough president, Marty Markowitz, and Mayor Bloomberg over whether or not National Guard troops should be brought in to help with the aftermath of the storm. Bloomberg and the NYPD did not want anyone with guns other than New York police on the streets. Eli Rosenberg, "Bloomberg: The National Guard in Coney Is a Bad Idea," *The Brooklyn Paper*, November 1, 2012, www.brooklynpaper.com/stories/35/44/all_martysnubbed_2012_11_02_bk.html. NRA officials unfamiliar with New York political folkways may simply have been baffled by the existence of a job called "Borough President."

169 *"The only way to stop":* Transcript: NRA Statement from December 21 Press Conference, *Hartford Courant*, December 21, 2012.

169 *armed guard in every elementary school:* New York City schools have school safety officers (over five thousand in early 2013, more than one per school). They are instructed to escort students to safety, not to shoot intruders. Over two hundred uniformed officers patrol dangerous schools. NYPD School Safety Division, Mission and Overview, July 2013, www.nyc.gov/html/nypd/html/school_safety/school_safety_overview.shtml. The idea, however, that every rural elementary school must have an armed guard, in case a crazed mass murderer might show up, seems far-fetched. Having police in urban

high schools has had deleterious consequences for some. When police are in a school, they can make arrests. City schools face disruption from unruly students. But police presence can also turn teens fighting in the halls from something that leads to a trip to the principal's office to the first step of a criminal record, with all the ancillary consequences. Erik Ekholm, "With More Police in Schools, More Children in Court," *New York Times*, April 12, 2013, www .nytimes.com/2013/04/12/education/with-police-in-schools-more-children-in-court.html?pagewanted=all&_r=0.

169 *newspaper headlines:* New York *Daily News*, December 22, 2012; *New York Post*, December 22, 2012.

CONCLUSION: "THE RIGHT OF THE PEOPLE"

172 *a point acknowledged:* See, for example, Lund, "The Past and Future of the Individual's Right to Bear Arms," 3.

172 *"There is almost no political question":* Alexis de Tocqueville, *Democracy in America*, abridged., trans. Stephen T. Grant (Indianapolis: Hackett, 2000), 123.

174 *A full scan of American history:* See Kramer, *The People Themselves*, a provocative look at the ways ordinary citizens helped shape constitutional understandings in the republic's early years. See also Sean Wilentz, *The Rise of American Democracy* (New York: W. W. Norton, 2005).

175 *"Public sentiment is everything":* Lincoln: *Speeches and Writings 1832–58*, ed. Don E. Ferenbacher (Des Moines: Library of America, 1989), 524–5. Lincoln spoke at his first debate with Stephen O. Douglas at Ottowa, Illinois, on August 21, 1858.

176 *"living originalism":* Jack Balkin, *Living Originalism* (Cambridge: Harvard University Press, 2011), 120–21.

176 *It did not hurt:* This point is argued in David Richards, *Fundamentalism in American Religion and Law: Obama's Challenge to Patriarchy's Threat to Democracy* (Cambridge: Cambridge University Press, 2010). Richards points out the traditional gender roles in Scalia's majority opinion, elevating as it does the duty to protect "hearth and home." Breyer's dissent pulls in modern concerns about domestic violence, 228–29.

176 *Justice Stephen Breyer has offered:* Breyer, *Active Liberty*, 17–19.

INDEX

Page numbers beginning with 189 refer to end notes.

ABOUT THE AUTHOR

Michael Waldman is president of the Brennan Center for Justice at NYU School of Law, a leading nonpartisan law and policy institute that focuses on improving the systems of democracy and justice. He was director of speechwriting for President Bill Clinton from 1995 to 1999, responsible for writing or editing nearly two thousand speeches, including four State of the Union and two Inaugural Addresses. He was special assistant to the president for policy coordination from 1993 to 1995. He has been a lecturer at Harvard's Kennedy School of Government and an attorney in private practice. His books include *My Fellow Americans, A Return to Common Sense,* and *POTUS Speaks.* He appears frequently on television and radio to discuss the presidency, democracy, and the Constitution. Waldman is a graduate of Columbia College and NYU School of Law. He lives with his family in Brooklyn, New York.